# Two Dingbats on a Spiritual Quest

ELLIE MAC

Published by ELLIE MAC, 2023.

# Dedication

Words are limited when it comes to sharing my full heart, but they are all I can use on this empty page to tell you, my children and grandchildren, how loved you are, and how grateful I am that you chose to be in my life and permitted me to be in yours. You have been on a journey with me from one continent to another, and done so with love and trust. You have been my truest teachers. You have had faith in me far beyond that which I ever deserved and are my greatest work of art. As for my amazing grandchildren, you are proof that what we call God has not yet finished with the planet.

Then there are my friends, who have listened to so many of my stories, not yet written, and also to incessant phone calls as I have tried to make sense of my life and philosophy.

And I come to those who have supported me in this process of writing. My friend Linda, thank you, and also my dear friend, Margaret Marcham, who has given me a set of wings to fly which no bird has yet trumped, constantly encouraging me on my journey, and constantly seeking and seeing perfection.

Most importantly, I am ever grateful to those who have shared their wisdom and dedicated their lives in service to humanity and contributed greatly to this book, H.P. Blavatsky, W.Q. Judge, Damodar Mavalankar, E.A. Neresheimer, and other great thinkers. The best parts of this story would not be possible without you.

# An Introduction

This is a unique story, about a Master of Light who skillfully uses direct contact, and the Power of Love, to accelerate His pupils along the road to freedom. Incredible gems of truth are shared, with great wisdom, power, and a great sense of humour.

You may *begin* by thinking that certain excerpts in this book are quite incredible, unique even, but I assure you, all that has been written, only shares the reality of natural law in perfect operation.

You see, it all started when Linda and I wrote *The Letter*. It's perfectly true, this letter changed every aspect of our worlds, and continues to throw at us adventure, mind blowing insights, and lots of laughter.

There is not one area of my life, and I know I speak for Linda also, that has not been impacted by the little piece of paper on which we wrote it, and I admit, it was not necessarily the wisest thing we have ever done. It was, however, the very action which would propel us forward, accelerating our lives, like we were drivers in a Formula One racing car on the circuit of a Grand Prix. It's been the ride of a lifetime.

# Chapter One

*Your current safe boundaries were once unknown frontiers.*
Unknown

I had no idea that within 24 hours I would be struggling for life, surrendering to death, and rising up with a stranger, and all because of the letter.

Looking back, it's easy to see the supposedly random events which brought me to that first 24 hours. Though it was also very clear the events I experienced were all part of a grand design that even the craziest of minds would have found difficulty dreaming up.

So this may sound crazy, but then again reality often is – especially in a life such as mine - but this is a story of a journey, my journey, and this is my personal invitation for you to join me. You'll need an open mind and if you happen to find this a challenge, just trust me, as sometimes I've felt the same way. By the time you've finished reading, you'll have your own opinions for sure.

Due to failing health during the winter of 2009, I made the decision to visit my daughter in Calgary and I extended the visit in order to take a few days to travel into the mountains for some alone time. I had been feeling extremely disillusioned with my universe, very disconnected with my inner-self and with my God, and so my prescription to be alone in nature seemed the perfect solution.

With the loan of my daughter's car, packed and ready, I made my way out along the #1 Highway towards Banff, with no real time restriction and no definite destination.

The big, blue, Alberta sky collaborated with the sun to give the impression of a balmy summer's day, but outside the snappy air froze the hairs up my nose and forced me to bundle on more clothing, something I disliked.

Along the highway I passed familiar peaks recalling Native stories of lost loves and Chinook winds and it wasn't long before the city was a forgotten past life, miles behind me.

Fresh snow had fallen the night before and though the thought had crossed my mind that maybe it was a little too late in the day for a walk in the mountains, I turned off the highway and about 10 miles into the valley I found a familiar parking area and stopped the car. I started along a path I had taken many times before and as always was looking forward to bumping into the odd cross-country skier or day hiker.

It seemed bizarre to me that one could encounter a stranger on a footpath in the middle of nowhere, and get into conversation quite easily without being perceived as forward or weird, and also without feeling threatened. Yet that same stranger one could meet on the streets in one's hometown and avoid acknowledging them altogether, why is this?

This day I encountered no one. There were footprints in the snow of a coyote or maybe a wolf, but either way this animal was to be my only encounter and being curious I followed. I've never feared coyotes or wolves so fifteen minutes or so into my walk I had the determination to find my potential new acquaintance, whose prints ran over a hill to my left.

The snow was deep and dry and I felt like a child playing in powdered icing sugar, sinking up to my knees and laughing all the way to the top of an incline. The view at the top was breathtaking.

For as far as I could see a white blanket lay stretched over mother earth while she slept her dormant sleep, and it seemed as if the undulating breath of a snow goddess had danced into the curves and valleys of her hibernating form.

As I looked to the left towards a line of dense forest I could see something moving, and sure enough the prints leading over to the trees were those of my lone animal.

I followed his calling card for some 45 minutes until I drew close to the remnants of an old Native sweat lodge. I stopped and stared at the one set of prints where the animal had entered, noticing nothing to indicate he had left.

I waited a moment. All was quiet. Anticipation punched at my heart. What was I going to do once I faced him?

Slowly I entered the lodge and looked around, expecting to come face to face with my playmate, but there was nothing. I sat down on a large rock totally confused. Outside the howl of an animal pierced the silence and looking out of the entrance I watched as my coyote disappeared into the forest.

It was an ominous shiver that danced through my body that late afternoon, a shiver which had I heeded would have halted any further pursuit. Instead I disregarded my initial instincts for it was all so thoroughly stimulating. He was calling me, taunting me to follow, and I did.

Like an owner pursuing her runaway dog I ran into the trees, and like my life so far I took notice of nothing but the adventure ahead. As I entered the wooded area he was waiting, crouching low and looking directly at me. I slowly approached, then he rose and ran, and so did I...after him.

After quite some time of playing 'catch the coyote' I stopped and sat on a fallen log and took stock of my situation. It was then I realised the foolishness of my actions. A steady fall of snow had covered everything, and to top it all off, I had lost my bearings as well as my mind.

Looking around I could see this foolish chase must have taken far longer than I thought, or was it just getting darker earlier than I had anticipated?

My elusive friend was now long gone leaving me in the company of shadows bent on casting a different landscape. Though I wasn't afraid of the dark, the ensuing night, like my lost coyote friend, had started to play hide and seek with me. I was getting colder and I had a sick sense that something, not my coyote friend, was out there waiting and this just added to the chill.

By now the sun had disappeared over some cold uninviting peak, the snow I was sitting on was feeling uncomfortably wet, and as night started to lay her blanket over the earth in preparation for sleep I quickly started to catch hold of the hem of fear.

I've no idea how long I wandered about trying to find my way back, but it wasn't long before the beauty I had viewed earlier became the bleak backdrop for my own survival show, and even though I kept repeating out loud "this is not happening to me," my attempts to stave off impending waves of panic were futile.

Finally I had to face facts. All was not good, I mean really not good. The sweat I'd built up had turned to cold shivers, and as panic began to take up permanent residence I began to play over in my head some of the survival shows I'd watched on television.

Still believing I wasn't far from my starting point I began shouting, loud and hard, hoping someone would hear me, that maybe, just maybe, there would be a lone hiker or a late skier nearby, homeward bound. Then I remembered my cell phone.

Scrambling into my small backpack I breathed out a string of thank yous to the god of cell phones, entered the number for my son, and pressed send. Nothing. I pressed send again and again but with the same response. The battery was dead. What now?

Any remaining remnants of composure quickly lost the fight against the force of my fear, and now pushed to my limit I decided to take the spiritual route. Calmly at first I started calling on the names of spirits, of angels, of anyone who might be out there who could help. Nothing! No sudden flash of insight, no guiding light, no guide at all, animal or otherwise.

Then my fear and desperation quickly turned into anger and that anger I directed at God. This Supreme Being, the one I had faithfully followed for years, was supposed to be aware of everything and I felt sure IT was aware of my dilemma now. So what was the bloody designer of the Universe doing? Where was the epitome of so-called love now when I needed it the most?

Giving up I began to cry and as months of frustration, vulgarities and undecipherable sounds spewed out of my mouth making little sense, I swore this big Kahuna was not having me dance the dance a moment longer. I screeched into the darkness, "you can take your bloody spiritual path and shove it, and shove it where *your* sun don't shine."

Finally I ceased the verbal abuse and accepted I was going to have to stay out all night in this bleak wilderness. So, settling by a circle of old trees, I broke some branches, placed a portion on the snow and sat down, then pulled the remainder over me and there I stayed, shivering.

My belief was that I had a better chance of conserving energy until I was found by staying put in my primitive bed, rather than continuing my disoriented scurry getting nowhere. So after sitting for some time, bellowing the odd holler, I laid my head down on the firs for a few moments to rest.

While I recalled how dangerous it was to sleep in the snow by now I was so utterly exhausted I didn't care. Though I was determined to stay awake until the sun rose I closed my eyes and in my false reverie fell asleep.

Somewhere in the depths of this sleep a comforting hand rested on my body, and though death also seemed to be beckoning me with her seductive lullaby, the familiar energy of this touch drew me back to life. Feeling disoriented and unable to gather my thoughts, I opened my eyes to see a dark figure of a man looking down on me and I could only stare at his face and sob. Someone had found me, now I was safe!

His gentle hand on my arm motioned me to stay put and with little resistance I did. He knelt beside me, placing something soft over and around my worn out body, securing me in a cocoon of caring, and I just accepted that it would be morning when he would lead me to civilization and safety.

Feeling perfectly safe and for the first time in many hours wonderfully warm, I slipped into the sleep of a baby rocked in the arms of its mother softly comforted in the warmth of a down blanket, and I was happy to fall back into this comfortable world of peace – utter peace. For now a gentle caress seemed to convey all was as it should be and a distant, gentle voice resounded through me. "You are safe."

How long I slept I've no idea, but a warm breeze tenderly touched my closed eyelids and I awoke. Gathering my thoughts, and myself, I rose and gazed around the still darkness expecting to see my Good Samaritan nearby, but there was no one, so I waited silently just staring.

What I noticed made little sense, for the bed I'd slept in with the few branches I'd placed under and over me was still the same; there was no soft covering to keep me warm and obviously no stranger.

# Chapter Two

*Everything you can imagine is real.*
Pablo Piccasso

Night was still loitering and a chill ran through my warm body confirming the heat which had kept me so comforted during my rest. I strained my eyes, in a pathetic attempt to pierce the darkness, hoping to see something, anything, any clue, that would explain what had happened, but there was only silence.

The area around me looked the same; trees and more trees; snow, white; sky, dark; shadows, grey; me, lost. Where had my Samaritan gone? Or, more to the point, was he ever here? I hadn't been prepared for any of this, not from the physical, the mental nor emotional standpoint, and God knows my spiritual point of view had gone out the window and was on a hike in some far off land.

It wasn't a sound, nor a movement, that caught my attention, but I knew something or someone was very close by, watching me.

Holding my breath, in an attempt to hear better, served nothing. The longer I held my breath the louder my heart thumped and the less I could think. I couldn't focus, I had absolutely no idea what to do and it was a mixture of resignation and seething resentment that spawned my whisper, "I give up God, I bloody-well give up. You go on and feed your endless ego. You just please yourself because you win." And not caring any more I let go. Instantly I was enveloped in an overwhelming calm.

Suspended in this surreal stillness I slowly lifted my head and looked around, and there, standing by a huge tree, was my Good Samaritan. He turned away and casually motioned me to follow him. In my relief, without question, I picked myself up and followed.

We walked for a while, neither of us speaking. For me it was shock, for him I have no idea. My mind started racing through all that had transpired since our first encounter.

The contrast in my circumstances, from earlier in the night, had automatically put me in a calmer place. Then I had a sudden thought and stopped. In all this crazy-making, where was he taking me? He continued on and I stood still. Further ahead he stopped and turned, then spoke.

"You are being invited on a journey into reality." He beckoned me to come forward and walk beside him. As I approached I stumbled on a raised tree root and in an instant he was by my side steadying me. His reaction was so incredibly quick that my reaction was one of shock. Gathering myself quickly I assured him I'd had a good dose of reality and that a further journey was not necessary. To be taken to my car was my only request. I certainly didn't want to consider any extension to my last, so many, hours.

Moving in closer to me he whispered. "My Dear, you requested this, remember the letter?"

There seemed to be a hint of humour in his voice, and as if the situation I had gotten myself into wasn't enough, my mind was now racing trying to recall any letters I'd written and to whom. With a warm smile he assured me all would be explained once we reached the cabin, and that this cabin was to be our first destination.

To bring some clarity here, I'm quite used to strange happenings. Over time my life has been saved on more than one occasion by miraculous means, and somehow, at the oddest times people have turned up in unexpected places to assist me. However, I was sure my new-found friend's reference to a letter I had apparently written was a mistake. I also felt sure it would be sorted out once we reached this cabin he was referring to.

We approached a modest hut, climbed the wooden steps and entered through the main doorway into a cosy, rustic living area. My host showed me to a seat, poured a cup of steaming tea, motioning me to help myself to the food already prepared on a small table.

If I had entertained the thought of being confused by all that had transpired so far, I was wrong. Confusion now hit a record high on my Richter scale, for it seemed, though I don't know how, that I'd been expected.

Attempting to collate some of the crazy thoughts bumping about in my head, I decided to ask his name. Before I could get the words from my mouth he answered, "it is Raj."

As he tied back his long, dark hair, I caught a glimpse of a smile. He stopped what he was doing and turned to me.

In an attempt to distract myself I diverted my attention back to the room. What I noticed was puzzling. Although the hut was well lit and warm, there were no light fixtures and no visible source for the warmth. I was acutely aware he was observing me so I faced him again, and then, as if lifting thoughts from my head, he explained.

"The power for the light, heat, and the food you see is supplied by a force, a power which supplies all in the Universe. It is the Divine, the Great Spirit, or whatever name you wish to bestow upon it. It is Truth.

"Our worlds are the effect of our own consciousness and when our individual consciousness is one with the truth, truth is manifest in our worlds. Humanity fumbles in the dark so to speak, only catching glimpses, manifesting in part, until relative truth is taken up by the light of absolute truth. Truth, My Dear, truly sets you free. Man has brought through the mind makeshift things, imperfect things, and this will continue until humanity wakes up and reunites with Source."

There was some resistance in me to the word God because of my life of late, and this rescuer of mine, with his fashion being that of a darker version of the generically accepted Jesus, also reared some resistance and questions. However, he had captivated me in a strange way. He stopped talking and was now smiling at me.

I was now feeling inordinately calm and safe, not something one would have expected considering the events of the past 24 hours, and though I had quite a few questions, for now I was content to sit in the warmth and eat.

He poured me another cup of tea then looked towards the door and excused himself. When he returned he entered with two very interesting people and introduced me to Nada and Francis.

Nada rested her cerulean eyes on mine and smiled as she moved gracefully past me. It was as though a butterfly had entered the room. What struck me the most were her features, which were in perfect symmetry. So strange, when something is perfect it screams out that perfection.

Francis I knew. Don't ask me how, but as He approached me I felt He knew me far better than I knew myself, and when He held my obvious stare with His gentle, violet eyes, I felt dipped in the fullness of total acceptance.

Was He the One who had assisted me on many previous occasions: when my car broke down on a deserted road through the mountains; the one who saved me from an out of control school bus; the man who had sat down next to me in an empty church and comforted me when I was shedding tears of grief? He didn't physically look like any of these persons but He was that familiar One.

Though both Francis and Nada seemed to me around 34 years old it was extremely difficult to pin an age on them. Raj mentioned later that they had been coming to, and going from, the Rockies, along with others, for at least sixty years. So the next question arose, who were these two and where did they come from?

Francis sat at the table and began to talk about the many calls I'd made to my Higher Self. He referred to them as calls rather than prayers, for I would often start with "I need you to listen here" or "I need an answer in no uncertain terms and not an airy fairy response."

He then referred to a letter I'd written some thirty years earlier and said this letter and my persistence had been the initiator of the situation I now found myself in. A letter I had written? What could I have put in this letter I didn't remember writing to have warranted all this?

Then a picture flashed in my mind and Francis smiled: I remembered. The content was vivid. Yes, I recalled writing that letter and clearly remembered my bravado as I declared my sincere desire to face all my Karma in this life, regardless of the consequences. As if this wasn't enough, I took it further in my own dramatic style, and summoned up from the depths of my heart, "hey, bring it all on God, bring it all on."

I felt foolish, but couldn't stop laughing, because I even remembered mailing the letter, and with no address, trusting it would be received. Then something else flashed into my mind. My dear friend Linda had also written the letter and I only had to look at *her* life of late to understand that we truly had been two dingbats, and still are two dingbats on a spiritual quest.

"It was debatable as to whether you were quite ready for this experience" He continued. "However, your persistence could not be ignored any longer. When enough energy is generated the desired result is actualized.

"But It was not your demanding which drew our attention, it was your commanding.

"A child stomps the feet to demand what it wants, one's Presence commands attention in a very different way. Think on this and you will have a better understanding of what I'm conveying to you." Francis sat for a while just looking at me, then He continued.

"At any given moment an individual is expanding or contracting. We experience expansion as awareness and when we are completely expanded we have the experience of being at one with all life. In truth there is only one life and with resistance gone we are able to interact with other beings and all forms of nature, in fact all life.

"Just as there are degrees of expansion there are also degrees of contraction. When man is contracted he isolates himself and this brings to him fear and suffering. When a man contracts enough he feels hatred, anger, separateness, he feels resistance to everyone and everything and eventually he may even be considered crazy. There is a way of getting out of this resistance by throwing it out. Cultivate no resistance to what you think, feel or see, this is what I am asking of you whilst with us, I am asking you to prove what I am saying.

"It is your choice at any given moment, in every circumstance, whether you contract or expand; you have absolute control over your attitude and it is your attitude that plays an important role in your decisions and consequently your life. Francis explained how more information would be given throughout the journey.

"After a good night's rest we will start our excursion into the mountains. Over our time together the light of the soul will illumine the mind, provoking new ideas, desiring new answers, and your mind will create new questions enabling the growth of the spirit within."

At this point, a week or so away seemed harmless enough. Francis continued.

"What is conceived is achieved and in your case has compelled the experience you are now having. With regard to this journey, you have free will to proceed with us or not." I had no doubts in me, I knew I was following and so did Francis.

So far I felt safe and excited like a child in her father's secure arms waiting for a surprise, and in my heart there was anticipation.

I came to realise later, it is perfectly natural to feel safe when in the presence of beings such as these as they have an innate ability to embody harmony and peace because they are harmony and peace.

I was shown to a modest room and as the door closed I flopped onto the bed relaxing into the covers, then I let my mind replay over and over all that had happened.

Finally I settled my thoughts on Raj and the familiar connection I felt. It was pleasant to recall his catching me, and thrilling to recall his strength, beauty and grace, though a little disconcerting to think he may be aware of it.

Could he read my thoughts? I hoped not. Was he aware of my feelings? I really hoped not. At times they verged on being quite indiscreet and yet, they also seemed so natural. I tried to let it all go, to drift into sleep which my whole being was really ready for, yet something inside said I would never be the same and it excited me, and all because of the letter.

# Chapter Three

*There are two ways to live your life – one is as though nothing is a miracle, the other is as though everything is a miracle.*
Einstein

The next morning, when I opened my eyes, I cautiously viewed my surroundings and with relief, rose to find I was still in the cabin not lying again on a bed of branches in some lucid dream. On a chair just outside my room sat a small bundle of basic clothing and necessities, and a note bearing my name.

Outside, our supplies for the upcoming journey were already packed onto horses and all I needed to do was to have mine added. At this point I didn't feel the need to ask the who's nor the why's, for there was something very natural about my absurd situation.

Nada, Raj and I gathered on the front porch where Francis greeted us and asked if I wanted to write a note to my family, which he said would be delivered at a later time. I hadn't voiced any concerns, if anything I'd forgotten, but he assured me all things would be taken care of and although it was early in our relationship I had no worries. I went back to the table, wrote my note and handed it to Him trusting a guide would deliver it.

There isn't much to tell you regarding my travelling companions. They dressed simply and had an ease about them, and I guess yes, they *were* different, though I couldn't put my finger on exactly why.

I ask you, the reader, wouldn't you stay around to find out more? Wouldn't you want to find out how sweet the carrots were?

I already had some understanding of gurus in India, teachers in Tibet, and monks who had left their Ferrari's retreating to a life of austerity in the Himalayas. However it had always seemed a little strange to me that so many gurus resided in the East, when it was obvious so many were wanted in the West.

Were my companions part of a new age group or religious order? I had questions around both of these. To me a new age teacher, preacher or even guru, is no different than the religious priest or minister of old. A rose is still a rose by any other name. Their followers would still be waiting for their latest revelation or 'new way'. Surely it's about finding that connection and relationship for oneself.

I had questions regarding the fundamental orders of any 'ism', around the 'giving up' process, denial and punishment, which quite honestly smacked of the old controlling order.

Was the giving up of one's joy and pleasure, replacing it with solemnity a prerequisite to finding this God? Is abstinence truly what a loving father would want for his child? Was this so-called God of the churches so fearful and demanding, and have such a fragile ego that he was needy enough to demand worship and sacrifice? Is this God so easily angered that to deny him would result in punishment or damnation? Could one really lose one's soul, and if so where did it go? The questions were accumulating.

No, at the onset of this journey I had expressed clearly what this God could do with his path, and I meant it.

I guess if humanity expects to have to live a life of austerity, or suffer for a 'so called' loving God, or to fulfill any set of requirements so as to not risk his wrath and damnation, then that's exactly what humanity will have to do until humanity changes its mind.

We started our first day's walk with the warm sun on our backs over a terrain that was flat and easy, and I was happy to follow behind Francis, Raj and Nada who appeared to be locked in deep conversation.

Before falling asleep the previous night my last thoughts had been of Raj, and now, as I ambled happily behind him, I found it easy to let my mind continue to wander into the unexpected attraction I had for him and elaborate upon it. But I was pulled up short by a mental monster, a cocktail of sin, which quickly changed my innocent pastime into a bog of guilt due to the old order of religion and indoctrination I'd been raised in.

He was so obviously a holy man or monk, and one only had to listen to him, observe his demeanour, to realise my thoughts of defrocking a man of God was not a good thing. I did chuckle though at my mental attempts at a modern day Thornbird.

Quickening my pace I determined to keep my thoughts superficial. Where was he from? How did he meet Franics. Then he stopped, turned, and made his way toward me.

For the second time I stumbled. Once again he was steadying me, however this time he held me firmly in his arms until my legs were stable.

"Do you have a balance problem?" He smiled, but before I could respond, he laughed so warmly I, too, found myself laughing. How at ease he made me feel.

"India" came his response, "and I met Francis some years ago when He was on a project in my hometown and when the opportunity arose, I travelled to Canada and settled in the Rockies to further my studies under His tutelage. Do you feel a familiarity towards me?"

His question shocked me. I tried to answer, but all my tongue could do was flap whilst making no sense, as it attempted to navigate my dried up mouth. All those thoughts I'd entertained about his body, and his seeming ability to know answers to questions I hadn't voiced. He had access to my mind!

For a moment his look seemed far away, as if checking in with someone or something, and then, in my head I heard him. "We have known each other a long, long time."

He walked a little way ahead and I observed how he moved with such grace over a terrain that seemed a white crusted replica of the moon's cold surface. Checking myself from fantasising was proving a challenge I was rapidly losing, and then he approached me again.

Keeping his eyes steadily on mine, I felt him searching for something, something inside me that I should know. His warm breath brushed my cheeks, my head spun and my heart punched in my chest, but then his smile caressed me gently and his words stroked poetry into my heart.

"The cohesive energy of love has brought us together again, and it's that love you're remembering. Some truths are difficult to see when caught up in this three-dimensional world, for our sight so often becomes fixed on the illusions around us. What we fix upon we continue to re-create. You could say we become masters of creating and reinforcing that which is an illusion. We become so caught up in the illusions we seem to lose our way in reality.

"How perfect are the opportunities offered in this world, for what better way could there possibly be to experience who we are than to immerse ourselves into what we are not? By experiencing this duality, we get to exercise the gift that separates us from the animal kingdom – free-will. Our choices carry us along the road to our effects and sometimes the effects seem to separate us and the Great Spirit. However, this is impossible, eventually we wake up."

His eyes held me in a suspended state for a little while and then he changed the subject completely. An onrush of feelings and distant memories I couldn't quite understand had started to make me feel self-conscious, so I was very happy at the subject change, but it left me pondering on what had just happened.

He explained he was studying, and I was curious as to what those studies were, and why here in the Rockies? I was unaware of any university close by. Smiling at my attempt to be clever, he said was studying life and who better to study this subject with than someone who was living.

For the next couple of hours we hiked steadily upward, and contrary to what one would expect, considering my level of fitness of late, I found the going quite easy.

My thoughts went to his reference of our knowing each other, though heaven knows where or when that could have been. I also felt sure that I would have definitely remembered.

However, what Raj had said regarding love was starting to stir emotions I hadn't known existed, and at this point, I wasn't sure I wanted to go there.

Beautiful is a lame word to express the sights we encountered. All around, the rise and fall of nature's contrasting body, her edgy curves and sharp beauty, her smooth valleys rising to mounds of wild brush took my breath away and at times I stood in silence as a child does when watching Christmas lights and stars, mesmerised by all her wild splendour.

It was overwhelming in many ways, my new view on nature, my new friends, and then of course, there was Raj. I felt a oneness with him I couldn't explain, and didn't want explained to me just yet. All I wanted to do was just be, and that brought me a kind of freedom I liked.

On a ledge, we stopped and viewed the scene back along the path we'd taken, and after food and rest we started the incline to the next cabin and our night's destination.

During our journey, I'd noticed my hosts seemed to have little need for water, food or rest. I felt sure they only partook as a courtesy, which I believe was to make me, and later, my fellow travellers, feel more at ease. It was a long and steep incline and one I would never challenge under normal circumstances, but I noticed things change for me physically, and I had a surge of energy that propelled and sustained me, so that upon arrival I was strangely refreshed.

The cabin they referred to sat on a large ridge, overlooking an expanse of crystal water, the hue of unpolished emeralds. This cabin was far from what I'd anticipated it to be. Nada said it was a retreat, little known to the outside world, and we would be using it for a while as a base.

Not ostentatious, though impressive, the smooth, solid wood of the entrance hall floor showed rings of age swirling in a dance. In the centre of the floor, a large, rose quartz, six-pointed star was expertly inlaid, each point directing towards a corridor, each corridor revealing doors to the various rooms.

Down one of the corridors came a tall, slender woman who seemed very excited to see me. Nada introduced Margaret and left. As Margaret escorted me down one of the corridors, she explained we had been friends for a long time. I must admit, it was like going down memory lane on some kind of 'this-is-your-life' TV show, packed with feelings of familiarity.

For sure, I knew her, just like I knew Francis. She helped me settle into my room and my feelings of familiarity became stronger. Yes, there was something with all my hosts that made them stand out, but Margaret seemed like a sister.

Upon leaving she turned and took my hands. "You are indeed on a journey that will push your boundaries, a journey that will open your mind to see with the soul, to hear, to touch, to enable you to listen with your heart and reach out from your soul to embrace life." She smiled, and she left.

My room was warm and bright, and, like before, I searched for fixtures, but like before, there were none. I knew I'd already been supplied with the answer, however, the human in me needed to keep searching, just in case. I put down my few things and rushed back to the receiving hall. I didn't wish to miss anything.

In the main hall, Francis greeted me and said he would be leaving to deliver the letter which I had written to my family. He requested I put the time and date on it, which I did, then He departed with a definite look of mischief.

At supper, I was introduced to Margaret's companion Alan, to Meta and Thomas, as well as other people who had been invited on this journey, though not in the same way as myself.

The food was sumptuous: tropical fruits, nuts, berries, bread, butters, juice and tea, all in abundance. There was no meat, and when I questioned Raj, he said they ate nothing that had conscious life. Thomas then addressed us.

"All power comes from the Great Source. There are no miracles, only that which you perceive as miracles, it is natural law in action. All you will experience in this short amount of time with us will at first seem sensational, until you become familiar with natural law in action.

"Life is limitless, and here, in this retreat, the One Life supplies the heat, light, and food in abundance. Two thousand years ago, a great teacher demonstrated this same law, little understood then, and not too much practised now. The Master said, 'He that believeth on me, the works that I do shall he do also; and greater works than these shall he do.'"

"On this journey we have but few requests. We ask you to put aside any conclusions until its completion and also that you keep an open heart. Your demonstration of this heart is the very thing that drew you here and we ask you to continue to be receptive throughout your time with us.

"This will seem to you like no ordinary excursion, yet it is one that is as natural as your breathing. It is one open to all souls, yet seemingly hidden to the many.

"We ask each of you to shed a light upon the path of others, to encourage them, so they, too, may embrace their own individual journeys along their way of truth."

He concluded his address with a smile just as Francis entered the room and sat at the far end of the table. Francis said he had delivered my letter and not to concern myself. Did I believe Him? Even though I'd been immersed in metaphysics and had some totally unexplainable experiences in my past, to deliver a letter, by hand, a few hundred miles in minutes, was way outside of my mental reach. I did what I was asked to do and placed my doubts in a cubby hole in my mind to revisit later.

# Chapter Four

The appearance of things change according to the emotions and thus we see magic and beauty in them, while the magic and beauty are really in ourselves.

During my wanderings the previous day I had come across a large precipice with an expansive valley below and, before retiring, I requested to be woken up in time to see the sunrise from this vantage point.

When I arrived, a few of my new travelling companions, obviously with the same intent, had taken up residence also. Finding a spot for myself, I settled in silence as the sun started her slow ascent. The mist beneath drifted across the valley like a large, drowsy fairy and I was quite content to dreamily drift with her, following the route of her soft caresses o'r the ragged rocks.

The world I had left behind seemed like a far off burden, with its troubles belonging to some other me. In this newfound freedom I was weightless and suspended. Thoughts drifted like the valley mist into and out of my head, until a thought dropped into my mind like a seed taking root.

"May the soul illumine my mind," I said to myself, and this thought persisted of its own volition.

This one thought produced questions, which then seemed to stimulate random answers, which then turned into more questions. The soul I was invoking was not just my soul but also a body of souls, a level of consciousness of which I am a part, where truth and wisdom reside. The original thought repeated again.

"May the soul illumine my mind," and the process continued.

Time, like the mists below, seemed to drift by and how long I was lost in this I've no idea. I orientated myself back to my surroundings and looked around at my companions. We were all suspended some inches above the rock.

"You seem surprised at this experience," someone said, "however all have the ability to rise above self-imposed limitations. Your mind became lost in the beauty presented to you and you allowed yourself to become part of nature. You became the gentle breeze dancing in unity with the mind of the Divine."

Trying to analyse what had just been said brought me out of my reverie, and with sudden sureness, my rear end landed harshly on the rock beneath me. To the side stood Francis and He continued.

"Meditation is a discipline and humanity, as a whole, is slow to add yet another discipline to their already perceived, limited lives. Some view meditation as a restriction of their time, but how far from the truth this is, for it takes the aspirant from the illusion of limitation to unlimited opportunities. It is an opening to the soul, a route to understanding and consciously connecting with Source.

"The noises of the outer world drown the ability to hear the still, small voice which sits quietly within, the voice of encouragement and enlightenment.

"The outer world is ever busy; it distracts and mesmerises and is quick to enforce and reinforce any pre-established fear and limitation, and is swift to create new limitations. An old adage says, 'if you always do what you've always done, you'll always get what you've always got,' and you are still here, right?

"There are many ways to experience Divinity, though as you have just discovered, some of these are reliant on outside influences and all outside influences are transient. That which is within is constant and subject to nothing, nothing, yet that which is without is fleeting and subject to fluctuation, to constant change.

"Some souls become trapped, searching for their experiences again and again, looking for the same scene, drink, drugs, or sexual partners, the something or someone they believe supplied their satisfaction, and when it is lost, they feel lost, because of the transient nature of all outside influences.

"Ignorance is not bliss, for oftentimes, in order to fulfil this desire, this divine discontent, one may turn to the nearest person, place, condition or thing, and at times this will court suffering. However, suffering is never wasted, far from it, for great mastery may be attained via this route and the soul will use these experiences to bring about enlightenment.

"Remember there is no such thing as right or wrong, for if that were true, it would prove a God of retribution, a God of fear and not a Divine Source of unconditional love. Cause and effect, action and reaction and sequence and consequence are the true laws. Deity is no respecter of persons.

"This is the way the Universe maintains harmony, balance and equilibrium, and if a cause were ever to be set in motion without a corresponding effect, the whole Universe would cease to be. Continuity and existence depends on this great law of balance and adjustment, not right or wrong or a judgmental God.

"The Divine Force is perpetual motion, always moving matter. The soul is where you may touch wisdom's hem and understand more of the truths I am addressing. But enough for now, it is time for us to depart."

# TWO DINGBATS ON A SPIRITUAL QUEST

It seemed to me, the last words from Francis touched many of the subjects which had recently been on my mind, and although he did not go into great depth, he gave me enough to 'whet my whistle' stimulating the desire to find out more.

We all left the ledge and prepared for the next leg of our journey. It was interesting to listen to the different accounts of why and how each came to be in the group, so when we were outside, I meandered over to two people I had not yet become acquainted with and struck up a conversation.

They were around 26 years of age and had been camping close to a tourist area in the foothills of the Rockies, near Lake Louise. On their last morning, while packing up to leave, a lone hiker passed by, struck up a conversation, and from that moment on they found themselves on a hike up a different mountain than the one they had planned. The lone hiker, I discovered, was Francis.

Were we the first group to experience a journey such as this? I think not. How many other people had been on one similar? How many others would be open to a journey such as this? Would you, the reader, be open to such a quest?

I realise my circumstances were a little different, having got myself foolishly lost, but had I really been lost? A rush of excitement rose inside with the realisation - if this was open to me, then this was open to everyone.

I settled into a steady stride, viewing all nature around me. I was grateful - grateful for my hosts, companions, life, and the mountains. For what 'til then had been grey and granite peaks, now seemed touched by the brush of a master artist. The wind was kissing my face and even the snow had softened the sharp edges of the rocks beneath my boots.

A popular saying is, 'if you've seen one mountain you've seen them all.' How naive is that? Even the same mountain showed me a different face due to the light of the sun, as well as the light within my heart.

How often we roll out clichés about life, making judgments based on our limited perspective and experience, then make further judgments based on our shaky hypothesis, gravitating to others who will reinforce our original error.

Now I started looking back over my life and began to appreciate the courage I was able to summon when facing my greatest fears and lows.

I also saw that no matter how many rejections, disappointments and lost loves I had faced, I still had the ability and desire to turn my face again towards that which had been the initiator of so much pain – love. Oh, what a capacity for love we have as human beings.

It was becoming clear to me how quick we are to see our own faults and the faults of others, something life has taught us no doubt. It was also becoming clear to me that we could quite easily turn the tide by taking the time, maybe at the end of our day, to review the incredible fortitude, resilience and love we have and have shared.

I had written the letter, written it with such faith and hope, and now, along with many other things, it was giving me the gift of seeing myself a little more objectively. It was giving me the gift of feeling more love. Clearly, I was worthy of receiving love in all its forms, and now I just needed to allow it to take me into the depths of passion.

After a few hours of hiking, I decided to stop to take a water break, leaving the others to carry on ahead. Whilst packing away my water bottle, I started to feel extremely uneasy. My first thought was to get to my friends and get out of the immediate area, though I had no idea what had caused such an impulse.

Before I could reach anyone, a deep, guttural sound drew my attention as a large grizzly bear reared towards me. Terror is a mild word to convey the paralysis that possessed all but my mind, which was already anticipating graphically my being torn limb from limb.

A breeze later, Raj was with me placing his body between the animal and myself and Francis stepped from nowhere speaking gently to it like a dear friend. The bear immediately lowered his large body, rolling like a puppy wanting a belly rub and the Master and the beast both played happily.

"Animals respond to fear with fear, and if they receive love they respond with love. Looking into the eyes of this brother one sees the Source of all life, and that is love. When you connect with the Divine in anyone you connect with Source and are one with Source, no harm can befall you. It is fear that begets fear, and fear will creep upon you like a thief in the night to steal that which is your birthright. This is Truth.

"Truth has been presented in many ways and in many cultures. Remember, TRUTH IS. There is no mysterious truth or metaphysical truth; it is either Truth or not. There is no deep truth or shallow truth, only Truth.

"We have perceptions of Truth according to our enlightenment and consciousness, Truth, to be Truth must be Truth. According to our consciousness and knowing of Truth comes the use of infinite power."

"So can you tell me more about the Truth around death?" I asked and Francis replied.

"What is the natural law regarding death? Of course, it is only the death of the physical that humanity observes, for you cannot die. Eternal youth is the Divine's seed, planted in the cells of every human. Decay is the result of disease. Anger, grief, fear, these are but a few of the emotions which encourage the ageing process, likewise, thoughts of love, joy and peace create youth. The aged body is but a shell, housing the pearl of youth waiting to be given birth.

"You celebrate birthdays as milestones of the ageing process – yes, one can say a celebration of the ageing process – when in reality all is a continuum of conscious existence. Oh, that you celebrate your perfection, this is your fountain of youth! It would serve humanity to focus on this alone, the conscious awareness of continuous unfoldment and growth.

"Consciousness evolves from within and always manifests without, ever supplied by its infinite Source into expression in the finite. The infinite cannot die. Death is the belief that consciousness loses its awareness, and immortality knows that consciousness always has awareness of its body, its own identity, it's knowing and truth. We can take this a step further and say that life is 'knowing' this dominion of immortality.

"One is free to create one's own reality, which manifests in his or her own health, finances, and world in all its aspects.

"*You* have control of your attitude, your thoughts, your mind, your being. Of course, you have free will. Ah, free will —.

"I will give you a practice for when you retire at night. The affirmation 'I am now a body of light and beautiful. I am the Divine child. Every atom, cell and electron radiates light, which now manifests in me perfectly'. Upon awakening say, 'I am in truth the Divine Alchemist, my body is the perfection of Divinity'. Continue with this on a regular basis.

"All have an inner alchemist who during sleep will start transforming those dying cells into the liquid gold of health and inner beauty. Say often 'The Divine alchemist is within me, I am the spirit of youth'. Say often 'May the light of the soul illumine my mind. My mind and my heart are filled with the wisdom of the soul and I am whole and harmonious through and through'.

"We must now continue on with our journey in order to reach our hosts at the appointed time". The bear went on his way and so did we.

We spent most of the day on a path that steered through a thick forest of evergreens curling around the edge of a mountain. There was something intoxicating about the smell wafting from the tall fir and pines, like open perfume bottles stacked on a shelf in a department store, tempting me to inhale deeper.

I noticed at this point a dramatic increase in my energy, and even though we had been trekking many miles now, and the altitude had been increasing quite steadily, I found my stamina mounting to match the challenge. As I walked alongside Raj I commented on the pungent aroma of the trees and also, it would seem, my newfound youth.

He smiled. "Nature loves to harmonise, which is why so many who are pulled down by the everyday stresses of life are drawn to her. They feel peace when walking in her woods and wild places."

I loved the way he put it. I did feel cosseted, even though at times it was terrifying, as my recent encounter testifies.

He went on to explain how the aroma of pine was beneficial for clearing the head and excellent at activating the mind. He further explained how the transference of energy from Francis was supporting me physically and would enable me to participate more fully in all that was to transpire.

I had another question for Raj; if we were already perfect, why would it take time to master perfection? It seemed a contradiction.

He smiled and thought awhile and said, "It is because you do not believe this to be so, you do not accept this to be so, or you would have embodied it. The only limitation is your mind.

"Do you believe your God would lose its essence and force once it manifested as dense matter? You are that essence. Take, for example, an ice cube becoming less dense, turning to water and then to vapour, or vapour to water and then to the ice cube. What was lost? The original essence is still present. The law is – and as you study the law for one portion of nature, you will find the law applies to the whole of the natural world. What you term God, I term the perpetual, as well as the uncreated motion.

"It is the only Deity I can acknowledge at this point in my evolution. Who knows beyond this? Who has experienced beyond this?"

We arrived at an opening in the trees where I stopped and gasped in sheer homage at the vision before me, majestic mounts, the Rockies in full splendour. A breeze pirouetted through the valley below, whipping up snow, dancing and kissing randomly all it came into contact with, resembling an excited lover. I, too, was being enticed by this vision, and I, too, was falling into love.

# Chapter Five

*And if this is a correct view of freedom, our chief energy must be
concentrated on achieving
reform from within.*
Gandhi

A few hours into our journey I found myself thinking
continuously about joy, and every time my mind wandered in
some direction or another, the word 'joy' would drop like rain and
wash over every other thought. This three-letter word was so
persistent it took root and grew into quite the realisation.

For me, and just for me, happiness seemed as if it was an outer
activity, subject to outer conditions, something that I experienced
when I received a kiss or when eating chocolate cake or visiting with
friends. Whereas joy seemed to run along with contentment and
inner peace. Joy was part of my nature, a part of the core of who I am.
It didn't seem to be subject to outside influence but was stimulated
deep inside when in service or when I felt gratitude. It was something
permanent within me, something which, even after going through
life's traumas, I would always seem to come back to; it was part of
who I am, subject to nothing, nothing.

Was joy an attitude? If that were so, then like all other attitudes,
it could be learned and with practice assimilated into my very being.
How powerful this realisation was, and all I had to do was apply
myself. Light bulbs were going on in my head; words and more

words illuminating the many cubbyholes where I had gathered symbols – words I had used all too randomly in the past to communicate with others. No wonder verbal communication could be so difficult at times. In many cases, we use the same words but we colour those words with shades of our own personal histories.

What a door this one word had opened. I soon discovered it had also taken hours off my journey, hours which had passed in what seemed like a second. Later I was informed I'd been introduced to the art of walking meditation, contemplation which obviously did not comply with the laws of time and space. Though I have to say, it didn't seem long before such philosophical thoughts dropped away and my mind wandered over to Raj as I watched him walking ahead of me. With every step I could see the definition of his body and the strength of his form moving effortlessly and with such grace. My thoughts stimulated feelings, seeped with softness for him, that I found hard to control. They also opened the door to another cubby hole of guilt, guilt for something unpermitted.

He stopped, gazed over his shoulder, held my stare and smiled. I caught my breath and stumbled. He didn't rush. While he was making his way to me, I quickly dug into the pockets in my mind to find a word, two words, a sentence, a diversion from the embarrassing situation I had found myself in.

He took my hands, moved in closer and whispered, "I do understand."

Steadying me against a tree, holding me so close I could feel his warm perfumed breath kiss my face. I found my escape.

"Joy," I blurted out. "I kept getting the word joy repeating itself." I blushed and he stepped back slightly, smiling.

"In yoga, cheerfulness is considered one of the austerities; it travels the same path as joy."

I queried his use of words here for I believed austerity was something associated with penance, with flagellation, lying on a bed of nails, something performed as a deluded torture of the mind, body, or senses. But Raj smiled, reminding me of the limitation imposed by words.

"In Raja yoga, 'tapas' and 'austerity' work the same. Tapas is Sanskrit and means 'to be on fire'. In yoga, the austerities include, even mindedness, cheerfulness, gentleness, kindness, self-restraint and sedative communion with the inner self. A person who has tapas has a full spiritual resolve, a passion, generated by the soul on fire, to achieve.

"Cheerfulness," he continued, "may be cultivated with discipline and passion to great advantage and goes hand in hand with joy on any true spiritual path. Some who embark on a path of spirituality believe it necessary to drop their cheerfulness, becoming convinced that solemnity is a prerequisite to holiness, somehow believing a loving God or The Brothers of Light would be flattered by such childish behaviour.

"Joy is an active principle of love, and part of the Great Spirit. Now, speaking of misunderstandings..." He placed his searching eyes upon me.

"There seems to be a misunderstanding around the word love, as if the giving of oneself is indeed synonymous with a lack of spirituality. How far from the truth this is, when to give of oneself selflessly is always in accord with Divinity. Giving selflessly towards any part of life is love in action and when love is in action, the giver undeniably feels joy.

"Far too many misconceptions and judgments are bandied about regarding the giving of oneself. Why, the prostitute is sometimes considered closer to knowing Deity than the long faced religionist!"

He smiled as if recalling something and I was wondering whether he had heard my mental admiration. Oh, I wanted death by avalanche at this point!

"Are you saying we should all go around making love, even to strangers?" I said flippantly.

His face shone with benevolent love and understanding, without a trace of condescension.

He laughed. "That might bring about far better results than one would expect. What do you think would happen if people started to love randomly? I wonder if those who would do harm would have quite a different challenge."

I had some conflict around his reference to the prostitute and the long faced religionist, but he quickly cleared that up for me.

He told me a story about a young woman who fell into a certain way of living, purely to support an invalid family member and her child. The by-product of this selfless service was her ability to grow very fond, and even love, her selected regular clients. The ripple effect of her love towards her clients encouraged them to live better lives.

Another story he shared was of the vicar's daughter, who grew up in a household of little to no love. This father consigned his daughter, along with his parishioners, as being sinful and inferior, for he believed piety and strict rule were the ways to the kingdom. They were clearly deprived of the basic principles taught by the Master Jesus that he so fanatically expounded.

Raj had used the words, misconceptions and judgments and I had fallen into both. He said more light would be shone on the subject later. We then caught up with the rest of the group.

By now, our party had come to a halt at a rock face and I watched Francis raise his hand. What I witnessed was not what I considered within the realm of normal, however, as promised, I observed. The rock face moved and opened up into an entrance of what looked like a cave. When we entered, what I had at first thought was a regular cave, was far from it.

Inside, the glass-like walls automatically raised one's eyes to tall ceilings covered with symbols, among which I could make out the different religions of the world. Though I know little of engineering, to present solid rock as if it were smooth glass on such a vast scale was a feat that would be quite the challenge even today. Once again, the natural glow that had given warmth and light in the first small cabin was present and emanating here.

You know, as babies, we grow in our communities becoming familiar with our surroundings, which for the most part are similar, and we rarely question what we become familiar with. As humans, we often reject what's outside our realm of experience and which isn't shown or explained to our rational mind.

Since embarking on this somewhat strange journey, a change had come about in my thinking process. Just because I wasn't familiar with these extremely different people and recent events, didn't mean they were not valid, as was being proven. No, for me, that way of thinking was no longer viable.

Moving further into the cave, we were greeted and escorted to our quarters by Margaret and Alan, who fascinated me. Although they had travelled a little ahead of our party and I hadn't had an opportunity to make much contact with them, they stood out in the group. I asked Raj what the itch was that I couldn't scratch regarding them. He was quite secretive but said all would be revealed very shortly.

We were asked to meet for supper in a large room off the main entrance, and with my few belongings deposited in my quarters, I made my way to the meeting place. 'Out of the world' experiences require 'out of the world' words, and no matter how much I use the inadequate symbols we call words, they will be insufficient in communicating all I found myself witnessing.

In the centre of the room around a large table were a number of high-back chairs covered in violet velvet. Many of our party had already taken up seats, so I quickly took mine next to Raj, and waited.

The light in the room intensified greatly as we sat in silence. Two figures, one Francis, and the other, a tall man with shoulder length hair and eyes as blue as Francis' were violet, stepped forward (from where I have no idea) and the light softened. I had come to accept my hosts as Adepts of an unusual kind, and if you, the reader, can appreciate this, you will be patient with my references. The tall man spoke.

"Love is the most glorious attribute of Logos. Inside all is the tree of life and the richest fruit on that tree is love. When fully ripened it will heal all of life's ills, every disease, every sorrow, every condition that renders harshness and pain, every perceived lack. It replaces all these with the gentle mantle of the Father-Mother's caress of perfection. It is the law.

"Like the wings of an angel, it reaches out with amplified joy to all who yearn, all who call, all who desire to be enveloped in the balm of Gilead. Come to me as little children with a truly open heart." He held his arms out to us.

"All here have been touched by this angel of love, whose outstretched wings reach hidden places, corners not seen. Love heals all, gives all, and is the cohesive power of Divinity.

"The love of the Absolute is beyond comprehension; it is ever accumulating unto itself and ever reaching out. It is endless, omnipotent, omniscient and omnipresent – this is a Divine Trinity of God's love. Love has a constant desire to search for inlets where it can heal the wounds of humanity. It is constantly bringing together people, communities, nations, and unites a fragmented planet.

"The Divine is in sheer joy when the individual soul returns home on wings of love, the return of the prodigal son. The tree of life within you holds the key to unlock the door to the treasure chamber of your heart, where love sits waiting to burst forth and proclaim your true freedom, where perfection is celebrated for the truth it is. All humanity will awake – they will awake.

"This journey offers you Divine opportunity to experience many things first hand, the limitless, the truth, the law, and for this I am ever thankful and in the service of my Brother here, who came forward on your behalf to request such a journey for you."

At this point, we were asked to give thanks for the food set before us, for the life giving fruit of love, and for the fact that this same opportunity, given to us, was open to all humanity. I looked at the table which had been filled to the full with fruit and nuts. In the hands of the Master was a loaf of bread. He blessed the bread and shared it among us saying, "Eat with me." And we ate.

"Ever reach out to the Divine, calling for the love of the soul to control your lower nature and guide you in the way of love," He continued.

"Approach the Divine with bold affirmation, secure in the result. Has it not been said many times, before they call, I will answer and while they are yet speaking, I will hear? Do not grovel, yet have faith that it is already granted unto you, for faith really does move mountains, as you have witnessed."

This made me think, among other things, back to the entrance of the cave when Francis placed his hand upon the rock and the mountain moved. He continued His address, much of which was for those attending, and with every word imprinting on my heart, never to be lost.

Then He said He would leave us to our feast and His parting words were, "I am always closer than your breath, and in faith on my word that it is so, would be the measure of seeing me and the fruits thereof." The light shone bright and he departed the same way he arrived.

We all sat silent for some time, basking in the warm afterglow permeating the room. I had been dipped into the heart of love, filled to overflowing with peace, and then wrapped in the blanket of wisdom. I knew I had been in the Presence of a Soul who had attained the pure consciousness of the Christ, and the word gratitude is too small a symbol to convey to you what I was feeling. After some time of silence, Raj gently touched my arm and without a word spoken, we all slowly made our way from the room to our own private quarters.

At sunrise the next morning, we gathered in the main hall, there were about thirty of us now. The majority were, like myself, ready to embark on the next leg of our journey; we had been together the previous night and shared a common bond of quietness.

As usual, our supplies were loaded on horses and we made our way out of the cave. Three hours or so into our journey, we arrived at a riverbank where evidence of a forest fire was still visible. Though on the far embankment the flames seemed to have died down, red-hot embers were still mapping the forest floor, making it impossible to carry on any further. Forest fires are not unusual in the large forest areas of North America, but the world I was now in was a world of unusual occurrences, and so this usual occurrence seemed quite unusual and it jarred me.

Francis suggested we make a temporary camp for lunch and told us that a party, headed by himself, would be crossing. He extended the offer for us to join them if we wished. He also said there was a bridge, two hours along the path we were following, which would lead us safely to our meeting point, where He would be waiting if we chose that route. The water was shallow and could be crossed with no difficulty at all, but once on the other side the risk of burning oneself, or of clothing catching fire, not to mention ground not touched by the fire, which could ignite at any time, was high. Now I found myself in an unusual situation, which was running more true to form and I was just a little fearful.

Six people, including Francis, approached the trees by the riverbank and crossed the river and then proceeded to make their way along the red, forest floor. They continued walking steadily, ignoring any sudden flairs, eventually disappearing into the trees. I was beginning to love episodes like this, for I was really starting, and I only say starting, to accept these seemingly impossible feats. Raj moved to my side.

"This is not a miracle, it is natural law in operation, however, I warn against attempting such feats until ready. Only self-imposed limitation holds a soul bound, and the lower mind controls with fear, establishing limitation in one's thinking.

"Those who have crossed the river into the forest beyond are no different from you, nor do they possess superhuman powers. No human is given more power than another. They have attained the use of power with right thought. Everyone can achieve all you have witnessed. Many have demonstrated this to humanity. All is within, and man's consciousness is the key, remember – you are free or bound by what you think."

I said I would like to cross but I doubted I could: part of my mind trusted, while another part was just as certain I would be courting disaster and I would burn my feet. Raj said he would be happy to accompany me if I decided to go the river way, and also would join me happily if I decided to take the alternate route to the bridge.

I watched as another group, headed by Margaret and Alan, waded across and stepped onto the embers, and then I took Raj's hand tightly. "I want to walk over too." I wanted to tell him I trusted him deep in my being, but I just held onto him, feeling nothing could possibly go wrong as we waded across.

Before stepping out of the water Raj stopped; he looked deep into my eyes and said one word. "Trust." I took my first step out of the water onto land, holding the hand of the man I loved, and we carried on walking 'til we met up with the others. I can't tell you the distance nor can I recall the intensity of the fire, for my focus was on Raj and the love I was now feeling.

I do know that I suffered nothing, no burns, no spontaneous combustion (I'm laughing as I write this) and my feeling of elation upon achieving this was way up in the skies. I also knew I never wanted to be apart from this man again. Whatever it would take to be with him, I would do.

# Chapter Six

*When man is serene, the pulse of the heart flows and connects, just as pearls are joined together or like a string of red jade, then one can talk about a healthy heart.*
The Yellow Emperor's Canon of Internal Medicine.

It was the noisiest time of our journey as a cacophony of voices vied for attention, each one getting louder as the excitement built. Eventually, as we all settled down, everyone gave his or her own special account of what happened regarding the forest fire. Although we had all witnessed the same event, our experiences were vastly different.

It was plain and clear that what had happened had nothing to do with the miracle syndrome, but everything to do with natural law - nature. Certainly I was the same person I was at the start of all this. I wasn't an instant adept or enlightened being. I hadn't displayed any tendencies towards walking on water lately, but by God, I'd walked over and through fire.

I knew it was I who made the decision to go across the river, and I who acted upon that decision, and I'm pleased to say it was I who stepped through fear into love. Yes, it was me who had just accepted the 'present'. After exhausting our stories, we continued hiking through the trees, up a steady incline, with most of us settling into quiet satisfaction, which I believed came from achieving something beyond our norm.

As the sun sat low on the horizon, we came to a clearing and stopped for a rest break. The surrounding peaks offered a womb fertile with a variety of trees and wild flowers nestling down to the centre. Filtering through this picture, smoke from tepees and other make-do camps wafted up in curls, and the aroma was intoxicating.

We started our slow descent, following a narrow path between some rocks, until we finally approached the outside edge of a meadow full of people. Making our way through well over a hundred of them, busying with fires and cooking, I was distracted by a sudden elevation of high- pitched voices. It was the children who first spotted Him, and screaming like banshees, waving arms, they rushed Him. Francis crouched low and within seconds disappeared under a full playground of eager children, climbing, jumping and swinging. He greeted them all, and it was obvious He was a child at heart.

At the far side of the dell, elevated slightly and carved into the face of the mountain, stood a three-story building whose imposing facade would actually have been easy to miss; so well camouflaged it's design mimicked the texture, colour, and curve of nature herself. Do you remember those optical illusion pictures of the sixties? The ones where you would see an image and then, with a shift of perspective, you could see a totally different image? That is what it was like looking at this landscape.

Francis turned to the crowd and there was silence. "Atma is, be content. May you act as a soul in all your ways."

We followed Francis into the stone building and met up with the rest of our party. After refreshments, we were shown to our quarters, where I flopped on the bed in clouds of contentment and slept for what seemed like days.

It was nearing evening when I rose and went outside to watch the sun finally disappear. As always, I wanted to familiarise myself with my surroundings, and as before, I discovered most of our party shared the same thought. Sitting quietly on a rock, I viewed the stars, which were just starting to appear, each one seemingly trying to outshine the others.

Whilst talking with us earlier that day, Francis had made a suggestion to practise the discipline at night of placing our attention on one star at a time, and every time our mind wandered, to bring ourselves back to that one star. I now sat and tried focusing on one star at a time, it was really difficult: my mind wandered to other stars, my mind wandered to other thoughts.

Francis said stars were like our thoughts, clamouring for centre stage, each one vying for attention. He said the act of focusing on one thought at a time cultivated a certain method of concentration, eventually leading to abstract thinking and connection to the soul, something the soul desired.

Most of us go about our daily lives focusing on something or someone, or focusing on an event which has just happened or is about to happen and we miss the gift of the present. If we invest enough emotion, which is energy in motion, we create a reality, which then brings the person, place, condition, or thing, into our experience.

If the thought is spiritually aspiring, we are uplifted, and if the thought is destructive, it will bring to our doorstep a corresponding effect. Both these reactions serve us. One gives us feedback we'll wish to recreate, and the other gives us feedback which will take us to different choices, if we're wise.

The following day after breakfast, we grouped outside and Raj suggested we mingle with the crowds. Walking past a small group of Indigenous people, I stopped to share some herbal tea with a woman from the Sioux Nation who was sitting quietly alone.

It was her first visit, and though there had been other gatherings previously, she had not been able to travel as the route was difficult and her sight was poor. It was her persistent faith which prompted her brother, who was not a believer in anything other than eat, work, sleep, to take the trek with her, so she could have the chance to receive what she believed would heal the blindness she had experienced since birth.

Some of these people had travelled great distances, with much hardship, so great was their faith. I reflected back on my world. How caught up we could get seeking doctors and healers and all manner of methods, all in an attempt to get well. I accept the great service the medical profession renders, but we put far too much emphasis on relegating our own personal responsibility, not looking to the cause of our effects, not looking to our own thoughts, words, and deeds.

At this point, I wasn't sure of much, accepting far more than I would've thought, and shelving new concepts and beliefs continuously.

Having drunk our tea and spent some pleasant time together, I said goodbye to my new friend. I continued walking, meeting up with a group who were making their way over to a stream, running to the far north of another large meadow. I followed the stream until I came to a huge waterfall, where crowds were gathering around a man standing in an effervescent pool.

"Celebrate your Christ-mass as your birth into truth," He said. "Let not your mind rest on the illusions creating disease, but let your soul illumine your mind and shine a light upon the way of others. You dip yourselves into these waters as a symbolic gesture of your dipping into the Universal Soul, and I ask you to continue to hold this immaculate concept for all, just as I hold the immaculate concept for each of you here.

"Hold in your hearts and repeat often, I am the resurrection and the life of every atom, cell, and electron of my physical body, my entire consciousness, being and world."

I saw bodies straighten, sight restored, sores vanish, and a man sitting sobbing. As I walked past him he tugged at my sleeve, he wanted to share his story with me. Through his sobs he spoke of his heart condition, saying his heart, his hard heart, was healed and he was free. He hung onto me still sobbing, uttering his gratitude, touching my heart profoundly. How interesting that he chose me to share with – I had been dealing with a heart condition before starting this journey.

He shared how for years his near blind sister had begged him to bring her here, and now he realised it was he who had needed the healing. I sat and watched as many filed by, feeling I must have entered a portal to a past time, a time of long ago, and I thought of the Master Jesus.

Raj was in the distance talking with a group of people, so I made my way over. Boy, I needed to understand some things, but for now, I wanted to know why this was hidden from so many. As I approached, not turning, he held out his hand to me and continued talking, and I sat.

"It is man's choosing whether he is to be, or not to be. Some, gathered here, who experience physical healing, will once again return to their old ways: ways of criticism, condemnation and judgement or other activities that do not serve. Once again, they will reap the results of their creation, manifesting disease.

"There will also be those who will rise above their past by staying in the truth they have experienced, and making the consciousness they have found, the first, the last, and their only thought. But this takes effort, this takes persistence, this takes a commitment to the way." He tightened his hold on my hand.

"The physical healings you are witnessing here draw your attention to the physical, but it is the inner which will sustain the perfection you desire to permanently experience, it is the inner which will manifest the result accordingly for each individual." Raj turned slightly to look at me.

"The man you see, whose heart is now free, has had a burden of many lifetimes lifted, and this in the blink of an eye. But it is the inner vision he now has, his enlightenment, which will sustain him like a staff on his journey, and I doubt he will choose to return to his former state. His physical pain was the outer manifestation of erroneous thinking, and now, anything less than perfection will fade in the light of the truth of who he truly is. Man, know thyself!"

After sitting awhile, I realised the healing I desired had nothing to do with any of my physical challenges. The problem was the separation my lower mind had bought into, and this big monster sat like a troll on the crossroads of my path. At this point, we regrouped with others from our party and continued our wanderings.

The day was filled with wonders: people, stories, their laughter, their generosity and their devotion. It was as if I had landed in what was a true revival church of the Divine, with praise echoing out of the mountain bowl like a volcano of love erupting over all.

# Chapter Seven

*The word of the Lord came to me, saying, "Before I formed you in the womb I knew you; and before you were born I set you apart." Jeremiah 1:4-6*

After supper, Raj and I wandered outside where fires crackled, carrying smoke signals towards heaven. As we wandered, I wondered. In the city, on those quiet nights at the end of a busy day, those nights when you're driving home and you look out towards the mountains in the distance, those nights when you feel there's a special something emanating from those silently standing silhouettes, was that moment of sensitivity providing a brief connection to these Adepts?

As we strolled, Raj reunited with old friends and welcomed new ones. Like all good parties, everything came to an end and people had started to look to their beds. Time was now being relegated into a reality where dreams ignored its presence, and tranquillity enveloped all life. Raj steered me to a clearing just as a figure emerged from the lodge, and mingling with those still lingering around their warm fires, the figure conversed with them like all were old friends.

By now, the seemingly abnormal was becoming quite normal. What I would've labelled in the past as the stuff of fairy stories was now becoming part of my everyday experience. My meeting with Advanced Souls was becoming more casual. My abilities to overcome things that a short time ago had seemed impossible, were now starting to feel possible. Don't get me wrong, it was far from casual, but I am trying to make a point here about the change I was experiencing. In truth, something had changed, and what was the change?

One answer to this question became very clear; it was simply a change of mind. I was now experiencing a world totally alien, yet, just as real, because I had changed my mind. If only I could apply this simple action of changing my mind to other things in life, how much easier it would be.

After making his slow, halting way through the camp, the figure finally sat on the last step outside the retreat and we gathered, like children eager to hear a goodnight story. This was the same person who had addressed us on 'love' at our last resting place.

"I say to you, take no thought of your life. What you shall eat, nor for how you will clothe your body. Life is more than meat and the body, more than raiment. Consider the ravens, they neither sow nor reap and have no storehouse or barn: and the Great Spirit feeds them, how much more are you?"

The words he spoke were familiar, where had I heard them before? My thoughts jumped from one place to another; in fact, I started to see sheep jumping over the gate and dozed a little. By the time I drifted back, most of what he'd said had been lost to me.

"But rather seek ye the kingdom of the Divine; and realise all things shall be added unto you. Fear not little flock, for it is your Father's good pleasure to give you the kingdom."

I remembered some of these words from my infant school and knew that I had serious questions regarding becoming 'as a raven' and not worrying about what I shall eat or put on my body, but true to form, before I could say anything, Raj answered.

"The Teacher addresses supply, and you are thinking of the results of supply. Let us look at an apple tree full of fruit. When the fruit is all eaten, the apples will grow again. Neither the apples nor the tree are the supply. Humanity concerns itself with the fruits, when it could step out of all limitation by connecting with the supply.

"Your supply always comes from the Universal Force, which is the only Force in the Universe. All your needs are met, always, and in all-ways, and at times not in the ways you would want or expect. When your consciousness is one with the true Self, you will know full abundance.

"There is no need to concern yourself with money or outer things, your thoughts turned inward to your true Self will manifest accordingly. By contemplating the analogy of the apple tree, one may connect directly with the soul. Please think on this when sitting quietly.``

I had experienced intermittent moments with Source via meditation, but was I there yet? Ha! I didn't think so. Raj had explained on one occasion how meditation on a seed thought spawns connection with the soul, and he further explained how it was this connection, which was the very thing I had been looking for in this life. He had also directed me to the work of The Mahatmas, the teachers of H.P. Blavatsky for more understanding of the seed thought process, and to the Ancient Wisdom writings for my further studies.

The Teacher viewed the crowd and I was wondering what was going to happen next when two women with two small bowls came forward. In one was bannock bread and in the other was a thick vegetable stew. He gave thanks then asked for the food to be distributed to all present.

I would like to say here, the bowls held enough for possibly six people at a push, however, all of us received food and had our fill. This reminded me of when I was in India some ten years previously and I ended up at the retreat of a local guru. What I witnessed was the same occurrence but on a much larger scale, and I wondered whether these events were more common than I thought.

After eating, the two of us made our way back to the retreat where we joined about thirty others in a simply furnished room. Chairs had been placed in a semi-circle and we sat, quite content to be listening to gentle music echoing from the distance. Each cadence gently and expertly stroked my heart 'til it was confident enough to break open with a mixture of emotions, none of which I could contain – nor wanted to, but which left me sobbing in sheer humility. I was feeling an intense reverence for the greatness of the One Infinite, Divine Life.

I sat contemplating how life would never be the same again once I returned home. I also knew many other people, like myself, were going to feel the 'call of the Rockies', which in reality would be the call of the Masters.

A group of people, including Nada and Thomas, entered the room and the music, which had been lulling us in the background, rose into a crescendo, it was as though thousands were gathering on unseen levels. Then, as the music melted away into oh so gentle, random notes, Francis entered the room.

Though it may be a challenge for the reader to accept exactly what I'm going to say next, I'd be doing a disservice if I didn't mention it. I could 'feel' and 'hear' colours coming from Francis, and also 'see' these colours as they emanated around the room, toning into a seamless serenade. When the music and colour ebbed, Francis spoke.

"We are grateful to be joined by some, who, out of great mercy, act as mediators between the perfection of the law and the imperfection created by humans. Step into your higher mind and dwell permanently in the mind of the soul. Step into harmony and peace, ever be in the service of all."

We stood silently as an organ played Cavellera Rusticana. I saw Margaret and Alan standing in a beautiful, mellow glow. Then Margaret spoke.

"Humanity, extend your vision. There is a higher life for you outside the Maya of your repetitive experiences. What is it that prevents you from receiving a greater truth than you now have? It is your brain-mind. What is it that prevents the steady stream of wisdom and intuition from continually flowing into your being? It is your brain-mind. And this mind, with its preconceptions, prejudices and all manner of feelings against this and against that, is a muddy filter that keeps out higher thoughts and higher intuitions.

"Is it any wonder that humanity receives only a glimpse of the mind of the Great One? The lower mind, with its silly thoughts and its trivial trappings, prevents the higher aspirations from entering in, for the two cannot reside in the same place.

"Empty the mind of all its small stuff so the spirit of truth and wisdom may enter in. Empty the mind of all its addictive patterns and passions and the spirit of truth will enter in.

"We who reside in the higher mind hold the immaculate concept for all, and desire to be one with the mind of all humanity, however, humanity needs to raise its game, so to speak.

"We are in service to the Presence within each one of you, and grateful to those who give constant service by directing light upon the true way, who stand ever ready to assist the sincere seeker.

"Be of service to all souls out of love, where love feels trodden, love anyway, where you are trodden, serve anyway. Love purely for the sake of love and love will sustain you always. This is the truth." Then Alan spoke.

"These things you have witnessed, will be experienced by all as they awaken to the truth of their being. I am the light of the world and I am in you and you in me. Step out of your caves and place the crown upon your own heads.

"Go forth *this moment* as the Christ, behave each moment as the Christ and all your moments will be created Divinely. I challenge you to hold this right action for 24 hours and see the wondrous results."

We sat in silence for some time as the Adepts departed, among them, Margaret and Alan: none of us wanting to leave, none of us wishing to let go.

# Chapter Eight

*Men are not moved by things, but by the views they take of them.*
*All is change; all yields its place and goes.* Epictetus

The event I just witnessed was both poignant and spectacular, and for the first time in a long time, there were no thoughts or questions hurrying around in my head, no place I wanted to be, no one I wanted to see. A cocoon of peace had been spun around us and I was immersed in my personal chrysalis of Deity.

It was the veranda by my room I retreated to. The sun slowly dropped on the horizon, the last remnants of campfires dissipated to smells, and the sounds of the night still echoed, mellowing, as of a soft breeze. Deity had donned the nightgown of nature, and I retired, in mine, to bed.

After breakfast, Francis, Raj and six others of our group started a day's hike to meet up with an elder from a local Native tribe. I was in delightful anticipation as we left the valley and hiked for about an hour into the next dell. We came across an old man sitting quietly in meditation, and in the distance red flames from an extremely active campfire spat sparks into the air. Following the lead of my fellow companions, I sat quietly observing the motionless figure until he opened his eyes and beamed at each one of us individually, then he started laughing.

His amusement escalated into a belly laugh causing his body to rock backwards and forward and I had no idea what was going on.

Francis and Raj started to break a smile and before long we were all caught up with the infection, and it didn't stop there. He rolled over onto the dirt holding his stomach, flaying his arms, and gasping for breath, leaving us to look on laughing through our tears.

Tin cups and a pot sat nearby and he picked himself up, poured cold tea, then handed each of us a container. In between giggles and a little composure, we drank. This old man, who Raj said was a holy man, shared some of the old ways, stories handed down from one generation to another, and every now and then he would stop, and just laugh.

He told us of people living so deep in the mountains they had little knowledge of our 'so called modern civilization' still living the old ways even today.

"The ancestors were conscious of the Great Spirit; they lived in harmony with nature, aware of their connection and inheritance," he said, and then he laughed again for a while.

Continuing on, he spoke about us being part of each other's completeness whether we were aware of it or not, and that it was our responsibility to search for truth and live it.

"Ignorance," he continued, "does not change one iota of the law." Pointing to the surrounding tall peaks, he added that we might see the mountains as separating us, yet they link us, for there is only one sky, one earth, and one stream.

"Some may believe they are separate from the Great Spirit, yet where I stand is holy and where you stand is holy, and Deity is in its holy temple: one body, one life, many manifestations. We just need to adjust the lens we are looking and living through," he smiled.

He arose and giving a good belly laugh said it was time for a sweat so we followed him to a dome shaped frame constructed of thick twigs. I remembered the beginning of my journey – with the sweat lodge and coyote, and a question rose. Who was the coyote, the trickster who had played with me? The holy man turned quickly and smiled at me.

Some of our group gathered up thick, heavy rugs and blankets, and as instructed, placed them over the frame of the lodge, while I, along with others, placed large stones into the red-hot fire seen upon our arrival. Then the old man took my arm and led me through the trees to a large pole.

Handing me a wad of tobacco, he pointed to the pole, all the time speaking undecipherable words and poking my arm as if he wanted me to understand something I didn't. Grabbing my shoulders, he turned me to face the north, east, south and west, pushing my arm directly to the sky and then pulling it down to the earth. Then he shouted more undecipherable words as he motioned me to place the tobacco at the foot of the pole.

I had no idea what he was saying or doing, but later Raj explained we were giving an offering to the Great Spirit, to the four directions, to the Great Father in the sky and to our Mother Earth here below. He gave me a cloth, miming to me to wrap it around my body, and then he returned to join the others. With absolutely no idea what was going on, I took my clothes off, wrapped myself in the cloth provided, and returned to the sweat area.

If it was cold I didn't notice, but I did notice my friends, minus Francis and Raj, were also wrapped in large pieces of brightly coloured cloth. The last of the hot rocks had been taken from the blazing fire and placed in the carpeted dome.

We all filed in from the left side and squatted on the ground. It was hot, very hot, I mean extremely hot, and I was pleased I had enough of the wrap to place over my head and arms as I settled into a comfortable position. Then the carpet at the entrance was lowered sealing us all in.

The holy man began chanting and the space grew hotter, hotter, and yes, even hotter. I thought about my situation. Here I was, squashed in this tent with eight other people, wearing only a cloth, in heat not even a roasting chicken would be expected to sit in whilst alive.

Clearly, the law of attraction was showing me something, for I had gone from one extreme to another. Death by freezing to death by roasting, what was it in my life that always seemed to scream for extremes?

Rocking seemed to help at first, and then I heard quiet, almost controlled, hysterical laughter, and it was coming from me. Other than the fact I had entered with others and could feel their bodies close to mine, I was aware of nothing but intense heat. I couldn't see a thing, let alone an escape route.

By now I was reaching for anything I could grab to draw over my exposed flesh in an attempt to protect it. I didn't care a hoot whether I was exposing another person to death by roasting. I really tried to bear the searing discomfort, but in truth, I was at the point of clawing my way through anything or anyone just to get out. I was now in fight or flight mode. Gratefully I heard Francis in my head. "You are not your body, focus on your breath not your discomfort."

Discomfort was hardly what it felt like, and I was ready to rip His face off, Teacher or no Teacher. But I did start counting through my teeth, one, two, three, four, five, six and So- Hum, So-Hum, So-Hum...then I was gone.

Everything swam, the chanting, the smells, the people, the lodge, my thoughts, even the heat. Suddenly I had a vision, followed by three more and all the while I was totally unaware of my discomfort in the sweat.

The next thing I was aware of was the carpet at the entrance being lifted, and we exited into the cool, fresh, open air. I looked up at the clear blue sky and watched eight golden eagles circling, one for each of us.

We all made our way back to the old man, who was sitting where we had first met him. I knew I had experienced these visions for a reason, I also knew I would be given the answers in due course.

We sat and listened to the holy man telling us how the sweat lodge was for healing, for clearing points in time and space. He peered into the distance, then looked at each one of us, explaining how important it was to spend the time contemplating our individual visions, then he started laughing. Like before, he laughed so loud and hard we couldn't help but do the same. I felt freer.

The old man explained how laughter was an invaluable healing agent having the power to break down negative energy. Negativity has no power other than the power we give it and laughter shatters any hold it may have.

I wondered why sometimes, when going through intense pain, either emotionally, mentally or physically, I have a tendency to laugh hysterically. Perhaps it is the psyche's way of keeping me healthy. We said our goodbyes and left our happy host.

# Chapter Nine

*Are you willing to be sponged out, erased, cancelled, made nothing?*
*Are you willing to be made nothing? Dipped into oblivion? If not, you*
*will never really change.* D. H. Lawrence.

My mind played over the four visions I had experienced, and all that had happened in the sweat lodge itself. What the old man had said regarding living as one, our perceptions of separation and fear, had hit me deep. My choices in life had created my life so far, and things were now going to change, it was time to knuckle down and apply myself.

It would seem my choices were simple: was I thinking of myself or thinking of the whole, choosing fear or choosing to act out of love, whether to die by heat or freeze to death in the cold (only joking). It is difficult to put everything into practice all the time, every day, but I had the determination now to work at it.

Being more conscious of my decisions demanded diligence. Many are the opportunities we miss, opportunities to choose unity instead of separation, to choose love instead of selfishness. Shining more light upon this would take me to a practice of cultivating this mindset and creating a new habit.

Of course I had certain concepts the wrong way around. My thoughts had been, 'if I become an Adept I could serve humanity better'. Now I realised that serving humanity first would lead to becoming an Adept. Of course serving humanity would be serving myself as we are truly all one. Is that selfish?

I read once that the space between one person and another is not really as we perceive, and that this space is almost all of everything there is. Compared to the volume of space all around, our physical forms are quite insignificant and the largest physical structure we know of is minuscule. I also read that if we took all the space away from within our forms, all the people on this planet could be encapsulated into one sugar cube.

If we are 99.9999999% space and we add that to all this space between us, we are joined at the hip by this very real subatomic world, and all that is not this space is but a speck. We are one. This subatomic world is alive and moving with thought, imagination, and information. Space is mind.

Now, even my mind can comprehend that where there is mind there is consciousness, and if there is consciousness, there is Universal Spirit. We are not separate, even if we buy into the illusion.

You, who are reading this book, are joined to me by this space, actually this space is a big part of us, the largest, most voluminous substance in the Universe, and if I affect that space, the effect will impact you, and vice versa.

How insular our lives can be, and it really doesn't serve us or anyone. We can be so unconscious to the affect we have on life next to us and totally unconscious to someone living in another part of the world.

Yet every breath taken on this planet impacts life, and with enough breaths in concert, breathing in unison, we can cause a wind of change that can affect many. Just think of all the possibilities to change the world now.

I reflected upon my journey and how being around these people, being closely influenced and interacting with them on a daily basis, had affected me and would go on to affect others. Was it any wonder I was feeling so good and achieving so much?

Through them I was experiencing oneness; I was becoming like them, though not to the same extent, yet. How important it is to be mind-full of choosing our influences with wisdom, and to share our minds with love, for as we give to others we truly do give to ourselves.

Back at base new guests had arrived, all wanting answers to their many questions. All I wanted was to retire to my reclusive balcony to think, so after supper I asked to take my leave.

Those solid mountains before me were not solid at all; they were space and a corpus of particles, resonating and moving together, constantly vibrating within a certain frequency of sound and colour, and oh what a sight, what insight. The purples in the sky swirled into candy floss, patches of white and silver clouds clung to the sides of silhouetted peaks, and all dipping into what may well have been the Great Spirit's own heart.

I closed my eyes and relived the visions I had been given in the sweat lodge, searching for more answers. I could hear Francis's voice in my head, "Stand back and detach yourself." I did so, and reviewed them once again like watching a movie. I opened my eyes and there Francis was. He smiled and we sat together.

During our travels, it became very apparent that these highly evolved souls were not devoid of humour; in fact, we witnessed many hilarious situations invoked by them that were funnier to me than a sitcom. I may well put forward these stories in another book.

Francis and I went over each vision, four past-life embodiments with the common denominator being Raj. Francis assisted me with seeing some of the reasons for my physical challenges in this life, and also some of the spiritual illusions I had immersed myself in.

Raj and I had experienced many lives together, but these four were highlighted. He had been a sun dancer, a Cathar priest, a sea admiral, and a servant to the ruler of a great civilization of a former root race. Sometime in the future, we would work together, I knew this, but there was a lot more evolving to do on my part, and how long would it take? Well, as I was learning, that was up to me.

Looking out over the mountains, I thought of the heart incident I had recently experienced and how perfectly I had created it along with other challenges. We are the result of all our thoughts, emotions, and actions, and also the result of the use or non-use of our will. What we think, feel, and do, moulds our character, a character that invokes misfortune or great joy depending on our standpoint, for we can only grow from the point we have already arrived at. We grow by changing certain parts of our nature to aspects that serve us better.

We must meet head on the energies we've already generated, we can't avoid them, even by death or suicide, and by meeting life with courage and the knowing that we have a new armour forged in truth we can create a new starting point.

Our nature is what we are born with, attitude is how we use what we're born with, and character is the sum of all our standards. We evolve our nature by applying the right attitude, and contrary to what has been told, our nature cannot be wiped aside by some saviour dying on a cross. Death by crucifixion cannot wipe out part of our nature, but that crucifixion can awaken in us a warrior, a warrior willing to embark on a journey towards that goal which is part of our true being.

As we modify our lives through our will, constructive forces soon overtake the old ways, and our lives become, regardless of outside appearances, lives on the path of peace and love.

It was Universal Law, Karma, which was affording me the opportunity to evolve. How wise it had been at drawing out my true nature. Now the real me was being well and truly aroused, and I was consciously coming to grips with and cooperating with nature. I realised this one step of cooperating with my returning energies,

Karma, was accelerating me along the evolutionary path as it does with all those who do the same. This conscious effort is well rewarded, my past was giving me greater opportunities, and all I needed to do was not shrink away.

Oh, how one can get so caught up with thoughts of Karma that it can feel like punishment. Francis said we re-embody with no memory, or at least little, so the soul may live a fresh round. The key is to take each moment as it comes by living in the now, constantly applying the attitude of love and service, which in turn creates another new moment. Let go of any thoughts of Karma; see each moment as a new opportunity for you to make a conscious decision for good. Love is God's will, God's will is goodwill, and goodwill is love in action. Francis entered my thoughts.

"The key is self-evolution. By taking personal responsibility for all our thoughts, words and deeds, knowing we create our own reality and thereby our world, and that no one else is responsible, we connect with the higher mind, and the higher mind is where we tap into our Souls' perfection. Thought itself is limited by the concept it is sent forth to embody. Truth is not a conception one cannot conceive the whole truth in a conception. We know that truth is, not what it is. The mind of humans is the vehicle by which the mind of Deity reveals itself.

"No matter how great a concept the mind has, it is limited, as it is only a concept, not all that 'IS'. All will be given unto man according to his knowing of the truth. Meditate on the question 'Who am I,' for this is a powerful tool for you to achieve further understanding on truth.

He departed the same way He came, leaving me with a myriad of incredible thoughts. If someone had told me these things some months earlier, or I had seen someone appear and disappear as Francis did, I would've booked myself into the nearest hospital. Now it all seemed so natural: but there again, it's supposed to be, yes?

# Chapter Ten

*What you see and hear depends a good deal on where you are
standing; it also depends on what sort of person you are.*
C. S. Lewis.

The next morning, a small group of people, including myself, were invited to go on the long hike into the Teton Range of Mountains. Like a vampire of the light, drawing on whatever was handed to me, I was going to take any and every opportunity presented to experience what I could. Who knew when this journey would end, so my attitude was to bring it all on. If I were honest, the only reason I would want to return to my former life would be for my family, as this life with my newfound friends was one of excitement, growth, laughter, joy and sheer bloody marvel.

Those who have experienced near-death can more than likely relate. Though they find themselves bathed in light and free from the bonds and limitations of the world, it's the world which holds their chosen loved ones that draws them back.

At 10:00 am we met outside. The supplies were loaded onto horses and Raj, Nada, Thomas and I, along with eleven others who were not familiar to me, gathered for the onset of our mammoth trek.

There were no illusions regarding the next leg of the journey, I was well aware it was going to be a long one. I laugh as I write this, because my past has been filled with illusions and, of course, my future will present yet more. We covered a great distance in record time, far more and much faster than I thought possible. Of course, all this was due to the abilities of the Adepts who were with us. I don't know how they did it, but I know they did.

My beliefs pertaining to time and distance had been challenged in this last while, with Francis appearing and disappearing, along with mountain treks seemingly far less difficult than they actually were. I was processing and accepting far more and shelving less. How things had changed since we set forth from the steps of our first cabin, at the beginning of our journey.

For sure I was keyed up and filled with excitement at the prospect of what was to come, until I looked up at one of the few peaks I'd been informed we'd be travelling over. The vision in front of me was alarming. Terrified of heights, the elevation of these high peaks made me realise the challenge was not one I was up for. No. Going around nicely was OK, traversing them was not. It was time to go home.

Now, reader, you'll have questions here. In the past I had mostly decided to push through fear. It had been the anticipation of something fearful that had kept me paralyzed or stifled my growth, and I had seen through this. Rarely did the perceived threat really happen. This feedback had given me courage, 'til now.

This was totally different. Even my mother, who didn't share my beliefs would say, "I believe she must have fallen off a mountain in a past life, she is so unbelievably insane when it comes to heights."

The thing was, I was terrified of heights, and I had done everything in my past to avoid ever having to confront this terror, everything, and I was not going to stop now. I had comfort in knowing our guides knew every part of these mountains, and they had proven time and time again that they had the superior abilities to achieve what we set out to do without ever compromising our safety, but it didn't matter. The simple truth was, I wanted to go home.

# TWO DINGBATS ON A SPIRITUAL QUEST

Just ahead, Raj was chatting with a group of people who had joined our party at the last stop, and so maybe I could distract him and convince him to take a different route with me or guide me home.

As I hadn't discussed with him any of the past life visions I had experienced at the sweat lodge, I decided to grab an opportunity to get him alone, to share. He looked so beautiful, and walking toward him my mind imagined the "what if's." What if he wasn't a sage? He stopped conversing with the group, turned, and stared as he made his way toward me.

I didn't know whether I would ever get used to looking into his eyes without feeling like a limp lettuce leaf, but I did hope I'd have a lifetime to try.

He placed his hand on mine and gently said, "I know, we will talk later, but for the present it would be good for you to focus on counting your breath. We will be stopping just a little further up the trail, and that would be a good time to talk." I took his advice and started counting, one...two...three, until we came to a ridge which skirted around the side of a mountain and we stopped.

There was room for one person at a time on this pass, so, in turn, each of our party carefully placed their body flat to the rock wall, and stepping sideways, manoeuvred carefully until they reached safety. Then it was my turn. All was fine, and counting my steps now, I began sidestepping around the ridge until I reached a very small crevice. Knowing it was such a small step over the gap, I looked down to find my footing and froze. Terror burst through every part of my body, pounding my thoughts onto my forehead, pounding my emotions through my chest, as I viewed the drop to hell.

Raj was just ahead and encouraged me to take one more step, assuring me all was well. Nothing, absolutely nothing, was ever going to make me move again. I found it physically impossible to do anything. Twenty minutes into my sudden and clinging love affair with the mountain, my mind tried to rationalise how safe I was. Nothing was going to happen to me. I knew I would never have been put in this position if I were not capable of dealing with it or overcoming it, a bit like life.

But it didn't matter. I sobbed, shook, screamed about how I wanted to go home, and how irresponsible and thoughtless it was for evolved people to put lesser-evolved people in this situation. I was going to die the worst death imaginable. I was not happy with anyone or anything, let alone myself for accepting this trip in the first place. And trip it was, a bad trip, without the cushion of any hallucinogenic.

Anger seethed with every pump of my heart and erupted in a flash of rage. Thoughts jumped randomly from one thing to another. Raj had been aware of this all the time, which was why he'd stayed so close to me. With heightened emotions I turned on him, swore at him, cursed him, and blamed him. He was the worst son of a bitch of a son of a bitch. Words stumbled over each other trying to find first place in the worst language ever out of my mouth in an attempt to hurt and shock him, and still I couldn't move.

All this time, Raj had his hand extended toward mine, calm, firm and strong, and all this time I spewed accusations and disappointments incessantly. I cried until my face was red and swollen.

I stopped my ranting and gazed tentatively at his hand, which under any other circumstance I would have taken, and then I felt calm white rage. This time the only person who was going to do this for me was me; I didn't need anyone's bloody help, not from any Adepts, nor from Raj, and certainly not from the Divine.

Two hours, yes, about two hours into this tirade, I lifted my left foot across the chasm, I prayed resentfully as I stepped over, sobbing with sheer relief as I fell into the arms of Raj. He held me close, firmly wrapping me with his body and kissing my head. He said nothing as he held me securely for some time, 'til I was ready to let go.

I cried as I recalled the way I had so unjustly directed my accusatory remarks at him. Through my sniffling, I calmed down and became more comfortable opening up my heart and sharing my innermost feelings with him, and he held me in his arms. Once I'd settled my tears and my heart, he turned me around and showed me the view from where we had started.

Raj was showing me this so I could see we had progressed a long way physically, but also to show me that we had come a long way together mentally and emotionally. Realising I had achieved much more than I had ever imagined, I turned and smiled into the eyes of the most beautiful man I had ever known.

He drew me close, into the shelter of his strong arms and gently whispered, "I love you. Do you know this? I love you."

I cried again, tears brought on by his words, as well as feelings of relief, euphoria and desire. He went on holding me.

Slowly, he released his arms and we quietly looked at each other. I collapsed into his dark eyes and raced through pictures of his past, touching events, feeling his emotions, which then became mine, hearing his words, which I absorbed, bouncing off his thoughts, each one taking me to further conclusions; brushing against his dreams, wanting those also, finally settling into the feeling and caress of his manifesting spirit. He lifted me up to his six-foot-two and gave me a gentle kiss before placing me firmly back down on my shaky legs and we went on our way.

When we caught up with our companions, no one referenced what had happened, but food was laid out and I was starving.

Since starting out on this journey, we had all been supplied with everything, and though at times I'd perceived danger, none of us had ever been in danger. I had been shown that all these fears of mine were unfounded and though caution would serve me, holding on to fear did not.

Fear is a dangerous lover who plays power games with our heads and dallies with our emotions, insisting we can only lose. It was fear that kept the negative thoughts revolving around in my head, keeping me stuck in my same old patterns, restricting my movement forward, and it had paralyzed my life.

What a waste of energy! How wrapped up I had become with the little 'I' and how much bigger I am. When I focused on Francis, Raj, or the beauty of the Great Spirit around me, I felt only love. And, yes, being with these people didn't take my fear away, but they did show me that with faith and love as my focus, I could move to other choices, and also move some of my own mountains. This knowledge would assist me as I journeyed onward, through and across these physical mountains, as well as the ones I only imagined.

I was pumped and ready for this. It was my time – in no uncertain terms. The terrain I covered in three days, and the heights I viewed the world from, was not normal for someone like me. I want to make clear the enormity of the task achieved, with no powers or siddhi's, as they're referred to in India. It's overwhelming how these Adepts have the ability to take us on such a journey with them. This is how they explained it to me.

We, man, have never been alone or been without a friend, for we have a line of Brothers and Sisters going on through eternity who carry the wisdom of the ages, the knowledge gained through trial and experience, and they are continually seeking opportunities to draw developing intelligences into considering the truths regarding the destiny of the soul.

These Brothers have always existed, and they all know of each other, no matter where they are in the Universe. When a cycle permits, they walk among mankind and are known by many. They are in all walks of society, functioning in an array of different areas, and they serve by sharing the knowledge they've gained of the laws of nature.

Primarily, they're concerned with the development and furthering of the progress of nations and organisations in areas such as medicine, government, law, and the environment, but they may be your neighbour or indeed, the stranger you may meet whilst on a walk in the mountains.

Sometimes we worship them, sometimes we crucify them and times we don't even notice them. There are times when an elder Brother is able to assist an individual by the transference of energy, enabling that individual to achieve wonderful feats not usually within their capabilities. Rather like me achieving great distances over great heights within a very short time.

They can continue this transference of energy for the complete embodiment of that soul if need be. This gives maximum opportunity for the person to attain greater enlightenment, and also, more importantly, to be of greater service. What love, what dedication, and what marvellous friends we have in the Universe.

The minds of man are now going through an alteration, which will permit us to advance to the place where it will be suitable for these elders to introduce themselves to our sight. They are constantly evolving, investigating and studying all the workings and truths of the Universe, and they know our innermost nature, who we were at birth and on our passing, and are also involved with the birth of a nation and a planet.

We reached a plateau above the clouds and sat down, although some of us had this newly found stamina, we were still bound by certain densities with certain limitations caused by our beliefs. Nada pointed to a set of peaks standing majestic and resolute, like sentinels guarding a secret only to be shared with those most ardent in their search. Though formidable, they called to be approached.

I thought of Sir Galahad and his quest for the Holy Grail, and how only a worthy knight could wear the shield and, with persistence, that knight could enter the most holy place and find his grail.

The clouds are broken in the sky,
And thro' the mountain-walls
A rolling organ-harmony
Swells up, and shakes and falls.
Then move the trees, the copses nod,
Wings flutter, voices hover clear:
"O just and faithful knight of God!
Ride on! the prize is near."
So pass I hostel, hall, and grange;
By bridge and ford, by park and pale,
All-arm'd I ride, whate'er betide,
Until I find the holy Grail
(Lord Alfred Tennyson) 1809-1892

We made camp with the setting sun and I lay back on the grass that carpeted the whole area, stared up at the stars and became lost in the sky. What did I know? How many skies were there? Was this a hologram? Was it all real? What was real? Who was I really? Why me for this journey? Why not me for this journey?

How many souls were lying also on the grass somewhere, looking at the stars, thinking the same as me? I was a speck, a dot in the cosmos; yet I, that dot, was needed to hold it all together, for if 'I' were not here, all would be so different everywhere. My every choice impacted every living thing, a whole planet, the Solar System and the Universe. Me, alone at that moment, feeling so small and so vast, and all at the same time.

Just before sunrise we continued on our journey, and as the warm glow of nature's heart spread gently over the cold peaks, Nada stopped and pointed. In the distance were the Cathedral Group of mountains consisting of the Grand Teton, Mount Owen and Mount Teewinot, creating what Nada termed the great pyramid. Nestled somewhere in this pyramid sat a retreat. It was an example of a glacial horn, calling from higher levels to all who were able to come for instruction and development. There were 38 open pathways to the peak, and Jackson Hole was at the heart.

Apparently, thousands of people make the climb each year, and some are given entrance into the retreats' grand halls, others, oblivious, enjoy the peace and beauty of nature. The retreat existed before the sinking of continents, more than twelve thousand years ago, a place where those who are Adepts convene and reside.

Sometime into the day's trek, Thomas stopped in front of an imposing rock face. There was a sense of something profound about to take place, and my heart felt as if it was waiting for Christmas and it was Christmas Eve, you know, that anticipation when all have gone to bed and you're waiting in the silence for Santa to come.

Thomas placed his hand over the rock face and it parted, revealing two large doors, which slowly opened. Pinching myself didn't change a darn thing, this was like something out of 'Ali Baba and the Forty Thieves' and he had just said, "open sayza me." We stepped onto a platform, descending some distance before stepping out into a large reception hall.

Tapestriesof geometric designs and likenesses of different people adorned the walls. In front of me was a large, magnificent tapestry made of silk and gems, which I later found out figured to the perfect likenesses of the founders of this retreat. The air was infused with a gentle light.

Raj made his way to me, and together, we slowly walked through this vast area as he pointed to the different symbols and pictures, explaining who they were and what they were. When it comes to spiritual development, it's logical that there are members of the human race who are going to be ahead of the game and can teach us something. Those who are ahead of the game we refer to as Adepts, Rishis or Mahatmas, and here in the west, Masters.

These advanced souls form what's known as the Brotherhood of Light bearing no reference to race or creed. Those of the Brotherhood have devoted their lives to showing us a way of truth, a way that's challenging and struggled with – until truth is attained. Here, in this place, was the wisdom of these Brothers, some of whom were residing deep in these Rockies.

A Universal hierarchy made sense: not one of superiority, but one of evolution, and until now, I'd had no idea how narrow my world had been.

It was Victor Hugo who said, "In the night I accept the authority of the torches, although I know there is a sun." For some, the Great Sun is too bright, and their hearts and minds prefer to follow the smaller torches, for they are easier to follow, to understand, and are less demanding. But as Plato once said, "All will one day leave the shadows of the dark cave, step out into the sunlight and stand before the light of their own Higher Self; all will know the mind of the soul."

We passed by many entrances, which led into different areas, each having a specific function, then we entered into a room with a gentle violet hue, and on one wall of the room was a large mirror. Raj turned to me.

"This mirror will show scenes relevant to you, and along with this disclosure you will see how the violet ray, manifesting as a flame, is used to change one's base metal into gold, one's lower aspects into the treasure house of the Divine. It is alchemy, yet, only according to what your Karma will permit."

I started to laugh, I wasn't sure I wanted some alchemical change, or to 'test my metal,' so to speak. I said to Raj this was getting fanciful, and I tried not to show my amusement; however, for some reason I couldn't hide my laughter and tears started to roll down my face. Surprisingly, Raj joined me and we continued laughing for quite some time.

He explained later how laughter was the result of the action of this freeing flame. We did become serious though. I stood in front of the mirror and soon found myself part of a scene being played out, in fact I was the main character.

Sitting at a wooden table, in a dark, cold place, I was writing with what looked like a quilled pen. In front of me was a small jar of dark ink. Panicking, I was rushing to complete my writing, though I have no idea what that writing was. From a distance, I could hear the sounds of voices and thuds, which frightened and sickened my heart. As the voices approached, and the closer they came, the more obvious it seemed fear took over.

I sprinkled the last of a powdered substance over the paper, and blew frantically where wet ink remained. I shook the excess powder off the page, and then closed the booklet hiding it under an old cloth just as a door was violently thrown open. Two men, clothed in long, black and cream robes grabbed my arms and took me from the room. I was dragged down a poorly lit corridor.

The scene stopped, and a fire of violet flame blazed up and surrounded me. It blazed endless shades of violet, purple and pink, erupting into the depths of indigo. I was bathed in its freeing action as it dissolved the scene around me, and I knew then, writing was to be part of my identity.

This incident, from somewhere in my past, had impacted me for too long. I'd found it difficult to put pen to paper for fear of repercussions when writing my truth, but what freedom I was feeling now! We left the room and made our way to the great hall.

In the grand hall, this amphitheatre of simple taste, sat a thousand or more people. Corridors ran off this vast hall, leading to other rooms and then sleeping quarters, and each quarter was uniquely decorated in gentle hues, vibrating a healing balm.

Nada had explained how many, who leave their sleeping bodies at night, travel in their finer bodies to this retreat to be instructed on the law and sciences, such as physics, medicine, and cosmic astrology, to name just a few. She also explained how the colours emanating from the various rooms were used for training individuals in the use of psychology, along with colour and sound, for healing, something that would be more understood and used in the near future.

We were shown to our quarters and then escorted to the dining hall, where we ate a good supper. I was feeling full and wonderfully tired as Raj escorted me to my room.

Holding me close, he whispered, "I am grateful that you eventually wrote that letter, grateful for you in my arms once again, and grateful for this time together." He kissed me on my forehead and I heard in my heart as well as my head, "Good night, dear." I slept like a child in the arms of the best mother in the world.

# Chapter Eleven

*You, yourself, as much as anybody in the entire Universe, deserve your love and affection.* Buddha

Raj was not present at breakfast, so I was happy to make my way to the library and take the time to sit quietly and reflect. For some months now, my world had been like a grand tale, a story, which, had it been told to me by another, would have been met with a measure of doubt. How easy it is to just discount something outside the box of our own experience, which temporarily closes the door to experiencing it for ourselves.

These moments alone were becoming valuable times of reflection for me, but soon the library began to fill and to my surprise, Raj sat by me.

There were no signs of an orchestra, but I definitely heard abstract music gently playing. There were no signs of strobe lighting, but a kaleidoscope of colour spun around me like Catherine wheels on bonfire night. Rays of red, orange, yellow, green, blue, indigo, and violet, then in the midst of this supernova, I got it. The whole show was me! My chakras were creating the colours and the frequencies were the music. I was witnessing my own 'orchestra', I was playing my own unique overture. I had no idea until then how beautiful I was, and how wonderfully designed and uniquely beautiful each person is.

Raj touched my hand and my focus came back to the auditorium, where the music of Faust, 'The Soldier's Chorus' was playing. (My suggestion is to listen to this piece whilst continuing the story).

As an electric blue light pervaded the whole auditorium, a man stepped forward. He was unusually tall, nearing some 7ft. His garments were quite plain, a long, open, white jacket, over a long, white tunic and pyjama-like pants, and upon His head was a simple, turban-like headpiece. He didn't have a microphone; neither did He raise His voice; nevertheless His words were strong, calm, and clear, and extremely audible.

He spoke of maya and the glamours which seduce the average person until the question is asked, 'who am I'. From this point the ego consciously climbs out of the pit of illusions towards the light of the soul. He also spoke of the temperaments of man, and how understanding these temperaments assist us in knowing ourselves as well as understanding others.

There are seven human temperaments, each with a colour and corresponding sound, and together they perform the harmonically convergent symphony of the Monad. We refer to these temperaments as rays.

The first ray corresponds to the Father aspect and has a driving force of will, courage, strength, power and determination.

The second ray corresponds with the Son aspect of the trinity; it corresponds to wisdom/love, compassion, intuition, generosity and inclusiveness, demonstrating a strong sense of unity.

The third ray corresponds to the Holy Ghost, the one who transforms. It is closely aligned to intelligence, being able to collate ideas. People on this ray like to fathom the mysteries with their abstract minds in order to help humanity, and so we have the philosopher.

The fourth ray corresponds to the beauty in all things, and harmony through conflict. We live in a world of opposites, our every thought, word, and deed has an opposing thought, word, and deed. War has meaning only if there is a concept of peace, and this is true throughout all life, as life is about endless dualities. This ray is constantly looking to harmonise these opposites and art is a way to bring a harmonising, balancing effect, art and music.

The fifth ray corresponds with the analytical aspect of the mind. Sharp, witty, probing, logical, this ray is the scientist, able to use the mind to deduce from gathered information to come to a logical conclusion.

The sixth ray corresponds with devotion and one pointed adoration. We see this ray exemplified in St. Bernadette, St. Francis, and Padre Pio, to the extent of manifesting the marks of the suffering of Jesus on his own physical body. They aspire to their highest ideal and show unwavering dedication to a cause.

The seventh ray corresponds with ceremonial magic, ritual, and the occult: all these manifest the design of this ray..

He also spoke about how we all reside in the body of a greater being, and how that body is evolving within a larger body. Correspondingly, we have millions of cells evolving within us, and I wondered if we appear as a cosmic being to those minute points of light, those atoms, cells and electrons, living within our bodies. Do we appear to those as a God?

He explained a little about the mathematics of the Universe, and how our atoms, cells and electrons are mini universes within the greater body – us. He spoke about how we are like atoms, cells and electrons in a greater body – the Planetary Logos. And so it goes on. He further explained how the Hierarchy of the planet was also evolving, constantly discovering more wonders of the Infinite

He shared valuable insights on Karma and how Karma was not fully understood. We have individual Karma and group Karma, and whilst we may evolve away from a particular thought, word, or deed that did not serve, we will all be given the opportunity to bring balance, harmony, and order once again into those areas.

There are records kept of how the energy of each ego has been used and at some point, the ego will have a burning desire to inhabit another body, referred to as re-embodiment in order to balance something in the past.

The microcosmic cell always desires to be in balance with the macrocosmic body in which it lives and with whom it loves. The Universe is always bringing about balance, always correcting the imbalance.

After speaking for about an hour, He introduced another teacher to give us an understanding of the vibratory action of the violet spectrum, the seventh ray. It was Francis!

He explained in detail the simple science of the violet, purple, and indigo spectrum and how, with application, so much could be accomplished in the way of freedom for humanity. We listened to Francis for some two hours, and I was coming to realise a minute portion of the challenges Masters face when presenting old truths in new ways.

Metaphysical Philosophy and the Occult, are gifts that have been presented to humanity throughout time, in many forms, and in many cultures. In fact all the religions of the world have their basis in the Occult.

However, this wisdom of the ages has been corrupted by some, and not really understood in general. During the times of old Christianity, the words occult and paganism had become synonymous with the dark arts, but this was not the case, this bastardization was, and still is, hiding a treasure house of true spirituality. At the close of the address, we stood together chanting a mantra and applauded.

Raj asked if I would like to leave and explore the countryside for a while, and whilst being more than happy to spend alone time with him, I wanted to be assured we would still be allowed back in when we returned. He threw his head back and laughed.

We strolled through a meadow of wild flowers and I noticed my favourite little blooms from home, forget-me-nots, blue flowers with golden hearts, and they were gathered in natural bouquets.

Raj stopped, placed his arm around me and drew me in closer. The tension between us was palpable and the electricity it generated surged up through my body in waves that needed release. I was nervous, excited and wanting, and he was totally aware and gentle.

Tightening his firm hold, he drew me even closer until I looked, then fell into the depths of his dark eyes. He spoke words which dropped into my heart yet rose as visions into my mind, and they were oh, so beautiful. He didn't loosen his hold, but gently lowered his head and smiled.

His love poured into me like a voluptuous water- fall powerfully washing away many of the veils and sorrows of yester-times and I felt the release.

Willingly my heart reached for him, he became the pulse dancing in waves through me. I breathed him in and he breathed me out, and I travelled into the bliss and satisfaction of his gentle soul. I was spinning in memories and wishes and at the same time desiring so much more.

Nothing could keep us from each other for we had been 'one' before and would be 'one' again. We were joined by an unseen umbilical cord, which had been stretched throughout time and space, yes our love was beyond death itself. Now I knew I had never been, nor would ever be, alone again. For a while, we wandered, sat, and shared.

Later, when clouds eclipsed the sun, we sat down on a soft bed of flowers, looked up at the sky and spoke of things I cannot share.

Today's words were spent, they were useless, neither of us desired to break the stillness., and as night gradually laid her blanket over us, we looked on as nature's breeze kissed the tips of the mountains encouraging wispy fragments of fading mists to flirt with their shadowy silhouettes below us.

The word 'love' seems so empty for the feeling I had been dipped into. Then he turned to me, touching my thoughts as he always did.

"I love you too," he whispered. He had taken me to a full definition of the word love, he had caressed me without the limitation of human touch, he had simply and purely loved me, and I him.

Gently laying me back, placing his body beside me, he tenderly stroked my hair. His perfume was of sandalwood, with an intoxicating sweetness, and my body danced, expectant, as he drew me into his sheltering form. His arm became tighter around me and my immediate present collapsed into his gentle gaze. I sighed, then, as I swayed suspended in surreal space, he firmly kissed my lips.

Tangled in the ivy garland of nature's tousled bed, we drank of each other, and united we danced through the inner space only those drenched in love are able to find. I was lost in a place where nothing was, yet all existed. Sun set, sun rose, lives came, lives went, we coursed with waves on distant shores wrapped in visions of distant dreams, my soul sang with his tunes, and, at last, I came to rest sobbing in his gentle caress.

My tears were the tears of centuries, of lost love, of past times, of the unknown; my tears were of joy, of absolutes, of pleasure, of indescribable emotions never felt before. My sobbing came from my soul, somewhere out in space, trying to get a Universe to understand without the use of words all that he meant to me. He kissed me again and I closed my eyes in peace.

Holding me close until the sun rose again, he turned to me and whispered, "I knew you were embodied in England but I had to wait for the right time." This was the first time I had ever seen Raj pensive.

"You have always loved the little blue flowers, and I have always given you a gift of these flowers every time we said goodbye, even in sleep."

He picked me a few forget-me-nots and gave them to me and I felt a shard of sadness enter my heart. Did this mean he was saying goodbye again? We stayed in that meadow for, I don't know how long, and then we slowly ambled back to the retreat.

# Chapter Twelve

*But when two people are at one in their inmost hearts, they shatter
even the strength of iron or of bronze.*
From The I Ching Ancient Chinese Text

Back in my room, someone had placed some extra clothing, including pants and a couple of sweaters of the most beautiful cashmere. On my bed sat two large boxes with a golden card placed on top with the words, 'To be opened tomorrow evening'. As I was inspecting the boxes, and if truth be known, was just about to peek into one, a knock came on the door. It was Francis.

"Ah! I see you have received the clothing. Good." He smiled. "We will be travelling early in the morning, to visit a friend near a neighbouring town. We will be staying overnight. Someone will collect the items you wish to take, so please leave them packed in your room. We will gather in the main entrance, after breakfast. Do sleep well." Then He departed.

Early the next morning, we set out with everything loaded onto the horses, including, to my surprise, the two mysterious boxes. Say to anyone, don't open those until tomorrow and it means, try and sneak a peek today, right? I amused myself with all sorts of imaginings and exercised great restraint. The boxes were by no means small and took up a whole ride, waddling from side to side on the back of an unsuspecting mare, gyrating in front of me like a dancer with enormous hips, teasing and taunting.

The hike was uneventful and quite easy compared to the terrain we had previously travelled, and it wasn't long before I could see the outline of a town in the distance, which someone said was Jackson Hole. I turned my thoughts away from the containers, which were courting my attention, and entertained myself by reliving some of my time with Raj.

Near late afternoon, we approached what looked like a large ranch, where cattle grazed lazily in an open meadow and horses roamed freely in two large paddocks. I could see a log home, with three glass gables to the front, and as we approached, there, standing at the open door, was a most beautiful woman.

There's a saying, 'clothes maketh the man', what absolute cobblers. It was not the plain, white blouse she was wearing, nor the riding pants and leather boots: no, it was her natural essence which exuded elegance, as well as intangible goodness. A poet once said, 'I had been dipped again in God and newly created.' This was how I felt around her.

She greeted Francis, then turned to the rest of us. "Please enter," She gifted us all with a beaming smile.

Inside the large entrance hall was a crystal chandelier refracting colours which danced off the walls in an attempt to make personal contact with all who entered. Two staircases rose, one on each side, to a balcony running across the top at the far end. Large vases stood in front of the white walls containing vibrant blooms bursting forth from their once contained blossoms. It all reflected perfectly the same effortless elegance as our hostess.

"My name is Portia, welcome." She waited for the last of our group to enter then resumed.

"You will be shown to your rooms, and, as the special event we have planned is rather soon, please take this time to freshen up and prepare. Anything you require will be supplied, so please ask." She turned and left, followed by Francis, Raj, and a few others, while the rest of us were escorted to our quarters.

My things, including my two mysterious boxes, were placed on my bed and again I was about to peer inside when, out of the corner of my eye, I saw Raj standing in the doorway. I wanted to know who our hostess was, what the special event was, and more importantly, what was in the boxes? He placed two fingers on my lips.

"Prepare for the evening." He smiled. "I will be back at eight."

I flung myself onto the bed. What's it all about, Ellie? How can all this be happening? How can all this be? Oh my God, what...are...in...the...boxes?

After showering, I went to my two special packages sitting on the bed and slowly opened the larger one, carefully pulling back the delicate tissue covering the contents. A shot of the darkest, aquamarine silk erupted forth, swelling over the sides of the box revealing a shower of tiny crystals that shimmered like droplets of dew on an azure lake.

To my utter surprise, when I lifted it all out, I saw it was a dress, as light as gossamer gauze, with the elegance of a couture gown designed for a ball. The fitted bodice was interlaced at the back with deep violet, falling to a full skirt, all the way down to the floor. In the smaller box, I found shoes and a shawl, all the necessary accoutrements for me to attend an elaborate function. Just then, there came a knock on my door, and when I opened it there stood Francis.

"I am so pleased you have had the opportunity to spend some alone time with Raj." He smiled playfully. "Many of your experiences may be shared when you return. They will give encouragement to those who believe in rigid rules which must be followed in order to experience the abundant love and the gifts of The Great One.

"There are no set rules, no do's and don'ts, no indoctrination requiring obedience to a closed minded God. No, only a loving

heart, an open mind, and just maybe, it might help to write a letter."
I felt blessed..

"The letter you wrote was an example of alchemy in its simplest form. You used the mind of the heart as a one-pointed laser, you actualized it in the physical by placing it on paper, and you even went to the trouble of mailing it. Such determination, Little One, such determination. Remember, one step taken by a life stream toward us, brings ten steps from us towards that lifestream.

"In a couple of hours you will again experience the joyful action of the violet spectrum through the medium of music." He smiled and departed and I returned to my boxes.

After donning the gown, which to my surprise fit perfectly, I looked in the mirror. In a million years I would never have bought such a dress, but it made me feel elegant, and I understood why women back in the day acted so charming when dressed in such finery. I too felt charming. Then I put on the beautiful, delicate shoes sitting by the box. They complemented the dress perfectly, but I eyed my Doc Marten boots, and there was no competition. So deciding to lace up my 'good old faithfuls' and place the dainties back in the box, I finished the rest of my dressing just as a knock came on the door. It was Raj.

He was breathtaking in a full-length ivory brocade sherwani, with a high Nehru styled collar, and buttons running down the full length of the long jacket. It was fitted, hugging his solid form, and his long, dark hair hung loose over his shoulders.

I was like a kid going on her first date and he laughed, motioning me to turn around. His warm hands gently brushed across my flesh, he kissed the back of my neck and placed a necklace around my throat. Turning me to face him, for a split second and only a second, I wondered if all this was real. Wrapping one arm around my waist, and the other to the back of my head, he kissed me again but this time on my lips, long and firm. My heart gave in to his sweet taste, I felt imprisoned in my flesh and hungered to lose myself in his soul.

In the distance, I heard words coming closer and closer, until I realised they were his words whispering in my ear. Steadying back to terra firma, I could still taste him. He took my hand and placed a ring on my finger.

"We have a marriage that originated from the heart of the Universe, one flame, one love, and we will return as such to the heart of all." He held my gaze, took both my hands in his and kissed my cheek. We walked, hand in hand, to the hall.

It was like entering a grand ball in an old movie, everyone was dressed in formal attire, most of the men wearing tuxedos and the women wearing gowns of opulent hues. Suddenly, Raj whisked me up and we danced. Waltzes rose like gentle waves gathering into tsunamis on a shore of sheer joy and the polkas made me laugh nonstop. As each waltz played faster, I became lighter and he held me closer, until I felt the full effect and action Francis had spoken of.

Many waltzes later, Raj escorted me to an alcove, perfect for watching those still dancing. My light-headedness I put down to the person I was dancing with, but whilst he was flattered and honoured, he said he couldn't take all of the credit.

"Waltzes lighten the heart and it's quite natural to feel lifted, even elevated, regardless of the boots." It had never crossed my mind to think of the boots, how funny they must have looked and sounded in a room full of finery.

We continued dancing until the early hours of the morning, then he escorted me to my quarters, placed two arms on my shoulders and kissed my cheek. He departed and I dropped my clothes and slept.

Raj and I spent the next two days together hiking, talking, and for my part, generally getting to know him better. He was the epitome of tenderness and showed gentle sophistication, which I believe was due to his spirituality. In short, he was the perfect gentleman and over our time together nothing caused him to veer from his serenity and peace.

He hadn't married, his profession was engineering, and at quite an early age, Francis had taken him under his wing, continuing the instructions of many lifetimes, to which Raj was ever an attentive pupil. He had been aware of Francis as his Teacher when very young, and I could see, though he never referred to it, that he had attained considerable enlightenment.

In the world I'd come from, there was much being said regarding ascension, and I was curious as to what these Elder Brothers thought regarding it all. So I asked and this is how it was explained.

"Paul said, 'Every day I die a little', referring to crossing out the little 'I' and replacing it with the big 'I'. The symbol of the cross is an old symbol, used before the time of Jesus. It is a reminder to the individual to transcend each moment.

"There will always be those who dangle quick ways to ascend, using the ascension carrot to entice others to buy their wares, follow their ways, or join their groups, and usually at a cost. And some misguided individuals set themselves up as gurus gathering around them vulnerable souls, who are all willing to become servants to a dominant ego.

"There are those who are certain of their ability to channel a Master or Adept. But ask yourself the question, why would a Master channel, when by the very act of being a Master, He has the ability to speak for himself. Childish.

"Some live in the illusion they can free a soul, or at least take another soul to a higher dimension. But ask yourself again, if this be so, do you not believe those who are further along the path of evolution, seeped in love's cause, would do this?

"A soul's journey is an inner journey dedicated to truth. A Master pianist may play a masterpiece for you and then show you how it is done. However, in order to do the same, you will have to apply the laws of music, work at it. No quick fixes.

"These Ascended Masters, as they are referred to, seem to carry on from the Christian churches, where the minions are plied with promises of being saved if they follow these self appointed gurus/ priests. No Master of Wisdom can or will do it for you." He smiled and continued.

"When one permanently transcends, it is usually by going through one's own personal Armageddon. In reality, one's only requirement is to awake from the dream, to realise that he/she IS. However, the process of awakening means coming out of a myriad of illusions. Wake up humanity to your inheritance, wake up." As Raj said this last sentence my head rang with the words 'wake up'.

"Many pathways lead to the Divine," he continued, "rather like the pathways to the Teton Retreat, and these ways are studied and practised in many religions, across many cultures. Every soul incarnated will reach its destination, and then the journey will continue again, with the soul entering new cycles. Even those we call Masters are evolving through spheres which they never knew existed at one time."

I had been under the impression that when a soul overcame time and space, or in other words ascended, all was achieved, but this didn't make sense now. If the 'One who we know little of' is omnipresent, omnipotent, and omniscient, then it has always been. Evolution will always be.

The Master Jesus didn't say, 'OK folks, been there, done that, ciao baby'. No, He would continue evolving, and still is. You know, we really don't think at times do we? We muddle along with our lives and forget to think, to examine things logically. No, I change that, we forget to think, period.

The day arrived to leave. Breakfast had been packed onto the horses so we could travel to a viewpoint, eat, see the sunrise, and make good time before sunset. Portia stood in the main hall. She bid us farewell and as I was about to leave she took my hand. I expected her to say something, but instead she gently placed her other hand on my head. She smiled and we left.

We reached our viewpoint just as the sun was rising above the distant peaks. We stood in silence. The rosy tinged sun climbed up into the sky, and burst forth colour like a can of spilt paint drizzling over the canvas placed before us. Magnificent! We ate and moved on.

Back at the Teton retreat, Raj suggested we spend some time alone hiking along some of the trails. On one of our excursions, we took a path leading to a small meadow not far away, a peaceful place of thick, lush grass, where perfumed patches of wild flowers made soft beds. He took my hand.

"Soon, dear, we will be departing, and you will be returning to your former life. But, just as I have been aware of you in the past, you will now be aware of me, and of course, we will connect whilst you sleep."

At first I felt lost when he said the word 'departing' as this equated to separation and losing my love when I had just found him. A murky sea of emotions washed over me, none of which I wanted to specifically identify, it was too painful and I was too confused.

But, I surrendered my old patterns, and decided to create new ones that would serve me better. I was becoming more peaceful and assured.

We discussed many things as we sat quietly amongst the flowers wallowing in Nature's aromatherapy, but the more time I spent with him, the more I knew I would miss him. There was something innocent about our relationship, and an expectation that was sensual, though not in the normal way. He was bringing out the poet in me and I knew he was aware of it.

We eventually made our way back for supper, and, as this was to be the last evening at the Tetons for some of us, I decided to get the packing of some personal things out of the way, so I could wander through our accommodation freely.

The elegance and symmetry everywhere was captivating. Glass goblets, embossed with gold and ruby, sat on a crystal shelf; they were the same in height and shape with no variations in colour; they were perfect. How could they have been made by hand? I came across a picture of Francis framed in gold; it was a photograph, yet something seemed different.

"Everything is precipitated, conceived in the mind of the One." It was Francis, standing by me.

"All is supplied from perfection, so all is perfection. It is the lower mind that conceives imperfection and therefore creates that which is imperfect. When your consciousness is one with the Divine there is no limit, your limited beliefs are your restrictions.

"When we view through your eyes, it is only to understand your needs. When one enters a healing temple, an enlightened healer does not see anything but the perfection that IS. All else is but an illusion.

"The Master Jesus knew this law and applied it. He did not say, 'Lazarus, I know you're dead and your body decaying, but if you can rise, it would be good'. No, He said, 'Lazarus rise'. Jesus knew the law He was operating within. When He said, 'You are healed', that one was healed. He was silent for a while.

"We need have no concern if the tree is bare, for as long as we are conscious of the truth that the law is operating, the tree will bring forth fruit after its own kind. All you see is but an expression of consciousness enlightened by truth. Remember this, for it holds a great key."

He referred back to the picture I'd been looking at. "It is indeed a photograph of sorts. It is a radiation, an electronic likeness, and a true likeness, yes?"

What Francis had shared with me over our time together was beyond anything I could have dreamt up, and I thanked Him. He smiled, slightly bowing his head, and departed, leaving me still wandering the halls. Later on, I spent some time in an area by myself, meditating until it was time to meet up with the others.

# Chapter Thirteen

*Whatever souls are made of, his and mine are the same.*
Emily Bronte

Raj and I met by the entrance of the grand hall and proceeded to our seats. There would be many, who, whilst asleep in their beds, would leave their physical bodies and travel to this retreat in their finer bodies. This finer body may look similar, but it would always display the inner beauty, which is more beautiful than one could ever imagine.

Sometimes, those who travel in their sleep are able to recall memories of their night, however all souls have a record on some level which can be recalled when necessary.

The auditorium was full with a mass of colour and a sea of faces, but something in the crowd caught my attention. I wandered over and saw it was Linda, with an emerald hue of energy around her. How youthful and vibrant she looked in her finer body, more ethereal than solid.

I shared a brief, very brief explanation of my more conventional means of getting to the retreat, which made her laugh, and of courseg she was aware of being asleep in bed and hoped she would remember everything upon waking. Just then, one of my favourite pieces of music started to play, 'Finlandia' so I returned to my seat and to Raj.

The tall man, Polaris, who had spoken the evening before, now addressed us.

"There are two paths to enlightenment. Some seek eternal bliss, and liberation from this world of suffering and the wheel of birth, death, and rebirth. Their aim is to become totally re-merged and reabsorbed in that infinite Source from which they came.

"But there are those who cannot enter joyfully into Nirvana and leave the masses of suffering humanity behind. How can they enter the ocean of bliss when they know full well that their fellow souls are trapped helpless in the swamp of pain and despair!

"Those who tread this path wish only to be of the utmost service to humanity. They have already decided that when at last their efforts bring them to the very threshold of Nirvana, they will turn their back upon it and renounce the Great Prize. These are the ones who follow the path of Renunciation. These are the Brothers of Compassion and Light.

"I will tell you a simple story, paraphrasing a small portion of the books put forward by H.P. Blavatsky.

"There was no time, and thought was not. Creation was not for thought was not. The Eternal Parent slept. There were no causes of misery, for there was no one to generate the illusion. Father, Mother, and Son were again one. There were no causes of existence, no illusion, for all illusion is a creation outside the Eternal Parent, and the Eternal Parent was asleep. The One existence slept boundless, infinite, cause- less, and though nothing was, nothing pulsated in eternal duration.

"The Eternal was unconscious, the Eternal was asleep. There was neither silence nor sound, it was darkness yet all light, there was only the Eternal breath, unaware of Itself, for It slept. It was a germ not yet stimulated by the ray. The Mother was not yet swollen; Her heart was not yet opened for the one ray to enter. Then darkness stirred. Radiating the ray into the Mother, it shot through the virgin egg. Six times the Mother swelled, cultivating all the elements needed for life, until the seventh swell. The swollen Mother opened like a lotus, which dropped the non-eternal germ to become the world egg, and the Great Idea was manifested. The Tree of Life had born fruit, and humanity tasted the apple of illusion.

"This is the love story of the Universe. This is a great mystery, and those ready to understand what I have said, will understand. Ask for further enlightenment on this in your meditation. Those further along the evolutionary path, those who you consider Adepts, are your brothers and sisters in service to this love, and it is only the illusions you have created, and continue to create, that show you otherwise. This unconditional love, given by those in service, I honour." The auditorium rang with applause. He continued.

"Love is the simple truth that is the awakener. One act of love generates unto itself more love, love mirrors itself out of love. The nature of love is to find any avenue to expand itself; it loves love and explodes with itself when the opportunity arises to filtrate into a dark place, providing a perfect stage to show its everlasting talents. To just say the word invokes its power and it is the only energy that binds for eternity, drawing souls together again and again as it is the law. To think the word changes the body of the thinker; to think the word with someone else in mind invokes the energy for another, to shout the word impacts your world around you and naught can be the same again.

"When it is the energy in motion, the emotion behind anything, it always achieves joy, peace, harmony and wonder. It continues to reverberate throughout time and space forever and it cannot be lost or stopped. It finds itself anywhere, searching, gathering unto itself its children. It is the silent watcher waiting, looking for one small niche, so eager is it. It carries with it joy, peace, harmony and plays with laughter, smiles and moments. It does not dance with selfishness, it does not sleep with the companions of cruel, but it will stay in the same playing field as these, waiting for the opening to shoot for a star. It is a powerful lover, caressing, soft and seductive, yet a laser that can open anything, exposing all.

"Contemplate *love* often and meditate often. As you contemplate love, new ideas of love will come to you. This will be love speaking directly to you and it will be your guide. Love will show you ways; it will show you new illustrations and ideas and will be your teacher. When one comes to you and says who taught you those things, be sure to tell them of your friend and guide named love so they, too, may partake of the wine of Dionysus and celebrate continuous birth-days. Celebrate often and at the close of your day think over where you noticed your greatest power, where you held the hands of your friend. Review your surrenders, then close your eyes and rest in the arms of your greatest lover." We sat in silence for some time and then he spoke again.

"The sweet perfume of love will caress all present, as well as those who come to know these words with a dispensation of healing in the heart." He bowed and departed.

Along with the feeling of being so vast, I also felt as small as a particle in a vast body. Blessed, loved, whole, pure, humbled before all creation, yet I was dipped again in God and new created. I was perfect, I was God, for I had looked on a perfect aspect of the Divine and I could not have done so if I had not seen it in myself. I could not speak, only feel, and that was overwhelmingly powerful.

None present desired to depart, so we all stayed for an hour or so and eventually left in silence. Saying nothing, Raj escorted me to my door, kissed the top of my head and I retired in stillness and peace. Lying on my bed, there were no words, no sounds and no movement. I was suspended in nothingness, which was everything.

What a great privilege to be chosen as a vehicle to share these words with you. I don't remember going to sleep.

Early the next morning, we all met in the great hall, and unlike the other times when we were embarking on a new leg of our travels, none of us spoke a word. For me, the previous evening was too sacred, with nothing to add. Words were irrelevant, and I believe all those present were touched with the same feeling.

Our time had come to leave this extraordinary place, and as a collective, we were subdued in more ways than one, so we said our goodbyes and quietly made our way towards the entrance.

I turned around to take a last look at the pictures and tapestries and took photographs with my mind, gathering memories of this wonderful retreat. When I had first entered this place, I had no idea who all these people were, but upon leaving, they had become part of my family. The entrance closed behind us and we were on our way, on what I believed to be the long hike back. However, I knew one could never be quite sure when it came to my hosts.

My fellow aspirants and I had one thing in common for sure, sadness. Who in their right mind, ha! right mind, would want to leave? Some of my companions were of course familiar with this retreat and also with our Hosts, having been with them before, but for the majority of us this was our first mind-blowing trip, how could one just go back to a relative normality.

We came to a clearing and were split into groups. There was a guide for each, and our group, headed by Nada and Thomas, including Raj and I, made our way down from the Grand Teton in a different direction.

A different route home had been charted, and I donned the dreary coat of sadness but it didn't keep me warm. I lolloped along like a lost beast in a barren desert, at this point, I would have welcomed a high ridge round a mountain.

It was too heavy a coat to carry for long, so I changed my mind, just like that. Then it hit me, and boy did it. What if I'd had a serious heart attack and was in a coma somewhere in the snow; was all this an illusion? What if it was worse and Raj was simply part of this illusion, and I was dead in limbo somewhere?

I could see the headlines in the local papers: 'Woman found dead in the snow after heart attack. Why was she deep in the wilds of the Rockies with a backpack full of empty chocolate bar wrappers? Due to the coyote prints all around the area, we can only assume she was feeding them and the situation escalated. Family informed.

Why should it matter if I was in an illusion, or even dead? Whatever was happening, I could choose to be in this so-called new illusion that had begun with writing a letter, or return to some other reality. Which world would you choose?

We journeyed on descending as we went, and within a week or so, we were back to the valley in the mountains' womb. The crowds were gone and over everything hung a mantle of silence. We were greeted by familiar faces, whom I remembered but had not been introduced to, and shown to our familiar quarters.

Later, when we met for dinner, we shared laughter, many stories and lighthearted amusements. We were treated to a cabaret of talents, and we also reviewed some of the hilarious events that happened to some of us along the way, which had us all, including our hosts, laughing so hard that we rocked in tears.

Oh, that all humanity could experience these Elder Brothers in such a free and loving way, instead of holding austere mindsets of pious beings with long faces, always ready and looking to punish us for our transgressions.

Nada came to me and talked about how she, Thomas and Raj, were going to start out early the next morning to visit an old gold mine and she asked if I would like to accompany them. The prospect was exciting (excuse the pun) so it was early to bed and early to rise and at dawn we were equipped and ready to roll. Necessities and overnight clothes had been packed on horses and to my knowledge, no time was set for our return.

We hiked our way out of the valley and through a gorge just as the sun reached its high point and started its descent. At one point,

I was sure we were nearing civilization, for there were people in the distance hiking. I also thought I heard a train, but within a short time all returned to the distinct enveloping silence of nature. It was no use timing our journey, as nothing was subject to time with our hosts, and space, well, I'd given up on intellectualising this unlimited Deity.

It was late when Thomas pointed up to a large ridge, part of a mining operation, and as we ascended a narrow path, a man dressed in a well-used hat and mud-caked mountain boots greeted us. His name was Simon and his home was built of wood and rustic. On the inside, it had a large fire burning in the hearth, two beds up, two beds down, a kitchen, a modest living area, and a bathroom, just the basics. He poured hot tea and as we ate some food, it became obvious that he knew my friends very well. Later, I was shown to a cosy room where, as usual, my belongings were already waiting.

Over supper, they discussed mining plans, and Simon expressed great uneasiness around his feeling that someone's life was in danger. Thomas explained how Francis was well aware of the situation, that everything was on track, and the mine would be up and running within a short time.

Plans and places were discussed, then, to my utter surprise, Thomas asked my views. Startled, was the word I used, and shock followed it. In fact, I wasn't sure why this excursion had included me in the first place, let alone why I was being asked my opinion concerning the mine.

"In a past embodiment, you were heavily involved with the mining of precious metals," Thomas explained. "Earth does not surrender her treasures easily, and though many believe the taking is up to the taker, I can assure you, she guards her treasures and will permit only so much abuse. She will then bring balance, and not always in the gentlest of ways, as natural disasters demonstrate.

"This mine is ready to release abundance; however, it is up to all those who have been involved in the past, as to how this story will unfold in the future, or whether it unfolds at all. Those who have come together, yourself included, have many times attempted a similar project and failed through disharmony of one sort or another. So here we are again. Karma has brought us to a similar situation once more."

It was explained to me that in the near future I would have an opportunity to do some future work regarding this project and others, and this preliminary introduction would give me a taste and feel for it. I had always had little attachment to money, no great ambition, no burning desire to be wealthy, but if a little more came my way, enabling greater freedom to pursue truth, then, thank you, Universe.

The thought entered my head as to how so many people spend inordinate amounts of energy desiring things, experiences, and people. Attachments and expectations can cause so much suffering, contrary to the belief that it will solve all their problems and heartaches. Many people look back on their lives and realise the worries and desires did zero to change their situation or satisfy the desire, zero. What a waste of energy.

Looking forward to tomorrow and feeling deliciously tired, I said goodnight, wallowed for a moment in the love radiating from Raj, went to my room, crashed on my bed, and stared at the full moon.

# Chapter Fourteen

I was sound asleep, but there was a mist, and through it came a very familiar figure, Francis. In my head, I heard Him.

"Meet me after breakfast at the entrance to the mine. Please wear what is needed for a leisurely hike." The mist turned to a bright light and he was gone. The dream left me a little confused, but I dressed appropriately and went downstairs.

Only Simon was at the table for breakfast, so I shared my vision of Francis and asked his thoughts on it. He said he had experienced something similar two nights previously and acted upon it. I was thrilled to hear this, so I finished my food and excused myself and made my way to the mine entrance.

Francis greeted me and we walked on together. Nature seemed different from when I had first set out on that very cold, eventful day, way back. If someone had told me, then, I'd be having a relationship with Nature the way it was going, I would've suggested they increase the dosage of their medication.

The weather was warm and the breeze had a rhythm that played in the background to the rustle of leaves and the song of the birds. The more I listened the more it impacted me, until, being so overwhelmed by it all, I stopped and started to cry. She had a heartbeat. Francis did nothing but wait.

She was alive. Of course I knew it before, but never took much notice. Resuming my step, I felt her life force pulsating throughout my body. I really didn't want to converse with Francis, wishing to be lost in the experience, but when we had trekked quite a distance Francis spoke.

"It is quite the experience, yes?" I knew what he was referring to and I agreed. After about another hour, He spoke again. "All life brings union to a responsive heart."

No more was said until we came to a small cave. It was like a little home, and we entered. There sat a man, crossed-legged, as if meditating. Though he was sitting I could see he was an extremely tall man, with long silver braids that hung on his large, barrel chest.

Outside, a crow ripped the silence with its sonic caw just as Francis motioned me to sit. Totally motionless, the man slowly opened his eyes and stared at me.

"If we recognize perfection," he said, "it is because that perfection is within us, and if we see with a critical eye, that very splinter is the plank we need to lose. The words of the Master Jesus are many, and meditation upon these words allows the blossoming of the soul to bear fruit in our everyday lives. When He said 'it is done,' it was done. When He said, I, and my Father are One, He was experiencing the Divinity within Himself, the same Divinity within all.

"What Divinity speaks to one, Divinity speaks to all. If I ask you to affirm an old mantra I Am God, what do you feel?

"Ask yourself, who is God? Do you see a man sitting on a throne of gold? Do you see an entity made in the image and likeness of you? When I refer to God, I refer to *That* which no man can fathom, I refer to *That*, for who is there who can report first hand the totality of the omniscient. Who dares?

"In the beginning was the word, and it was the breath of creation. For the breath to go forth it was first conceived in the mind, and who was this who had it in mind? And what of the omnipresence of this Creator?

"If God is everything, the Absolute, the Divine Principle, then God is everything bar none. There is nothing that is, was, nor will be that is not the Absolute. Oh, the ignorance of those who deign to utter - they know. Children at play.

"You are a manifestation of the Absolute, and the evolutionary path opens the lotus to show you this gem. Think about this. When you say this mantra, 'I Am God', you are identifying with the perfection inside the heart of the heart of the heart, the way, the truth, and the life inside everyone and everything.

"One meaning of I Am God is I Am Silent. When giving this affirmation, I Am God, notice what it shows you, and notice where your belief in the separation from your Father-Mother lies. This mantra will give you much and teach you well.

"When affirming, know it is the Divine self that accomplishes. In any situation where fear stands on your doorstep, this mantra will dissolve that fear, and it will project the Godself in its place. Some may believe this mantra blasphemous, but what does one care for the childish concerns of others."

He closed his eyes and in my head, I heard him speak. "Settle now into the mantra." I closed my eyes and started to repeat the mantra, I Am God.

It was hard, all manner of old programs surfaced, some I recognized and some I didn't even know existed. I stumbled over the words and felt resistance start to form steel barriers in my mind. It was hard believing myself bigger than I thought, and hard believing myself better than I thought, but that was the key, it wasn't me I was referring to when I said I Am God, it was my Source.

Gently, my Native friend's voice mellowed into my thoughts; gently he encouraged and repeated the mantra with me, until I lost him and there was only myself.

When I opened my eyes, it was dark and I could see his motionless form as a silhouette only. A gentle touch on my shoulder alerted me to Francis who was still standing at the entrance; I rose and joined him outside. A large black crow circled silently above as He placed his hand on my shoulder again, and in an instant we were back in the living room of Simon's cabin. I didn't speak nor did Francis. I retired to bed.

Most of the old schools say a mantra given by a teacher to a pupil should not be shared, and at first, I was concerned about sharing this mantra, but thinking more on the teachings I had received of late, the question I asked myself was, why? Was it out of fear? What could possibly be the result of anyone using it, enlightenment? None of the reasons for keeping it to myself seemed valid and all of my feelings said it had been given for me to share. It's such a simple exercise and can bring profound results.

Outside, a bird with A.D.D. sang full volume, so I had no choice but to rise, and whilst getting dressed, I noticed it was not only this bird vying for my attention, but all of nature had decided to turn up the volume.

My world seemed fresh and sweet, like a piece of fruit just picked off a ripe tree. The colours in my room were vivid, quite unlike my previous perception of them. Odours of woody dampness and crisp, clean pine, mingled with the smell of coffee, and all seemed extremely alive in my 360-degree universe.

In between sipping coffee, I shared with Simon my excursion to the old man in the cave, and the mantra, just as Raj and the others entered. My surroundings, the colours, the smells, and the noises, became so intense, to be honest it was all a bit too much. I wasn't sure what was happening, but above it all, the sound of Raj's deep tone echoed in my head.

"Take one deep breath and relax." I did. "Now focus on one sense at a time and be with it, familiarise yourself with it, and discover."

With one deep breath, the chatter of those taking their seats for breakfast faded, and listening to Raj's counsel, I was able to isolate the colour, and more astonishingly, the musical note of each person in the room. Emotions started to swirl around the room like a thick soup, but then I was able to isolate each emotion, matching it with its owner.

Thoughts seemed more predominant than words, easier to understand. What amazed me the most was the potency of each person's true smell. Then, as quickly as it came, the intensity left, and I was once again only aware of the chatter in the room and the discussions underway regarding the plans for that day.

It was a superb exercise, I had never before had such control of my senses nor had they ever been so acute. Throughout my life, I had been bombarded with vague, scrambled signals, and, from being a baby, I had to learn how to function with this bombardment of signals, not unlike most people. No wonder life on earth can be difficult at times. No one had ever shown me how to take one thing at a time, but no one around me knew how to either.

By the time I had put aside my thoughts and had become more involved with the talking taking place in the room, breakfast was over and we made our way outside. The others walked on ahead, but I wanted to just stop awhile and cherish this glorious morning. Raj stood with me.

"Your senses became heightened giving you the ability to tap into information normally out of your sphere of access. It's not telepathy, it's harmony. It's not sixth or seventh sense, but your five senses in a higher state of awareness. You can hone this skill."

We made our way to the entrance of a mine. I was expecting some underground cave, but instead we entered a rundown building with a mass of old machinery. According to Raj, the machinery could be repaired, and little was needed in order to start production. But my mind was not on the mine.

I needed to be alone for a while, so I excused myself, and left the building to wander over to a grassy area where I could see the valley below. I was more than excited at my newly discovered skills and wanted to experiment further.

Relaxing into nature's live picture show before me, I tuned into the birds, rustling leaves, and the chatter of life around me. I realised, just like the periphery of one's vision, there is a periphery to sound. Closing my eyes, in my mind I drew a circle around the furthest sounds I could hear. Beyond that circle was absolute stillness. Then I practised keeping my mind focused on that circle of stillness. Until then, I'd thought silence was the absence of sound, but in truth it's a presence, the presence of silence.

With imagination and desire, I could tune my senses still further. I could tune into individual frequencies, hearing each bird and animal, knowing where each one was located. I continued to do this until I touched a circumference of, I was told later, was around a mile.

Then, I heard a train rapidly making its way towards me and I was startled. I jolted out of my communion with nature. I turned to see Nada and realised she had been assisting me in this exercise all the while. We sat together on the grass and she shared a few things.

Nada was raised without a mother from a young age, and being the eldest, had chosen to stay at home to serve her father and siblings. Her brothers and sisters received the love and nurturing they needed from her, not only to survive, but also to thrive. She focused on their perfection, protection and success in all their endeavours, and held the immaculate concept for them all. She had no formal education.

As the children grew and left home, she became free to pursue her own dreams. She met Francis and was tutored by Him. What a beautiful soul, and dedicated to the service of humanity.

Storm clouds started to congregate, and as thunderclaps echoed through the canyons, we made our way back to the cabin to sit around a fire and talk. It's quite funny that everyday me, with no special qualifications, living in a quiet town, going shopping, coming home type of person, should be in the middle of the Rockies discussing high finance and gold mines with beings that walk on water, and manifest feasts. Nada turned towards me.

"You see, you have a past history with mining, coupled with your non-attachment to money; you are the perfect candidate for a mission."

"But I don't have money to be attached too." I laughed.

She smiled and nodded. "Precisely."

I think I missed a point somewhere but with the evening coming to an end and feeling deliciously tired, I excused myself and retired to my room. I lay on my bed and fell asleep to the rhythm of the rain dancing on my window.

I was in the cave sitting with the old man again, asleep in my bed but awake in another state. He opened his eyes.

"The lower mind thinks, going through likes and dislikes, making decisions based on the past, creating futures just in case. It sets you up for disappointment and also pain. The mind is addictive. If you don't believe what I say, ask yourself if you can give up thinking.

"The lower mind needs to be in control, and you believe you survive if you use your mind thus. And so it is that the mind covers up your present, the present, the gift given to you by the Creator every sacred moment.

"By keeping you in thoughts of the past and thoughts of the future, you become lost in your lower mind, your lower ego.

Remember, you are consciousness, not lower mind, consciousness can exist without thoughts, but thoughts cannot exist without consciousness.

"So now, close your eyes and listen to your thoughts. Who is this doing the listening? Yes, you are, you are observing your thoughts. Observe all your thoughts – see them come and go, like wild animals to a watering hole. Yes, you are observing them coming and going – who is this observing your thoughts? You are. Who are you? You are not your thoughts, you are the observer. Who is feeling fear? You are. Are you that fear? No, you are the observer of that fear, so let it go, why hold on to this, it is childish.

"Eventually the wild animals will stop drinking at your watering hole and the pond of the mind will be calm. With practice, you will drop into the space between your thoughts, the space where I am, where peace resides, where the soul sits.

"Yes, consciousness is the key; all that is exposed by light, becomes light. You have shone light on this, and in your 'now' you are illumined and free. Choose your 'nows' wisely. You may choose freedom at any time, literally."

I sat in the cave with this old man for I don't quite know how long, but I awoke refreshed. The sun spread her warmth throughout my room and morning kissed me. I washed, dressed, and went downstairs for breakfast, after which we rallied outside. As always my wonderful friends had already seen to our belongings, the horses were loaded and we were ready to roll.

I know my fellow travellers could have made the trip instantly, the same way Francis had demonstrated, but this was never broached out of courtesy to me. Also, I must say at this point, these evolved souls would never use energy for the sake of it, indiscriminately, but rather navigate our world the same way we do.

We said our goodbye in order to return at a reasonable time and I lingered to the back with Raj, happy to be close.

On the journey back to the lodge in the valley, Raj touched briefly on the subject of our visit and the conversation of mining. He explained that having a gold standard as a form of trade was far more desirable than the current paper standard, which left the power in the hands of the few to manipulate the lives of the many. Greed is only the result of fear, and if one is at one with the Universal, fear is not part of the equation.

The return journey was effortless and my energy level was high, my fingers tingled with life and my legs were boundless. Is this what it is supposed to feel like when the Great Spirit breathes into our bodies? Surely it is always flowing and flowing like this! Then why have I not experienced this before, why don't we all feel like this all the time? Why, when it comes into me as perfect light, do I manifest it less than perfect? It's a matter of choice, but I'm still contemplating this wonder, and also viewing the screens of my mind that I've allowed to steal my 'present'.

# Chapter Fifteen

*The most beautiful experience we can have is the mysterious. It is the fundamental emotion that stands at the cradle of true art and true science.* Einstein:

Once we had settled, Raj asked me to go for a walk. Though I was feeling nervous, it was in a good way, so I took his extended hand. Only a fraction of who this man truly was had been shown to me, and though he was always understated, I knew he had reached a level far beyond my ken.

He saw past my physical form, my foibles, and had the ability to see who I truly was: the part of me I hid well. I permitted this. With certainty Raj was taking me on a gentle journey to the heart of the heart of my heart, and it was a journey I needed.

The skies of Wyoming seemed crammed with stars all dancing for the limelight, and now and again something unknown would move across the horizon, and it all happened whilst the rest of the world slept. The Universal hand was reaching out touching my heart, as my hand was reaching out touching the heart of the Universe.

Those places, referred to so lovingly by our hosts, those places where love pushes through to manifest more of itself, were now appearing in me as Raj gently caressed my heart, my soul, and my spirit. We had shared our most intimate corners as we opened up to each other, and I was grateful for the cocoon spun from the purest love.

Later, while sitting on a soft blanket of grass, he shared some of the wonders he had seen on his travels, and I shared some of the crazy moments of my life. He drew me closer and spoke gently, sharing his insights to the power of music, Cavalleria Rusticana being his favourite. I thought I heard the piece playing, and I recalled intimate moments we had shared in meadows such as this. He drew me closer still and whispered.

"Life may separate our hands, but will never separate our souls."

His heart was the heart of a poet with a will of steel, his mind was the willing slave of Truth, and his soul was pure. Yet a sadness in him placed a pearl on the altar of my heart, and I knew this amazing man had touched my pains, my anguish, my highs, my lows. I knew in that moment, I had been spared so much and he had carried so much for me. The knowledge made me sob silently, and I knew he could feel this also.

We sat and talked about little things and large loves. After some time, he asked about my plans once I returned to my 'normal' life. Of course, I had none. My circumstances had changed considerably due to my not working, and with no income the possibilities were different.

Before this trip I would've answered this question a little differently, but now I was looking forward to what the future held and I was happy to go from there. I knew that life offered everything and it was entirely up to me what script I chose, where I wanted to act out my play, and who I wanted as my main characters and extras.

Raj suggested I write. Not being a writer, my first reaction was shock, but on our walk back to camp I chewed over what he had suggested, remembered my experience with the violet flame mirror, and thought yes, he's right. Maybe there would be others who would benefit from my words and the great wisdom shared with me. Maybe others would write their own letters and embark on an unusual journey, though not in the same way as me.

We arrived back and reluctantly I said goodnight, retiring to a heavenly sleep, snuggled in memories of Raj and thoughts of possibilities.

The next morning we ate a sumptuous breakfast, always the freshest fruit and delicious nut milk, fresh baked bread, and tea. I love tea, my day begins with tea and ends with tea, and, I might add, these friends of mine accommodated this delight of mine abundantly.

After breakfast, we said our goodbyes. I was freer than I ever imagined one could be, and cares, well they were not part of the vocabulary in this here and now. However, I had a feeling for home, a strong pull to see my wonderful family again, a pull that in many ways did not seem logical.

Those who have experienced 'near death' describe the place they go to as peace and perfect love. Yet something inside draws them back to their earthly life, to their families and loved ones, even to the relative pain of living. Despite everything, it is the love for those left behind, and sometimes the inner drive to fulfill something further, that overrides their desire to stay. I now had such a pull.

Raj, Nada, Thomas and I, along with others of our party of fellow travellers, left the peace and beauty of the retreat, and whilst slowly meandering behind them, I took the time to review my life: the past, present, and how I wanted my future to be. Raj had planted himself in my physical world, what was this going to be like now, how was this going to play out in my world?

So much had transpired. It would be impossible to put into a book all the events I witnessed, let alone the radical changes in me. All these transformations were going to affect my world, would those who had known me before these changes be comfortable around me? Come to think of it, was I?

What I witnessed had impacted my emotions and consequently changed my mind. My mind change begot different decisions;

different decisions begot different actions, which begot different outcomes. If you always do what you've always done, you'll always get what you've always got.

These mind changes were going to affect all my subsequent thoughts, not like a stone thrown into a pond, but like a boulder smashing into the ocean, and I knew the reverberations were going to impact my family as well as my friends. You, the reader, by now, I'm sure, will have your own feelings around all this.

I noticed others on this journey were in the same quiet mode as myself. We were not the boisterous bunch we had been at the outset, and in silence, we continued for about an hour. Then Raj came over to tell us we would be stopping at a local village, where we would be staying the night as guests.

It was not long before I could smell the aroma of smoke and cooking and as we came around a bend, I caught sight of campfires burning. Five or six families, each seemingly involved in either preparing or cooking food, sat in happy chatter and children, playing, screamed with laughter.

As we approached, they stopped what they were doing and raised their arms and voices, rushing to welcome Raj, Nada and Thomas, as well as the rest of our party. We were royal guests, and in turn, the families had their chance to spend alone time with my favoured friends.

While this was happening I mingled amongst the children and talked with some of the women who had wonderful stories to tell regarding my companions.

Although these Great Souls seemed to be little known by us in our modern world, in this other world, this hidden world, they were welcomed and loved as family. They never referred to themselves as different, and certainly never referred to themselves as Masters, but I realised they were highly evolved Beings, and they were residing in The Rockies.

As the evening came to a close, we ended up around a large fire where people sang and tired children lay their heads in the laps of their mothers. Older children lay blankets and fell asleep cradled by the breeze, their young ears listening to the lullabies of the gods. I, too, felt cradled as I placed my head on Raj's lap and fell asleep, warm and extremely content.

The smell of cooking woke me, and I was greeted with a smile of love. He hadn't moved all night. The fresh dew had kissed the grass, and crystal droplets were caught on the threads of webs being spun by spiders. An eagle soared; its haunting screech echoed through the landscape. All was well. We ate and readied ourselves to leave.

Even though it wasn't necessary to supply food, the families packed supplies for us, and with final farewells, they waved us out of the valley as we entered into the last leg of our journey back home.

# Chapter Sixteen

*You are an aperture through which the Universe is looking at and exploring Itself.*
Alan W. Watts

The outside world was approaching fast and my head felt thick, as if I'd been drinking too much heavy wine. I found myself in limbo, suspended between two worlds, the finer I was leaving, and the denser I was returning to. These two worlds, seemingly so far apart from each other, were physically divided only by a group of mountains and a mass of separate thoughts, just as the old holy man at the sweat lodge had said. Oh how right he was.

It was becoming clearer now, that the vow I had made in a prison cell never to write my truth again was childish. I had to write now, I was not afraid anymore. A book written with the truth, as I had experienced it, would be the one way I could attempt to bring these two seemingly separate worlds together, for those with ears to hear would hear, and those with eyes to see would see. Maybe by reading my account, more would desire to take the road less travelled, like myself.

Raj took me to a clearing in the trees and cloaked his arms around me and I felt swathed in sadness. I knew our parting was imminent, and it was a gut-wrenching heart felt grief. My mind could rationalise how we'd never be apart, in truth there was no separation, but every atom of my being knew I was going to miss the touch, smell, sight, humour, excitement, bliss, incredible tension infused with expectations, and the sheer "being" of Raj.

I was torn apart before it happened, my heart was on its way to being ripped out, and a void would exist where his smile should be. My ears would lose a tone, my sight would lose a dimension, my taste and smell would lose enthusiasm. He knew, he felt me.

Held in his tight embrace, I felt him also. He permitted me to be sensitive to his thoughts and feelings just as he was to mine. Raj was me.

Gently lifting my head, his tender smile melted all prior thoughts and feelings of loss and I started to regain unity. I had only touched a minute portion of him, this I knew, I also knew that he had cloaked much for my sake. It was not the way of these Elder Bothers to flaunt.

Eternity would not be long enough to be held by him, but just as everything comes and everything goes I soon became aware of our physical separation once more. I heard his whisper.

"Dearest, this will always be. I am you, you are me, and while a part of us will continue to experience this physical world, seemingly separate, the highest part of us knows we are one in eternity.

"This you know and have experienced. We are one life dreaming the dream. We linger here for a moment in time, yet we re-embody ad infinitum. Through endless time we experience everything, we grow, we stumble, we learn, until eventually we reach the stage where we are ready for greater truths, greater responsibility. But the journey never ends, never. Nor can love." We stood together, considering the valley below.

This was only the beginning, he assured me of that, and it was thrilling to know there was further work to do together, but I wondered how I would know when, or how, or what.

Like always he lifted my thoughts from my mind, threw his head back and laughed. His beautiful features made an indelible impression upon my memory that very moment.

He truly was a handsome man with a handsome soul, he was a soul awake and I was just flowering. He didn't speak this time but I heard him, and I knew that when the time was right, I would be with him again.

We returned to Francis and I said my good-byes to others who, like me, had experienced the excursion of all excursions, and now had an amazing story to share. Francis, Raj and I walked on alone passing a tearoom, where the everyday chatter invaded my space for the first time. Further along, hikers made their way with cameras and walking poles, all eager for their time with nature, and thoughts sprang to mind of the times I, too, had driven to the mountains to get away from it all, camera in hand, oblivious.,

The familiar site of Lake Louise stood before me and all too soon my journey's end was looming. As we passed a group of school children, a little girl ran up to Francis and hugged Him about his knees. He bent down and I heard her say she loved Him. He whispered into her ear and she ran back beaming.

The journey didn't begin nor end with me. Many would enter these mountains and connect in a real way with these wonderful Beings, and I was aware that many would experience more than I, because of the love in their hearts.

People have travelled all over this planet of ours in search of gurus and teachers, seeking experiences and answers, and many books have been written with truth expressed in a slightly different way. But there are those who wait for that one soul who resonates with brotherly love, to take one step towards them and they then take ten towards that soul.

How could I ever look at the so-called ordinary lives of ordinary people in the same light again, for there truly may be angels or even Masters walking among us.

We arrived at a bench where a group of tourists were flashing cameras and happily chatting. Francis greeted them conversing in

Japanese. He turned slightly toward me, and I knew this was His farewell.

There were many tears from me, no words. Raj and I walked on and eventually entered the lobby of a nearby hotel. A room was ready for my night, and I accepted it all without question. I smiled and laughed at a mini distraction happening in the lobby but the laughter was a pathetic mask hiding the urge to scream.

Raj held me for the last time. Memories of waltzes, the excursions we had taken alone, oh, the moments filled with beautiful tension as I waited for his discovery, his arms, his love, his being, our soul. As he kissed me tenderly on the forehead, I could taste the sweetness on my lips. I drank in his aroma of sandalwood and I watched him leave. I went straight to my room; I wanted to be alone.

When I opened the door, the room was infused with the sweet aroma of wild flowers, and vases overflowing with pink, blue, and gold blossoms welcoming me back to my old life.

Alone at the head of the bed was a small bouquet of forget-me-nots and a letter. I cried with such love, I cried with the welling of too many emotions in my heart to understand or explain. I read the poem over and over, and fell into a long sleep.

The light came into the room, it was time to wake up and get up, but I was very reluctant to make any move at all. I wanted to stay holding onto every last moment, nestling into reminiscences, and snuggling into my soft bed of warm memories. Halfheartedly, I gave in and slowly opened my eyes. Shocked, I could do nothing but stare.

Like a crazy woman, I ripped at my bed trying to make sense of what I was seeing. My hands raced over the surfaces around my head and body, I listened for any noise, anything that would give me some indication as to what was going on.

It was a sickness, that's what it was, a sickness had grabbed me, but I was breathing, and soon all would be OK. I sat, teetering on the verge of total mania and tried to replay some of the chronological events I had experienced, from the coyote to the hotel. Oh God, what was this asylum my mind had taken me to, or was I the main character in a grand cosmic joke?

What I was seeing around me was ludicrous. I sat alone, totally alone. My mind was muddled, but I had enough of my marbles together to know that no physical illness was causing this condition. My thoughts jumped like crazy animals. Trying to orientate myself proved impossible. I knew I needed to concentrate, to think about my last nine months, the last two days, even my last night, but my mind was losing the plot completely. What was the date? Where was I? And Raj? How was I so warm? What happened? Nine friggin months, I mean nine friggin months. Please someone help me!

Gradually, I began to accept my bed was on the ground with broken branches under and over me. Sitting up, I touched the cold snow around my warm body. Here I was, still lost in the foothills of the Rocky Mountains after chasing the coyote trickster with abandon. My drama had resumed.

There was no sense or logic to any of it so I was determined to wait until I had found my car before trying to work things out. As I rose, I noticed a bunch of beautiful blue flowers with little yellow centres. They had been placed for me to see them. I wept. My forget-me-nots.

It wasn't long before a familiar feeling seeped into my thrown world, Raj was with me. Raj was real. Though I couldn't see him I felt his presence. Skillfully, he pieced back some of my scattered psyche. Though I was still having some challenges with the whole picture presented to me, the light dawned slowly, on this, my new day.

I had just spent a very real amount of time, travelling through the Rocky Mountains of North America, yet, I'd spent one night in an isolated wilderness on a bed of twigs. I knew with every fibre of my being that my Teachers were real, and very present, though the situation I was in was still a mind blowing mystery I could not understand.

My Teacher had wonderfully employed a coyote, the trickster, who had lured me so cleverly to play like a child, and it was he who guided me into a wilderness of discoveries. It had been Raj who had stepped out from a dimension dancing with ours, and it was Raj who knew the rest. More than that I had no idea.

We were a group of normal folk, me and my fellow travellers, but we had joined up with these Adepts and walked together along the same path for a given amount of time. And though we walked through a world that existed at the same time as you, the reader, it would seem we were in a totally different space.

There was no panic now, only certainty as I made my way to where I thought my car was parked. There was a ski track in the distance, and a cross- country skier raised a pole, saying hello.

As Raj had intimated at the hotel, (somewhere in my dying, or was it my sleep) my car would be waiting for me, and it was: where I'd first left it. The tank was full, the engine started on the first try, and I began my journey home.

Along the open roads, I viewed the edge of the mountains through the trees, guarding their secrets well. Back in the world where I now found myself, all seemed so illusory; people were already busying themselves, seemingly getting nowhere fast, and everything exaggerated my slowness. The further I progressed along the road, the further down from the peak of my experience I came, and I found it necessary to stop at intervals to wander into the trees.

Once again, I was on the stage with my tragedies, my comedies, and my loves, and it would be played out as my own life experience. The distant shore I'd left I hadn't, the time I'd spent I didn't, and what about my fellow travellers and their journey alongside me? How long had it been for them? Were they even real?

To say I was confused, well reader, ask yourself if confusion wouldn't be natural? Now I also found myself in limbo, suspended in a space neither here nor there. I couldn't work out time, and my head couldn't put into any kind of order the events I'd experienced.

Had I been dying, and all this was one of those near-death experiences, or was I in a kind of limbo experience, one where I had left my body to rest, slipped into a dimension where time was not the measure, and space was in some parallel universe? I couldn't think and stopped trying.

# Chapter Seventeen

*Knock, And the door shall be opened Disappear, And He'll make you
shine so bright Fall, and He'll carry you up to paradise Surrender all,
And He'll give you everything.*
Ellie Mac

I arrived in Calgary at the front door of my daughter's house later
than anticipated, much later; in fact, it was 5pm. by the chime of
the hall clock. It seemed like a lifetime since my travels began, and
though I had a story to tell, I didn't know *what* story to tell. And you
know, amongst it all was the truth of it all, the teachings, Francis, and
of course, the love I could not deny, Raj. I wanted to hold onto my
thoughts and feelings for a while and savour the flavour of my
spiritual banquet.

They were thrilled I'd arrived at the appointed hour, which
scrambled my brain cells again. The meal they had prepared was
just being set on the table – and it was doing my head in. Their
timing was crazy, but Matt, my daughter's husband, explained how
Francis had popped in again and informed them I would be arriving
at precisely 5pm.

I had to sit down, I had to breathe. It seemed that once more I
was to be challenged, a common state of affairs for me.

"What do you mean, Francis came to you? What do you mean
again? How do you know Him? When did He arrive? How did you
know the exact time to set the table?" The questions kept coming.

As far as my family were concerned, it was very straightforward; Francis had arrived the first time, saying He was an old friend, and gave them the letter I'd written at the onset of my journey, which, if you remember, He had asked me to mark the date and time upon.

When he delivered it, He asked Matt to make note of the date and the exact time of its delivery. He told them it was an experiment, and knowing I loved this sort of thing, they played along. Francis explained how I'd met some old friends and that I would be staying overnight in the mountains, but would be arriving at their place the following day. Having set their minds completely at ease, He departed.

The second visit was about an hour before I arrived. He said He was passing Calgary and wanted to let them know I would be arriving home at 5pm. He then handed them a package to be given to me and departed.

Sarah, my daughter, went to a drawer and took out the piece of paper on which Matt had written the exact date and time of the arrival of my letter. It had been delivered immediately upon my handing it over to Francis, way out there in the boonies. It had my signature on it, with the date and time, plus a mark I'd secretly made on the back, in the bottom right hand corner, just in case.

I went over to the mantel and picked up the package, wrapped in beautiful violet paper with a small, gold card attached. I opened it. Inside was the picture of Francis, or should I say the electronic likeness of Francis, the one I'd seen at the retreat in the Tetons.

I held it close to my heart, and though I was happy to be back with my adorable family, I knew one day my soul's journey would continue with my spiritual family.

As I went to wrap the picture back into the paper, a small bunch of dried forget-me-nots fell out.

There have been many books written about near-death and out of the body experiences, however, I can only propose to you that somehow I travelled along a path with Masters, I also propose that one of these Masters, Francis, entered my secular world, showing me and my family, that they are indeed very present, walking with us when permitted.

Two letters had impacted me – one written long ago, which initiated this journey – and the one delivered to my family. It seemed obvious the pen was the way to go for me.

Where we come from determines where we end up, and if we don't like the outcomes in our lives we can make different choices, and a change of perception can change suffering. With the heart incident I had experienced many moons ago, I hadn't caught on too quickly, but it had afforded me an opportunity to change my mind, as well as change my heart, and that was going to now change my life.

Returning to normality had its challenges. I had so much to think about.

Later that morning I listened to the news, and was affected by a terrible act of violence. The incident highlighted for me the world I'd come from and the one I was now in. Two extremes playing out on two different stages, and the only difference were the choices made. Of course it's all evolution, the choices are made according to our consciousness, and our consciousness is ever evolving towards the vision we hold in the eye of the mind.

It was becoming very clear to me, how some of the petty angers and frustrations I'd demonstrated in the past, along with little retaliations and irritations had impacted more than just the person, place, condition or thing I'd aimed them at. My little microcosmic outbursts were contributing to the larger macrocosmic picture, and the question was, how was it affecting the world? How was I adding to the overall picture? Was it a picture of beauty worth looking at, or was it a picture that was better relegated to a darkened room like the picture of Dorian Grey?

I asked myself, had I added to the anger on this planet, had I added to the energy used in the terrible act of violence that day? You may not follow me with this thought, and in truth, I'm really not bothered; you may just brush over this, but I urge you to think seriously about it.

I made a very deep commitment that day: to be mind-full of my decisions, for they impact all life. I am determined to try to make choices that serve love, as love is the only energy worth serving.

I wonder though, if those beautiful young souls who were tragically taken and harmed that day, gave us the opportunity to find more love and compassion? Let's face it, sometimes it takes a tragedy to bring people together, to assist us in finding our brotherhood. I am ever grateful to them and honour them.

On route to the airport, I made my way to see my dear friend, Linda, the friend whom I had recognized at the retreat in the Tetons. Did she recall her visit to the Tetons; did she remember anything of that night? I still needed answers, so I took a taxi to her front door and knocked.

Over the years we had developed a relationship of love, trust, and giggles, we had experienced some wacky moments, joined many crazy clubs, and peed ourselves at untimely moments. We share a bond of soul sisterhood, and to date we've experienced more in one lifetime than the average person in twenty. I knocked again.

As the door opened, we jumped, screamed, and hugged each other, something even mature women do, then she looked me square in the eyes. "Frick Ellie we need to chat, I'll put the Lapsang on."

I followed her into the kitchen. As she poured water over the strong smelling tea bags, the aroma of newly smoked kippers brought back memories of days in Cornwall, memories curling up with the fishy brew.

We had a ritual. In the past, she always said, "I love the smell of this tea," and I would always answer, "I love the taste of it." This time we just sat there.

"You know how I routinely call to the Masters before I go to sleep at night," she said as she poured. "Well, I don't always remember much, but this particular night I did, and it was an exceptional experience, where I actually saw you in my sleep."

She explained how she had been dozing one afternoon, and it seemed to her she saw Francis. The mention of Francis was something of a shock to me, I hadn't said anything as yet about my recent crazy adventure, but I kept quiet as she continued. Whilst dozing, the vision of Francis invited her to join Him, and being true to form, she responded with a resounding, yes. Then suddenly she woke up. Though she felt the encounter was very real, she passed it off as a catnap without the catnip.

That night, whilst asleep, she saw Him again, and He was standing by a table where people were lining up to sign a big book. He asked her if she would commit to a project, and again true to form, she said yes. After signing the book, she found herself, in what she now knows to be a retreat in the Tetons, and the rest, well, 'tis history. She looked at me and I knew she was searching to see if I was aware of the book, and I was.

"I get goosebumps when I think of how we're supported and guided in life by these Masters. Seeing you at the retreat gave me the proof I'd been calling for, proof that some of my nights of dreaming have truly been trips into reality." She smiled. "Now, enough of me, tell me about you, but first let me put on more water for more tea."

We sat sipping our brew, recalling our individual memories of the Tetons, and we sat silent also, not wanting to share some of the personal moments given only for ourselves, and we were content.

A puzzle created by the Great Spirit may not be seen for the true picture until the last piece has been placed in the correct spot.

Leaving people behind was something familiar to me lately, and it was with tears we hugged our goodbyes. Our friendship was not subject to time or space, as we always carried on where we had left off, and always with a pot of tea.

Now, on my final journey home, I desired nothing more than to be alone, away from crowds and traffic, stores and artificial lights.

I hadn't spoken about Raj to anyone, neither my family nor Linda, and I didn't wish to mention him in idle words, nor let him out of the door of my heart. I didn't want to share him for I knew it would hurt more, and I already hurt some.

In my little home on the island, I would be able to sit in my reverie and my pain, and I could also go over what had happened, or try to, although I wasn't sure if that was really possible. I also knew, by being alone, it would be easier to connect with him, my love, Raj. And, of course, I lived in hopes he would come to me.

When I arrived at the airport, I requested the back seat by the window, and once in the air, I reviewed those magnificent mountains full of life and adventure. What was my life going to look like in my future? I knew now that I was the creator of what would be; the future would be what I had in mind, literally.

Looking down, I knew Francis would be guiding the next soul onto a pathway into reality, or at least encouraging them to write their letter, and I fancied I was again being held by Raj, cosseted in a greater love than I ever thought possible.

The flight attendant was a gem; she ended up sitting by me, trying to console me in my constant tears. It had all hit me and hit me hard, the leaving that is, and as she handed me tissues, I told her parts of my story, the easy parts, and all because she was willing to listen.

She may have thought I'd had one too many or was on some form of medication, either way she was with me. At times, when I managed to utter some coherent sentences, I thought I saw a look of wonder come across her face, and she would look out the window.

There are many things that impact a life, birth and death being two of the most poignant. However, I had been shown that life in the secular world is the greatest teacher, and the reason we come here in the first place. It's all those daily happenings that inhabit the space which fills in the time we're allocated that afford us the greatest growth.

If we have an open mind, we automatically call for more. What that more consists of depends on where our mind is. If we have an open heart, we automatically consent for more love to enter the heart, and the Universe always rushes to fulfill that call.

Writing the letter said I had faith, I lived in hope, and I wished to be permanently in charity, and I smile now, for it's unimportant whether I had written out of true faith, or just bravado, I had written it, and with courage.

# Part Two

# Chapter Eighteen

*We are what we repeatedly do. Excellence, then, is not an act, but a habit.*

Aristotle

There are adepts, Masters as we refer to them, who have obtained control over themselves and the forces of nature, and have also guarded the sacred writings in the past regarding the Spiritual Powers of man and the only way man can develop these powers. But I ask you, did these adepts succeed in developing their powers all at once?

Is it possible for a person to climb a tree without proceeding step by step? Can a person reach the top of a building without any means to do so? Do you expect a child to walk before he has learned to stand on his own two feet or to be an orator before he has learned to speak?

Are these not perfect illustrations sufficient to demonstrate that in order to succeed well in anything you must proceed gradually? A thing done rashly is a thing usually imperfect.

If you see before you the goal you wish to achieve, will you give up simply because you did not achieve it the first time? No, you would summon the courage within you to step in the very footsteps of these adepts who discovered the true path of Spiritual Enlightenment, a path that is woven as a thread of mystery within all precepts and doctrines on our planet.

These footprints are still preserved and can be found to this day, and many guides who have placed their feet within these steps are in the process of attaining the same ends which these pioneers/elder Brothers have. The footprints are clear and can be seen vividly by anyone who cares to look.

The question naturally arises as to where can these guides and adepts be found, and the answer is of course, everywhere. But are they accessible to all, can anybody employ them as other guides are employed, and what are the costs for their employment? Money? Don't make me laugh! The fact that they retire from the busy world necessarily proves that they do not care for anything pertaining to it.

That being said, what else then can induce them to come to you to guide you on the path? Why, it is the living of a proper life, which a man ought to do. But what is that lifes?

With all the writings of old, and I mean old, with all that has been shared by those further along the evolutionary path, the answer is always the same: we must consider the whole of mankind as one Brotherhood, and *Try* to live as such, for the whole of creation has emanated from the eternally Divine Principle which is everywhere, is in everything, and in which is everything.. Their motto is '*Try*'.

# Chapter Nineteen

*Upon passing over the first question he was asked, "Did you find joy?"*
*The second question was, "Did you share it with others?"*
Unknown

Raj, who had been my companion and was still my love, was a loss I had not come to terms with easily. Spiritual logic ha! Don't talk to me about that. Is there such a thing? Well anyway, spiritual logic said he hadn't left me but you see it was that human part of me that haunted me so.

In amongst all my recent self absorption I had that itch you can't quite scratch. It was as if something was trying to touch my consciousness, and that *something* was wanting me to touch back.

Eventually I decided to follow Raj's suggestion to write about some of my experiences in the Rockies, but also to embark on more serious work, work on myself, and this included my little attempt at alchemy, well not really alchemy, let's say the art of manifestation.

And so it was that on this particular evening whilst sitting at my computer, that old letter, which I had duplicated with Linda so long ago, began to conjure up its magic again.

Upon finishing my writing for the day I started my ritual. I sat in the half-light, same place, same chair, reminiscing about my recent parting from Francis and Raj. I was daydreaming.

The room became suffused with a gentle glow. The woody scent of sandalwood wafted around me curling memories into my head.

He was close, and with every practice he was getting closer. I had been deprived of his essence, and now he was the warm, perfumed atmosphere caressing me.

Now some of you reading this may feel I was verging on the edge of black magic. I have asked myself this. No, I was practising the art of manifestation. I was attempting to grab the attention of Raj wherever he was and bring him to me.

I would conjure him up in my mind. I would bring back the memory of his smell, his touch, anything that memory could give me, until I was again with him. But of course, it was only my imagination, a conjuring trick.

It didn't matter to me whether I was on a flight of fancy; I found it comforting sitting in the dimness with his fragrance taunting me.

On this night though, my thoughts drifted and turned towards all I had been given so far in my life, the good, the bad, and the extremely ugly, and an overwhelming sense of gratitude brought me to tears. Gratitude took over any sense of desire for Raj and gratitude became my driving force. Motivation drives the will.

Questions filled my head. Why was it that the Masters hadn't attempted en-masse what they had shown me? Why hadn't they manifested and shown others what I had witnessed? They certainly had the ability to do so, and it would certainly help with the evolution of humanity quicker than it was helping itself. Then, as clearly as if standing in front of me a voice spoke, arresting my thoughts.

"The Master KootHoomi addressed your main question very beautifully in one of the letters he wrote. The letters you will come across at a later date. Let me share with you as best I can his words.

"The success of an attempt of such a kind as the one you propose must be calculated and based upon a thorough knowledge of the people around you...as for human nature in general, it is the same now as it was a million years ago: prejudice based upon selfishness...

What then would be the results of the most astounding phenomena, supposing we consented to have them produced?

"However successful, danger would be grow- ing proportionately with success. No choice would soon remain but to go on ever crescendo, or to fail in this endless struggle with prejudice and ignorance killed by your own weapons.

"Test after test would be required and would have to be furnished; every subsequent phenomenon expected to be more marvellous than the preceding one. Would the lifetime of a man suffice to satisfy the whole world of skeptics. ...

"What of the hundreds of millions of those who could not be made eye-witnesses? The ignorant – unable to grapple with the invisible operators – might they someday vent their rage on the visible agents at work.

"In common with many, you blame us for our great secrecy. Yet we know something of human nature for the experience of long centuries – ay, ages – has taught us. We know that so long as science has anything to learn, and a shadow of religious dogmatism lingers in the hearts of the multitudes, the world's prejudices have to be conquered step by step, not at a rush. As hoary antiquity had more than one Socrates so the dim future will give birth to more than one martyr...

"All this is old history, you will think. Verily so; but the chronicles of our modern days do not differ very essentially from their predecessors. And we have but to bear in mind the burning of supposed witches, and sorcerers in South America, Russia and the frontiers of Spain – to assure ourselves that the only salvation of the genuine proficient in occult sciences lies in the skepticism of the public.

"I conclude by reminding you that such phenomena as you crave, have ever been reserved as a reward for those who have devoted their lives to serve."

I sat in the silence and sandalwood, I also sat in the *extreme* exhaustion I had been feeling all day, then the final light of the day faded. I closed the door on the room and retired to bed.

Being too tired to think, I decided to wait until morning to consider the how, the why, and more importantly, the whether, regarding the voice I had just heard. Yes, in the morning. Then it happened.

Slowly slipping into that place where one is neither quite asleep nor awake, I became aware of his familiar fragrance. The touch of his love reached into my soul and gently lifted me out of my body into a world he was more familiar with.

In that pre-dream place we spoke, Raj and I, not with words but with consciousness, I was content. Time meant nothing. Time was a distant invention of a troubled mind and I was inside the soul of everything, everything I ever wanted. There had always been us, him and me, and now in this half state I had found him, or should I say, he had made his way to me. Or was it a dream?

But suddenly it was all interrupted by a sharp pain in the cavity of my chest which jarred me away. The searing pain I recognized, and when it travelled down my arm, I panicked. A mantra kept chanting in my head, one I had heard before, 'heart attack, heart attack, heart attack' and I bought into it completely.

Alone on my bed I was locked in my own hell, my eyes were sealed to the waking state and now very open to another world. My breath searched in panic for an avenue to escape, any avenue, and I screamed but no sound came. My body felt broken, smashed and aching, and it was only the sound of wings that interrupted my nightmare. The sound drew closer.

Ahead, darker than pitch, a large figure moving with great hush came toward me. Ice flooded my veins and a smell of sweet dankness filled my nostrils, and as the spectre approached, with one gesture of its huge wings it expanded into a dark magnificent being.

Tall and imposing, his chilling stare looked down on me with calm compassion. His eyes, deeply set into large bony sockets, showed quiet love, and now for some unknown reason I craved more of his coldness.

I instinctively knew he could numb my terrible pain with his gentle and quiet condolence, yet his form was one that would strike terror into the minds of those who did not know him.

Expanding his grotesque form, cocooning me with silk wings oh–so–gentle, he lifted me into his loving arms. My pain eased as his breath dropped words into my mind.

"You see, it is living that can be painful but never death. When I take you in my arms I dip you into forgetfulness or into a river of memories."

He was right. I had been dipped into the balm of pure love with all pain and sorrows fading into a background of nothingness, and now I was feeling nothing short of peaceful stillness.

Then there came a voice, a strong voice I recognized and loved which reverberated like an echo in a cavern. It was Raj.

"It is not her time."

The imposing dark form pulled back his raven wings of coldness and turned to Raj. Death's kiss was sweet but even in this place Raj had found me and his kiss was sweeter. I tried to rush to him but could not move.

In the twilight of this no-place they looked at each other and spoke in silence, and with the same sound of raven's wings darkness lifted his cold veil and Raj pulled me close. Before I could do or say anything he whispered, "We will meet soon, I promise."

Slowly slipping away from him and entering my body once again on the bed, I heard his words. "Remember, I am always with love.

I couldn't wake up; I couldn't move; my body lay on the bed. I was in pain again. Raj's voice echoed in my head. "Remember it is through our hearts we connect."

Sleep captured my tired body gently caressing the wounds of my heart and kissing softly my bruised soul. She rocked me as if I was a baby, carrying me towards distant shores to heal and slumber and I remember nothing more of my night.

I woke up exhausted and just lay on top of my bed. The pain I had experienced in my chest and down my arm had gone, and though it seemed like another heart attack I was feeling so much better than before this incident happened. One thing I knew for certain was this, I had encountered Raj as well as an awesome entity and now my only desire was to find out more.

# Chapter Twenty

*Life asked death, "Why do people love me but hate you?" Death*
*replied.*
*"Because you're a beautiful lie,*
*and I'm an unknown truth."*
Unknown

Being immersed in the light of my hosts whilst journeying through the Rocky Mountains had carried me to incredible heights, and now, with this most recent experience, I felt I was being dunked into another strange realm, one inhabited by a weird but beautiful grim reaper.

Of course, I realised there had to be a reason for all this but I had no idea what that reason was, as yet. Then two very unexpected emails arrived: the first was from my dear friend Linda, and the second from an old friend I had not seen in quite some time. These two emails portended a massive change.

Great news, Linda was travelling to the UK and wanted me to consider going with her. The second email was sad news. An old friend, Jane, was seriously ill and had requested I come to her as soon as possible in Scotland. I sent my replies. To Linda I said I would meet her at a later date, to Jane I replied I would leave immediately and boarded a flight to Scotland.

Upon arriving I was driven to a large country estate and shown to the bedside of Jane.

I had known Jane for many years and she was one of those friends you don't see often but the connection is deep and lasting. Part of one's soul.

Weak though she was, she motioned the nurse to leave us and once alone she took my hand and I leaned in closer.

"You know, don't you?" Her weak breath brushed my face and her words sounded familiar.

"You know about the other side?" She squeezed my hand and silently pleaded with all the life I could see left in her eyes.

"You have trust right?"

Yes, I did know, I did trust. I knew that the other side, as she referred to it, was a place of beauty and a place where dreams could be experienced as a joy uninhibited by the dense human form, where one could go forward eventually into a realm of peace and bliss.

As we sat holding hands, my attention was drawn to the window where a branch was loudly banging on the pane, and on that branch sat a raven. In the time it took to blink, the bird transformed into a large spectre who gracefully unfurled his shadowy form as he approached my friend. This was the figure I experienced when having my heart incident and I was familiar with his form.

Though in his gaze there shone a terrible power it was full of compassion, and though his heart burned cold it burned with a passion that was beyond imagination.

His dark wings eclipsed her form and he slowly raised his head and looked deeper into my eyes as if searching for something, and then he spoke directly to me.

"I come to lift the weary traveller from the limitations of the human form. I am the eclipse of all light and I bring the sleep that soothes. I dwell in the shadows cloaked in my sombre vestments, but those who truly know of me know my light and my means. I am the one you desire the least yet the one you will come to love the most.

This I am. I speak not with words but with the gestures of the mind and with the connection of the soul."

With one large swoop he enveloped my waning friend, and as light shone she released her grip on my hand and blissfully smiled at me. Then she closed her eyes to this world and as the light subsided they were gone. Her lifeless shell lay limp on the bed.

I sat for some hours and went over and over what I had witnessed, and knew there was not only a reason I had to be there at her passing, but also that there must be a bigger picture about to unfold.

Later that day I wandered through the grounds. It was a remote place forested by trees rooted in their own beds of purple heather and the path I was on wove through to a cold loch. Quite a way along I stopped and turned to view the imposing stone mansion I had just left. It was a true monument to past Scottish traditions, and now I was part of its story but also about to create another chapter in my own.

Standing by the shoreline I was content to listen to the hypnotic flow of the water and a thought came into my mind. Where was my friend now?

"On the level where her emotions reside," came a voice into my head. This was interesting. Yes, there are many of us who hear voices, and some are classed as mentally unstable, some are told it may be the still small voice. Well this was neither. This was a definite voice I could hear but no one was there. It continued.

"Death is the laying aside of the physical body, and it makes no difference to the higher self than does the laying aside of an overcoat to the physical person. Having put off the physical body, the ego continues to live in the astral body until the force which has been generated by such emotions and passions that she had allowed herself to feel during her earthly life have been exhausted." By now I was well aware this was not me talking to me.

"The character of a man is not in the slightest degree changed by death; the thoughts, emotions and desires are exactly the same as before. He is in every way the same man minus his physical body, and his happiness or misery depends upon the extent of how this loss of the physical body affects him.

"So you see there is no such thing as death as it is understood by the masses and generated by the fundamental churches. There is only a succession of stages in a continuous life; stages lived in the three worlds, one after another. The time spent between these three worlds varies according to how man advances along the path of enlightenment."

"Where are memories stored?" was my next question. I was enjoying this and I wanted more. Sure enough there came a response.

"In the vicinity they blossomed. And in response to further questions the answers will be given in due course, once you arrive."

Arrive? What was this voice referring to? Arrive? Where? But of course I had been here before, standing on the edge of an unknown precipice, the question was, was I ready to jump? You bet I was.

Sitting down on the grass, I placed my back against an old oak and waited for things to continue. I waited a long time. I must have fallen asleep for when I stirred, the stars were ready to take their nightly dip.

Have you ever noticed that by a large body of water stars give the impression they are dipping into the distant horizon. But back to my story.

A soft breeze played around my shoulders so I stood in order to make my way back, but before I did, I made my way to the edge of the lake. Closing my eyes I did my little ritual I used to do in the evening at home, the one to bring Raj back to me. I visualised him, his smile, his embrace, and summoned up the memory of his aroma of sandalwood, which now wafted on the breeze.

"I want you to hear me in your heart always," I murmured. "I want to be that whisper in the background of your everyday life, my love no matter where you are." A voice replied.

"Ours is an unconditional love that has surpassed time and space, there is no need for words My Dear."

I felt complete in this self-created alchemy; I had no desire to move so I just stood in silence. For a moment I thought I felt his arms slowly enfold me and then I turned to leave.

He smiled and my legs gave way as they always had. He pulled me in closer and his stare took me quickly to those secret places only we shared. It was Raj, solid, real, as real as I am now writing this at my desk. It was him!

Undecipherable noises spewed from my mouth in a most ungainly manner, and of course true to form I turned into snot girl. He held me close to his heart, then lifted my chin, lowered his head and his long dark hair curtained us. What I had dreamed of, what I had accepted would never happen again in this life, just had. He held me close.

Of course I had questions. "Scotland? What? Why? How? I don't understand?" He placed a finger on my lips and as I looked at him I lost myself in his timelessness.

Oh lover, my thoughts resonated, I wish to lose myself totally and cease to be. With you I am everything. I see suns, moons, oh universes. I see you! Yet they mean nothing unless they are propelled to their glory by the power of this love you stir within me. Oh such famous words.

Back at the old lodge we sat on the secluded balcony of my room, and he, as he always did, patiently waited 'til I had finished my ramblings which, believe me, took a while.

Of course he already knew most of what I was sharing, for though he would never impose on my privacy he had always been aware when my heart and mind called out to him.

After exhausting all capacity to open my mouth any further, my tongue unable to move due to the excessive workout it had gone through, he took my hands in his and shared why he was here. Scotland was the place for his next mining project.

When we said our last goodbye we never discussed where the 'us' of our relationship would be. Certainly for me, I would never wish to intrude upon his privacy and accepted totally Raj was active in another world I knew little of. However now it seemed I would be privy to an outer part of his world, and I was grateful.

He was a first ray soul and his journey on the path of service was the first, last, and only thought in his heart. But as he had been asked to oversee the opening of a mine in the area, and my dying friend had requested my help, it opened up the perfect opportunity for us to meet again.

It was the same with him as it was with Francis, every opportunity opened up avenues in all directions and no time was ever wasted. I am fully aware also that if I were not up to scratch in some way, Raj would continue on regardless and that is as it should be.

A friend had asked me once why a Master would decline to take on any aspirant as a disciple and now it was clear to me. The Master would be responsible karmically for those students, and that is a large cross to bear if the pupils are not ready.

Indeed if that Master had a hundred or thousands of students who were not ready it could be a nightmare. Can Masters have nightmares? No, I think not, but you get what I mean.

Unlike ordinary men the Master's mind lives wholly in the spirit, although he may be in the physical when desired. The Masters do not ignore the conditions of daily life; they fully sympathise with the struggling masses of humanity, but the higher cannot stoop to the lower; the lower must see the heights above, and scale them if he will.

It must never be thought that the Masters are our creators: they are only inspirers and educators. They have undoubtedly a human side to their characters but it is so inseparably blended with the higher spiritual nature.

We spent the next little while together, as I had been invited to extend my stay, and I spent those days creating memories and pockets of pure love that I could place in jewel boxes inside my heart. Then one evening as we sat by the blaze of a log fire, he said work was to begin and it was time for serious study on my part. He had his serious face on.

"Dear, you are an earnest inquirer who persistently banged on the door of the Brothers and as a result Francis banged on mine. You really couldn't be ignored anymore."

He smiled and looked into the fire as if listening. I loved this side of him, the pensive, quiet and reserved man, the man who had hidden parts and secret worlds.

"Now the door is open and it is up to you. All who have been earnest in their endeavours have been rewarded for their labours with knowledge and certainty, and this will continue.

"The path is glorious, however fraught with perils, but the sincere traveller must at some point embark upon the steep climb where at times it may appear that he is seemingly alone. However this is only an illusion.

"It is imperative that you continue to search with a questioning and open mind and not become ensnared by the glamour of those dangling mediocre truths, and teachers clothed in the guise of gurus." He sat quiet for a little while and then continued.

"A note was found in Madame Blavatsky's room after she discarded her physical body. It is truth and I would like to share it with you, it goes like this.

*'There is a road, steep and thorny, beset with perils of every kind, but yet a road, and it leads to the heart of the Universe. There is no*

*danger that dauntless courage cannot conquer, there is no trial that spotless purity cannot pass through; there is no difficulty that strong intellect cannot surmount. For those who win onwards there is reward past all telling – the power to bless and save humanity; for those who fail, there are other lives in which success may come.'*

He sat quietly and I knew he was seriously reflecting on something, however what it was I had no idea. Sitting with him in the silence gave me time to review the profound words of that amazing woman and they resonated within me.

"Your adventure a while ago clarified for you that Teachers of the Ancient Wisdom reside in other parts of the world, not just in India and the Himalayas. You were also given a window into the Truth that they have control over themselves and also those forces in nature which they guard.

"As a result of your opportunity many doubts you may have entertained regarding those Masters, if you wish to refer to them as such, dissipated like phantoms and were replaced with fortitude, trust and a daring created in faith. Remember that for many years some of the proofs you received were of an objective character, what a blessing, but earned.

"Be mindful, my love, with your writing. Many things that would be very satisfactory to me may not be satisfactory to you or to your reader. But we both must do the best we can to share what we can with the little we are permitted to give.

"And, yes, you will indeed have the opportunity to write once more."

I knew, that what he was contemplating was more than he had shared, but I also knew it was not for me to ask.

# Chapter Twenty One

*You can't cross the sea merely by staring at the water.*
Rabindranath Tagore

And so it was that I entered the schoolroom. Raj and I met every morning after breakfast and he shared wonderful insights as we wandered through nature. It seemed that there was quite the group staying at this wonderful home of my late friend, and I soon discovered they met each evening together.

And so it was, that after one of our wanders, Raj mentioned to me that there was a meeting in the west wing of the home. That very evening after supper, as night drew down her skirt covering our day, Raj and I entered the library to continue our chat but this time it was to be in a group setting.

It would seem this home of my late friend had for years been the setting for many meetings. These meetings consisted of folk such as me, as well as esotericists, scientists, artists and those of different religions, and in all the years I had known her, I had been unaware that she was even involved in such matters. This showed me how unaware we can be as to the presence of angels and great souls.

The evenings continued with one extra guest, me, and at one of these meetings Raj spoke.

"Who we refer to as Jesus, said, 'I and my Father are one,' he also said, 'for in Him I live, move, and have my being.' And I ask you now, who is this 'Him' the Master refers to? Meditate upon this for it will open you up to great insights.

"We too, are a greater being, a god if you like to the multitude of life forms evolving within us, our own living cells. You would do well to meditate upon this also." Raj wasn't caught up with the sound of his own voice.

At times we would sit in silence after he had shared and this gave us the perfect opportunity to be with our thoughts. For me this way of studying was brilliant, for it opened up the space to think and gave me time for a higher principle to come forth from the soul and enlighten me directly.

The Ageless Wisdom he was imparting was a revelation. Why hadn't I known there were seven bodies for example and not just three, and why hadn't this wisdom been more available to me through my New Age search?

Yes I needed to study more and this was obvious, for having the experiences I had been given was all well and good but what happens when the experiences stop, what would I be left with?

So as the scribe let me share further with you some of the insights as clearly as I can recall them.

"There are seven bodies," Raj said, "all interrelated. Of course, we are all familiar with the physical body, but then there is the etheric body, the astral body, the mental body, higher mental body, buddhic, and Atmic.

OK, I feel sure that by now you're thinking too much information for one chapter, trust me, I thought so, too, my head hurt, but just read on as it is an explanation about you, yes, you! The mandate over the door of an old temple was *Man Know Thyself.* I will attempt to share his words further here.

"The etheric body is the matrix, and is very close to the physical body. The etheric body has centres called chakras, likened to flowers, and each chakra is connected to our physical nervous system by a funnel which extends some four to six inches. These chakras generate energy.

"The astral body is sometimes referred to as the emotional body and is the body usually seen by clairvoyants with its array of colours within an egg formation. All our emotions in varying degrees are generated within this body. It is possible to cultivate this body, and when a certain degree of ability is achieved one may be sensitive to the energy of trees and animals and other living things.

"This astral body is part of the astral dimension, just as our physical body is part of the physical dimension. It is possible to become fully aware on this plane when sleeping, though many are only partially aware, bringing back when awake only a vague memory of what may have transpired during sleep. In some cases we may call this dreaming.

"The mental body is where our thoughts reside, and like the other bodies, it, too, has a dimension of existence, the mental plane. It is the lower mind that responds to our thoughts and coalesces the matter in this dimension to eventually create the form we have been thinking. For with each thought we are moulding it into a reality, and when we repeat the same thought over and over it is more deeply impressed upon the astral light.

"These are our four lower bodies, and the higher three are the triangle aspect of our being referred to in some teachings as the Father, Son, and Holy Ghost. Brahma, Vishnu, and Shiva."

My mind was overwhelmed with this information he had shared, for what I thought I knew I now realised had been so limited and had errors. With all the groups I had come across, all the New Age gurus out there, one would have thought that I would have found such teachings before, but I hadn't. They must have been limited just like me.

My monkey mind started with its incessant chatter telling me I had wasted so much time on limited ideas and limited gurus, and now my brain cells were locking down with so much new information and I wondered whether I had taken it all in. Raj addressed this as it seemed others had the same thought and one person voiced this.

"Becoming caught up with wanting more, trying to grab anything under any circumstance, only creates more grabbing, so why not let that one go. Let trust take up the space of mindless chatter, all will be stored on the higher mental plane and for now that should be enough."

Our meeting was called to a close, so feeling deliciously tired I rose to go to my room. Raj being the perfect gentleman escorted me and just stood in the doorway smiling.

He pulled me in close and I rested my head on his chest. His heart beat strong and his warmth infused me like cosy flames from a fire, then he lifted my chin in the way I loved and looked deep into my eyes. This was enough. To have him look into my soul said everything. Yes, it was enough.

He made it clear this trip to Scotland was for study and growth. He also assured me our contact would be different, closer in the future, and to trust – again that word – trust. I trusted him with my soul but as he emphasised the word trust again, I felt uneasy.

Pulling me in closer he just held me then raised his head to the heavens. I became overwhelmed by a feeling of sadness, and such sadness I was unfamiliar with, and I thank Universal love in action dear reader that we don't have knowledge of our future, for if we did it would be to live in dread.

"Embrace the journey you are about to embark upon my love. You will need to dive deep to find that pearl which will be created on the bed of life's adversity. Take courage in knowing you are never alone."

I didn't understand then what he was saying but I understand more now. He retired and left me to my room.

My night was restless and upon waking I had a vague memory of listening to someone speak amongst a crowd of people, but I only had an itch I couldn't scratch again so I rose.

Raj was not present at breakfast, but then his life, other than when we were alone, was involved with mightier things and I could only speculate. I didn't even know who Raj really was.

I had touched his soul: he had taken me to mine, and I discovered beyond that I knew nothing. I did know I wouldn't be able to contain my body if he allowed me entrance into his world completely. I was not yet ready for such a light. But our relationship encouraged self-reflection for I desired to be a better person since he had arrived into my world, and that took effort and commitment.

He had said to me once that human love was maya and I disagreed with him; however he explained further, and I have to say now I agree with him fully.

It is maya, because it is troubled with illusions and also engenders illusions in us. Some sentimental people think the love they are experiencing will last forever and it doesn't, and they sometimes think their loved ones are different than what they are and they're not, and this is maya.

Maya doesn't mean it's not there only that what you believe is true is seen with unclear vision. It's not as it seems. Our disappointments are nurtured in maya and we can never have peace whilst we are under its influence, when we cannot see with a discerning eye.

In my twenties I married a man and believed that all was perfect and we would spend the rest of our lives together in harmony and love. I discovered some years later it wasn't and so we didn't. What we thought was perfect wasn't and the reality of it was very different. Maya is a temporary illusion, for nothing is permanent except the Absolute existence which contains the one true reality.

Most of what is termed love is not, it is maya, but this doesn't mean what we are experiencing is non-existent. Maya is a condition in which things appear to be something they're not, it is a state in which we see things as they are not. Maya engenders illusions in ourselves and also encourages illusions in others.

Being in relationships is one of the quickest routes to enlightenment for it gives the opportunity to break through the thraldom of maya and to step into the one reality. To do that with a partner is courageous.

Here are some of *my* observations around a few things, and some may think me quite crazy. I may be off my rocker but my thoughts on the road to enlightenment have to begin somewhere.

I bumped into a friend one day and she looked as miserable as hell. You see the man she was in love with, I stress the word love here, had not called her for over a week and she had lost all her sense of humour. Basically he was happy somewhere else and obviously she was not happy unless he was with her. It came back to her that he had met this other woman for coffee and kissed her. She was mortified. Now ask yourself, is it not strange that her whole happiness depended solely upon him wanting to be with her and no other?

Bear with me here for if it was love she was feeling towards this man surely she would be happy that he was happy. To be frank it is jealousy aroused by possessiveness that incites such suffering, call it what you will. This can be destructive for anyone on the true spiritual path. What should it matter to us how the one we love comes by his or her happiness?

Being caught up in the glamour of the illusion that love is about possession and jealousy can be destructive, and though you may laugh or even cry at what I say it is the cause of much suffering in the world and we serve ourselves and others better if we're honest with our observations. To be brutally honest it was childish.

# TWO DINGBATS ON A SPIRITUAL QUEST

How often have I heard friends say they love their partners so much that they would do whatever they can to make their partner happy, Yet when they see their partner happily engaging with someone or something else they feel it's the end of their world or at least their relationship. Not really love but Maya, the illusion of love.

What they're really saying is, I love you so much that I want to be the sole person to make you happy to the exclusion of everyone else, and when someone or something else makes you happy misery will be the result, and usually for all concerned.

Please don't misunderstand me, fidelity in a relationship is a most wonderful virtue to be admired, but not exacted.

Raj spoke to me about morality one time, explaining that there is sexual morality, which is what many consider important, but there is a higher morality, fidelity of the mind and also of the soul, and of far more importance.

He explained that when the body dies the physical links are severed but the emotional and mental links continue and repeat again in future lives. And so it is that we face our infidelity or fidelity, which brings further opportunity to find love or stay in our pseudo counterparts, Maya.

So back to the story. Our group continued to meet and we spent much of our time discussing things like illusions, seeing things differently, and all this time in the back of my mind I couldn't help but feel there was an added reason for these particular topics.

This particular night I walked into the library and Raj was sitting alone quietly watching the blazing fire. He was deep in a somewhere that was nowhere for me. I sat quietly near him and soon found myself staring into the flames also, entranced by the gyration.

Slowly raising his head he looked at me, and, mingled with the love he always gave, I felt something else, something heavy and it shook my inner world. This evening he was carrying a burden that was hidden behind his tender smile and there was no way of me knowing. In silence he walked me back to my room and opened the door.

With him on one side of the threshold and me on the other, without the use of words I shared my heart. I knew he understood but he stayed silent. Turning to leave he stopped and stood motionless then quickly his arm was around me and I was infused with my desired drug – him!

Effortlessly he carried me to a space that was his, and oh so tenderly he returned me to the space that was mine. He raised me to my tiptoes and kissed my forehead, then my eyes, and then placed one small forget-me-not onto my upturned palms.

He was leaving but only for a little while, but this leaving was not the deep pain I knew he was feeling and hiding so well. Motioning me to go to my bed he then quietly closed the door behind me.

Little did I realise at that moment, life was going to take me on another spiral, one which was not so common, one which was going to plunge me into darkness.

# Chapter Twenty Two

*I was not afraid, I was born to do this.*
Joan of Arc

For some weeks now, I had been in my Scottish stately home studying and generally getting to know the area. Raj had left to work on the mine and I had more alone time.

After a day's hike with some of the people from our group we returned to the notice that on the weekend there would be a 'ceilidh at the castle'. So the following day I borrowed a jeep and drove into the nearest town with the view to buying a tartan wrap.

Delightful would be the word to use for this little village, with quaint stone cottages and stores taking up the front parlours. Everywhere I drove, and very slowly I might add, men raised their hats in a gesture of courtesy and women waved as if I were a long lost friend. So testing that friendship I parked the jeep to ask where I could buy a tartan wrap for the festivities at the weekend.

After many invites for tea, I took up an offer from one lady who insisted we share a cuppa with shortbread in her garden. Even with her strong Scottish accent I managed to understand some history of the area, stories of magical Celtic circles, and she also referred to a gold mine that would soon be opened further north.

She said the engineer in charge was very well liked and those who had worked with him in the past, including her brother the foreman, spoke of a certain something he had that seemed to draw folk to him, and of course, I knew first hand whom she was referring to. Before I left she handed me a beautiful tartan wrap.

On the night of the festivities I donned my docs and also draped the gifted wrap around my shoulders just as the sound of bagpipes wound through the corridors as if knocking on each door. Then a knock came on mine.

Dressed to perfection in formal attire with a waistcoat of the same tartan as my shawl, stood a very tall man. His raven hair hung loose onto his shoulders, his smile was full of mischief and he held out his arm for me to take. Never have I flung myself into the arms of another human being so enthusiastically, but he caught me. Yes it was Raj.

Life is so full of laughter and love and it was the Gay Gordons that took me to my breaking point. Laughing from beginning to end cramped my stomach so much it was impossible to take another leap. Raj looked on with great amusement but then the waltz came and it was in his arms I lost all time. One waltz after another we spun and I never tired. We whirled as one lone Dervisher entering into a trance of utter joy. As the evening wound down he escorted me outside and down to the lake.

"No matter how many times the water leaves the shoreline, it will always return. So it is with us"

In the trees, lanterns hung like fallen stars, and in a grove lay a blanket and a low table full of fruit. He was 'a romantic' in many ways this love of mine, even if it was all for my benefit. We sat and ate and shared then looked at the heavens.

When the time came, when even nature's heartbeat seemed to have stopped, we both sat in silence and I noticed him studying me. There was an intimacy to this part of him. I had no secrets, only a desire to let my heart be vulnerable, no matter what: something I had never done in my past.

"Tomorrow, I am meeting with some people further north and would love you to accompany me. There will be others joining us, though it has not yet been decided what routes we will be taking. There'll be no need for you to worry about provisions, all will be taken care of."

"When will I have to be ready?

"5.30 in the morning." He smiled. Absolutely delighted I rose, eager to get back and start preparing, but he caught my hand and pulled me back down.

"You're too eager, come here." Pulling me closer he held me tight, and in a world of unadulterated bliss he took me to places beyond my ken. Some time later he dropped me off at my room and whispered, "5.30am in the hall."

Breakfasted and well tea'd, those of us who were departing gathered in the hall and within half an hour we were off, our path taking us north. However, at a certain point in the journey Raj and I veered slightly off track.

Ahead, snow laden peaks towered above the dark blue crags beneath. Small waterfalls trickled towards smooth edges and dropped onto the accumulating ice below creating a wonderful rhapsody. It all said one thing to me, 'cold,' and I was not much into cold. However I found a wonderful distraction.

Moving just ahead of me was a piece of art, a model for Michelangelo's David, and revelling in my warm but indiscreet thoughts made me forget the coldness. This was until the object of my reveries came to a halt, turned, and with a slight smile shook his head. Hot though he was, I shivered remembering once more where we were and I had to gather the few elements of decorum I possessed and focus on my steps.

It was an easy thing to leave civilization behind, The temperature gave us the clue we had climbed to a much higher altitude. Raj pointed to a dot of a lake in the distance.

"Three more hours and we'll stop for the night." I made it.

A small cottage sat near a slight overhang looking down onto the lake, and as we entered the front door we were greeted with a dancing fire in the hearth, some bread and butter on a large wooden slab, fruit in a bowl and a big pot of tea.

This was going to be a special night, Raj and I alone. Just to be held 'til the sun rose was something I was excited about. Then I heard a sound outside which distracted me and I went over to the door and opened it. There stood my teacher.

I have read of the devotion pupils have for their Spiritual Teachers and I can attest to it. I had no idea where my head was but I ran and flung myself at His feet and held them. He stood holding His arms extended with a look of utter shock. Gaining some composure I let go and He gently touched my arm suggesting I rise.

"Your devotion is overwhelming" He turned to Raj, smiled and then sat at the table.

"So, here we are again and the question is are you prepared?"

I had no idea what I was to be prepared for but affirmed I was. Like, seriously, who would say no to Francis? Like, 'well now, let me see, hem, not too sure about that one, but I'll get back to you.' I responded quickly with a resounding yes.

The biggest blessing I had received from both my teacher and Raj were not the experiences, which had been amazing, no, it was the love. This love was changing me on all levels. I listened to all that was shared until Francis departed and then I fell asleep with my head resting on Raj.

The following morning as I awoke, I discovered I had been placed upon the long sofa and wrapped in blankets. Raj was waiting outside. We made our way to meet the others we had separated from and our destination was the Munros, 282 mountains over 3,000 feet high.

To my mind, this was going to be another Rocky Mountain deal with Francis and Raj, and as it would transpire, quite a few others. But you see we really have no idea what we're embarking upon when we take that first step to anywhere, do we?

We started our hike early, myself lagging behind, and after about an hour my attention was drawn to the right to a quick flowing ravine we had been following. Hiking, parallel to us, on the other side of the ravine, was Francis with some of our original group.

However as I looked ahead I was rather surprised to see Raj and Francis in deep conversation.

I stopped, looked back over to the ravine again and went into shock. There was Francis still with the other group.

Automatically rushing ahead to reach Raj, again I saw him in deep conversation with Francis and as I approached them both I was in quite the panic.

"I think I have altitude sickness and I'm going to die if we climb any further, like, my head might explode. I've seen it on TV, well, not heads exploding, but you know what I mean."

This was one of the times I witnessed Francis laugh so loud and Raj asked me why I thought such a thing - did I feel physically unwell? Of course he was trying not to laugh himself, I could see it. I actually felt fine other than my delusion, or was it an illusion. but I had panicked.

"Dramas, oh life's dramas." beamed Raj. "You had presented to you a sketch that didn't fit your framework. A framed Renoir would serve you better if I'm not far wrong?" He smiled playfully and continued..

"There are many things in this world that propose a mystery or miracle, but as expressed many times, much that cannot be explained is a demonstration of natural law in operation. No mystery, no miracle. Of course maya loves to pose, she will constantly vie for your attention and cloud your vision, hiding the truth."

Raj took me aside and we wandered over to a severely steep ridge that looked over the ravine. Torrents of clear water boomed below with a constant agenda to find its destination. Raj, being ever mindful of my height sensitivity, kept me back from the edge.

He slowly turned his head and with his gaze intentionally motioned me to look towards the other group across the ravine. I followed his direction, and as I looked at them I saw Francis bend down and light their fire with something that glistened in His hand.

Looking behind me quickly I checked where Francis was, or at least where I thought He was, and sure enough He was standing a little further down behind me lighting our fire. He placed a silver lighter in His pocket and turned away.

With no idea what had just happened I looked over at the distant group and He was not there. They were all warming themselves around a blazing fire.

"We don't spend our lives performing party tricks to fan our own egos," Raj said, "however, there are times when we give demonstrations to encourage.

"We give you what you want so you want what we want to give you." It made perfect sense to me, but I said I hadn't asked for phenomena. "Precisely," he replied. Francis had departed.

Everything I had witnessed so far would always be explained, or the penny would drop eventually and I would understand what was meant. I decided not to dissect the incident but wait for the mechanism to kick in.

"What the masses term a miracle, we demonstrate as natural law. We've discussed this before. Meditate and listen, the answers will come."

I felt as if I was Luke listening to Yoda, and he read my thoughts and laughed. Refreshments were ready; we ate, drank, put out the fire and continued on our way.

# TWO DINGBATS ON A SPIRITUAL QUEST

We travelled onward to bare slopes where the action of the wind had blended pockets of snow with clumps of grass encased with frost. Patterns of pristine white clouds and banshee mists danced down from the elusive summits and it was glorious, this Scotland.

By now we had experienced the full range of mountain weather and terrain. From driving rain to the warmth of the sun, from gentle slopes to vertical cliffs and cornices of snow. We had covered acres of rocky sharp ground and mile upon mile of thick flora, and it was magnificent.

Similarly, we had used different methods to navigate it all, from trailing along ridges to traversing heathery inclines, and at times we even slid down patches of snow. It was fun, yes, our hosts, Raj and his supporting team, looked on as we had fun. Does that surprise you?

Around us always were the views, constantly stunning. These remote highlands stood out because of their sheer grandeur. Peaks rose like sentinels around us while some remained vague and ethereal on the horizon. Long lochs stretched far off running away from us but at the same time enticing us to follow. All of nature was wishing to be noticed. I was feeling high.

Our day ended as the last light started to settle below the horizon and it was not too far ahead that I first spied the magnificent old castle, a fitting retreat here in the Munros.

This was some castle. Have you ever been to an old building and felt that though it presented itself as stone or brick it was a facade covering a world of memories and alive?

Patriotism welled inside me, yet I'm not Scottish, but I could understand very well what it was that spawned such bravery in the folk of these parts. History had been brutal here but this had also been a haven for a diversity of life. The romantic windswept highlands presented this castle as a statement to the nobility of its ancient people. It had stood the test of time and endured battles with courage.

A butler met us by the enormous oak door and announced the Laird would be in the library when we were ready. I wondered who or what the Laird was. Truthfully I didn't know what a laird was.

Our rooms had been appointed and we all arranged to meet in the lobby at 6pm so I retired quietly and crashed on my bed. I hadn't done any hiking since my trip to the Rockies and I didn't realise how tired I was. I fell into a deep sleep this night, and a totally new experience was waiting for me.

A light mist gathered around me. I began to feel a presence. Though nothing was indicating I was moving, I felt as if I was being propelled forward at great speed. Then, as suddenly as the mist had gathered, as I slept, it dissipated and I viewed a different scene. This was not something of the past nor something of the future, but the present. With a presence of light, close to my left shoulder like a guardian, I felt safe, however in front to my right was a large billboard, one that very clearly showed menace and carried an energy of threat and danger.

Two men holding large guns glared from the dull, dirty poster, and words not of any language that I knew were scrolled across the bottom. I took my eyes away from the billboard, and looked at the long road that stretched forever across the dry rubble. It didn't take a psychic to know I was in a far-away land.

There was no audible voice but I knew by the words dropping into my mind that it was time to go forward, and with just that one thought we travelled with great speed to a line of trees in the distance and stopped. Like a shaven patch on a scarred head a circle of trees had been cut away, and as I planted my feet down on the land I found myself surrounded by high wire and guns.

There were more of us than I first thought, like a gathering of light, and I can only assume I was light also.

When I had a thought the answers came, and the first thought I had was where the heck am I?

"There is work to be done and our work is to focus."

My heart was already engaged because the sight before me was pitiful. In front of me were little children. Though they were thin and dirty they had created a game with little bits of rubble and stone and they were laughing together just as little ones do. I made my way over to the group who were squatting in the dirt. Then I heard. "Our work is by the gate."

I was dumbfounded and near to tears. Before me was a depressing picture of children in a dismal cage and I was to leave them. By engaging my emotions, even for a moment, I had become stuck.

"Focus." I heard.

I knew I was not to let my emotions take over so I let go of the depressing image presented to me and imagined light surrounding the whole situation. I refocused my thoughts and joined the others by the gate area.

Three emaciated men stood talking and I swear one turned and made direct eye contact with me. I knew by my thoughts that I was to focus on intense light and hold it, so I did.

The gate opened and the last vision I had were of the three men, who, without turning once, walked out into the forest. The mist then enveloped me and I was once more aware of being in my bed, half asleep. It was now morning.

What had I been part of? I wanted to remember everything so I kept my mind focused on the last vision. I needed proof. And then I heard clearly.

"You will have the proof." I woke up fully.

On coming out of the shower I looked at the clock and it was 5am in the morning. I had slept all through supper and all through the night, I was shocked. Dressing, I decided to make my way to the loch. Leaving the front entrance I found Raj waiting. Talking incessantly with him about my adventures was becoming a pastime for me and all the way down I told him everything about my night, as if he didn't know, he might not, so I did.

"Well if you were informed you would get the proof, My Dear, you will." That was all he said. Funny?

That evening, after a grand supper and when everyone had gone off somewhere, I followed the sound of faint voices to the wing at the back of the hall. A small TV sat on the counter. I felt I had intruded into a part of the castle that was private, so I started to leave. Then I heard a news flash on the box and stood riveted.

"The three men will be arriving soon. We hope we may get a few words with them before they...oh, here they come now" said an announcer. Assaulted by flashing cameras and voices came the three men. The announcer resumed.

"Please keep your questions short, as you can appreciate these men have been through quite the ordeal."

A reporter asked how they came to be released from the camp they had been held in for three years and one of the men, who was quite weak, responded.

"We have no idea what happened, the gate just opened." There was silence as he became emotional. "At first, we thought it was a trap, we thought they wanted us to leave in order to shoot us. However we had nothing to lose so we walked through the open gate and kept walking until we entered a wooded area. Then we ran. We were waiting for the bullets." He stopped and lowered his head overwhelmed. "But nothing came. We have no idea how the gate opened or why." With this the men were escorted into a waiting vehicle.

They were reporters and had been captured about three years earlier and taken to a camp, it was assumed they would eventually be used as exchange hostages. These three men I recognised as the men in my sleep.

# TWO DINGBATS ON A SPIRITUAL QUEST

As I stood trying to piece things together a hand touched my left shoulder and I quickly turned to see Raj. Only then did I realise the one taking me that night as I travelled to this camp, was him.

"Let's walk. In general people have the belief that those a little further along the path are super beings." We walked further and he became silent for a while.

"Ascended I believe the term is, but then what? The journey is never ending, it is forever." He stressed again the word, 'forever.'

"Forever is hard to grasp due to the tendency of man to place the omniscient, omnipresent and omnipotent into a mental box labelled 'concept'. There has always been a hierarchy, there will always be a hierarchy. All life is evolving along various paths towards Brotherhood and Union, and then the journey continues beyond into unfathomable realms that even the Mahatmas cannot comprehend.

"We are all in the body of the Planetary Logos which of course is part of a larger body, that of the Solar Logos, which in its turn is in an even larger body, the Universal Logos, and so it goes on infinitum. Why even the cells evolving within you believe you are the Logos.

"It is impossible to grasp the fullness of the word infinitum but forever is the soul's journey, and as you journey through forever you will encounter everything in every way. Remember a concept is never the whole truth. Contemplate these things and answers will pour like liquid gold from the cup of truth and wisdom."

He walked me back to my room and we entered. He closed the door and my heart took a cue from his heart. I was happy just to rest quietly in his arms.

Many times, we danced to the melody of love. Our harmony bounced off stars like gems on a cymbal sounding our own unique chords in harmony with the notes of the Universe. He was an exquisite lover.

When we were together like this he never just touched me he embraced all of me. His kiss was never a mere pressing of lips, his touch never just the coming together of two people, it was a union. With him I would break the confines of my prison anchored so brutally at times in my limited physical body. This freedom he took me to was where I forgot the little affairs of my own small heart and stepped into the heart of all. He told me this would happen, and I believe him.

An awesome realisation came to me, of how those who are further along the path sometimes surrender a part of their freedom to assist another soul in service out of the purest love and with the purest intentions. This divine romance we were in was the result of many lifetimes and for most of these lifetimes he had been in service to me.

As I write this dear reader, I would endure a thousand lifetimes in order to transcend my limited being so as to free him. Of course it all sounds so romantic and I never considered myself that, but I never promised this book would be anything other than my story, told my way.

"My love will always be with you my dear, with no expectations, remember this," he whispered as I fell asleep.

He didn't leave me that night but held me in his arms whilst I slept, and when I awoke he was at the door. He smiled whilst quietly leaving my room. On the pillow next to me was a beautiful note, a poem, and his words were of love and I felt warmed.

# Chapter Twenty Three

*By the dim light of an accidental lamp, tall, antique, worm- eaten, wooden tenements were seen tottering to their fall, in directions so many and capricious that scarce the semblance of a passage was discernible between them.*

Edgar Allan Poe

We had our routine, the guests that is. We would meet in the library at 8am, break for lunch, and the afternoons were informal. After supper we would resume once more in the library with our Teacher. But things were about to change as the following morning we were moving to a location near one of the distant peaks. After breakfast we met outside and with all prepared we set off.

Scotland demanded attention, not in the brash way of a continental playground or the intense bustle of a metropolis. No it was with her rare beauty, her rough edges full of life and colour, one could become seduced by her natural beauty. The heart of this country was dotted with pockets waiting for someone to discover them. One of these pockets was like no other I had visited before.

We approached this particular wooded area with enormous trees that stretched arms upward towards the sun. They were magnificent. We could see as we walked across the forest floor, roots like little old ladies fingers that had gnarled their way through the undergrowth winding to and fro supporting and keeping it all together. The light shot through branches showing up the lime on all the soft moss and buds as well as the heather and small flowers, and the colours reminded me of stained glass windows. This was a place of fairy stories and more. However whilst taking all this in something to the left caught my attention.

He was there and about three and half feet tall, motionless, and peering at me in just the startled manner I was peering at him. A little man with a long beard, rosy cheeks, and oh please don't crucify me here dear reader, a hat, yes a hat, and it was green.

Then he popped behind a tree quicker than I could question and the whole moment was over. I fell. Raj hadn't saved me from that fall. As I turned my Samaritan was looking at me laughing and I stayed on the floor 'til he had gotten over his merriment. I rose, rubbed my butt and joined him and the others.

Humour runs along with joy, it was told to me once, and it does. In my experience with those further along the evolutionary path than I, there were no long-faced religionists, there were no austere solemn or out of reach gurus ready to show me inferior to their superior. No, I have only been met with constant love, endless patience, and boundless humour.

Over food and tea we shared some stories, and then the chance arose for me to ask about the gnome. Was it a gnome? Was I experiencing some form of altitude sickness again?

"Gnomes, sylphs, fairies, djinns and the like, are the Soul of the elements, the changeable forces in Nature, acting under one immutable law," offered Raj.

"With undeveloped consciousness and bodies of plastic mould, they can be shaped according to the conscious or unconscious will of the human being who puts himself en rapport with them.

"They are said to have etheric bodies that are composed of etheric matter, a type of matter much finer and purer and composed of smaller particles than ordinary physical plane matter. They are usually seen when the third eye is open.

"Devas help guide the process operations of nature. Such processes are the evolution and the growth of plants. Their appearance is sometimes perceived as coloured flames about the size of a human being, however at times they can be enormous and take on a form one would call angelic. There are smaller, undeveloped, minor angels, called nature spirits, elementals and fairies, and these all come under the guidance of the Devic Kingdom.

"This kingdom is on a separate line of spiritual evolution called the 'deva evolution' or sometimes referred to as the 'angelic path.' As their souls advance through the process of reincarnation they will all evolve eventually as devas. Their process is no different than that of human evolution, for all life has a hierarchy.

"The Devic hierarchy has been involved from the very beginning of this planet with the creation of nature, and are presently involved in, and working closely with, the human hierarchy.

"In fact we all have a Solar Angel that is very near to us, they have actually given a part of themselves to help us evolve, they are in our service so to speak. The part they give to us is the part of divinity within them that has been growing for endless years and the reason they do this is to help us evolve.

"We owe a great deal to the Solar Angel and to the Devic kingdom who are constantly attempting to bring about balance where humanity has wrought such havoc in nature. Though very real, they're not always seen, however this old forest is the ideal place to peer through the window into their world."

I appreciated all he was saying, however I became distracted with something else. You see we each have our own perfume, our own smell, and Raj's was always a light but heady sandalwood which I couldn't get enough of, and just at this moment I found myself inhaling rather deeper than I had before. He turned to me.

"Do you have a problem with your breathing, My Dear? Is the journey too much for you? Would you prefer to go back and rest while we continue on?" He smiled.

No matter how much time I spent with this man, I still became embarrassed at my little human foibles though they seemed to make him smile. I cut him an embarrassed and dirty look and he just laughed.

The dying flame of the day shot its last glimmering tapers across the land, and further in we came across a most delightful small stone cottage, one of many rustic places dotted throughout the forest. This Bothie was to be mine for the night. Local landowners offer them as resting places for any passing traveller, but of course in our case it had all been pre-arranged, more to the point, pre-ordained.

Later that evening, after supper and lots of tea, we sat around the large warm fire pit chatting and laughing and like a vision from the woods, Francis joined us.

"Have yourselves a restful night for in the morning we will split into two groups. Our journeys will take us on different paths." Then he departed.

Immersed in the descending cover of mist, wrapped in woollen blankets, Raj and I sat together on the moss and heather outside the little cottage and eventually I fell asleep in his arms.

The next thing, I was looking down on my body lying on the moss asleep and motionless. It was weird but Raj was by my side. As we walked, leaving our bodies behind, I heard intonations which pulsed louder and louder.

A little way in the distance rose a tall light, a force of energy that exuded rays from its upper body, outward and upward, just like long hair blowing in the wind. Then I heard Raj.

"Neither male nor female the being is free, free from the ties of reproduction and the dense physical body that keeps us bound."

This being was Devic with piercing eyes of power I automatically respected. It seemed from another world but in fact it was from another kingdom working along with ours.

As it pulsed towards me it sang a chorus of thoughts into my mind, I felt a part of this nature: we were connecting. But with this overwhelming connection I experienced first hand some of the losses nature was experiencing. I became very saddened.

"The harmonising work of nature is endless and these beings are constantly bringing about balance and bliss, constantly repairing all that humanity in its ignorance is destroying."

Raj smiled and we walked on. We walked over to where the fire was still burning and watched the colours unfurl like the wings of exotic birds dancing up towards paradise. "The workers of fire," whispered Raj.

These were the salamanders, the willing servants of the great fire devas with the power to scorch rocks, yet pirouetting like playful children. As I watched them, their hypnotic gyration made me light headed and I was back in my body again and knew nothing 'til morning. When I awoke I was in my cottage, in bed, snuggly warm and getting hungry.

Our next day's hike was uneventful 'til we came to a small village, and walking right through to the other side, up a winding incline, we reached the old country seat of a rather interesting man. The approach was stunning with an arched bridge giving access to the main building. Later I found out that a number of important relics had been housed within its walls and chief among them was the Fairie Flag and Cup of an old clan.

Legends, however fantastic or far-fetched they may appear to be, are rarely without some trace of historical fact. When a relic survives to tell its own story, that at least is one fact it is impossible to ignore, and the flag of this old established family was just such a relic. Fairy stories can sometimes be difficult to relate to fact, or so it would have seemed to me before this trip.

As we approached via the stone walkway the storybook atmosphere of the whole place struck me. The surrounding green moat and the triangular layout of the whole place showcased each corner capped with a turret or two. By the double oak doors stood a man donning what I considered to be the tartan of this old family, and he welcomed us into the big hall.

A blazing fire burned in an impressive stone carved surround whose design forced me to look up to the well-worn coat of arms obviously placed there many moons ago. After we took off our outer clothing, he slid open two heavy oak panels showing a room of books, tapestries, oak furniture and the biggest, old, wooden chandelier I had ever seen. However it was the smell that caught my attention, it was a smell I knew – but didn't, if you know what I mean, it was a memory from somewhere.

Francis greeted Raj and they went off elsewhere, and the rest of us followed the man into a dining room where we were fed and well tea'd.

My room was up a curious left-handed spiral staircase, which I discovered later is extremely rare. In old castles the staircases are more often built to accommodate right handed men who may at some point need to wield a sword as they climb. So it was obvious the owner at the time of construction was left-handed. It's amazing what one learns when one studies with an Elder Brother, only joking.

My room was spectacular and located in one of the smaller turrets. Out the window was a view of the loch and inside was a four-poster bed with big soft pillows and brocade curtains. I threw myself on the bed, a princess in her castle.

Wandering downstairs I found a wonderful oak room (we were permitted to wander), and I tapped at the panels to see if there were any hollow sounds hiding secret passages. Startled by a voice behind me I turned to see a woman wearing a long tartan skirt.

"There are," and she took my hand and escorted me into a very small library. She stopped in front of a shelf covered with Theosophical works, removed a couple of books and placed them on a table. Then she reached her hand to the back of the shelf where the books had sat, and slowly the whole panel moved. There behind a wall of books was a corridor and we entered.

It was that smell again, the familiar smell which had caught my attention earlier and it was wafting down the corridor. They say that smells are linked with memories and sometimes we recall the smell but not always the memory.

We entered an open chamber where documents and old papers were housed, then she lifted an envelope with a red seal off the shelf and placed it in an old box.

There was my memory. This was the same smell in the library where I had found the letter I replicated some time ago, and this box was the same as the one that was sitting next to it.

Was the envelope she had put in the box *the letter* that Linda and I had replicated? How could it be? She then picked up two books titled "The Secret Doctrine" and handed them to me and continued talking.

"Of course in the past most secret passages were avenues of escape leading to safe places in the woodlands," she shared. All I wanted was to see the box and the letter inside, all she wanted was to talk more about Theosophy.

"Madame Blavatsky presented teachings from the Ageless Wisdom and the society was called Theosophy. There is a misconception regarding theosophy. Some think it a religion, some a cult, and there are some who call themselves theosophists, who give verbal homage to a written word leaving behind the true essence."

Inside I was screaming, I wanted to see inside the box.

"Theosophy encourages brotherhood and open-minded inquiry into world religions, science, philosophy, as well as the arts. It encourages respect for the unity of all life and assists those willing to explore spiritual self-transformation and abstract thinking without judgement." I was still screaming inside, for I wanted to see inside the box.

"This path is for the serious seeker. There are those who call themselves theosophists who entrench themselves in the doctrine becoming veritable libraries, but if one fails to embody the essence of the true meaning it is empty.

"Calling oneself a theosophist or belonging to a lodge is not an automatic entrance key to the door to Mastery." She motioned me to keep the books.

"Ageless Wisdom is contained within those covers and although you may find parts challenging at first, it is the theory of the gradual evolution of humanity over a timespan of millions of years.

"Each step in human evolution is called a root race, of which there are seven in all. It is a masterwork covering cosmic, planetary, and human evolution, as well as science, religion, and mythology with corroborating testimony from hundreds of sources.

"Questions constitute the path so ask many, and persistence is a quality necessary to scale the mountain so be persistent." I was persistent, I was screaming a question inside, I wanted to see in the box, but just then the gong sounded and we went to the larger room.

Though our close party consisted of four, with of course Raj and at times Francis, in this larger room were many I had not seen before.

We were all from various backgrounds, like Russia, India and America, and it wasn't long before the conversation became very lively. That was until a sudden stillness came over us, it was as if an angel had just walked into the room.

# TWO DINGBATS ON A SPIRITUAL QUEST

We all quietly found our seats; it was so automatic, without words or notice. This was curious; it reminded me of the hundredth monkey theory though on a much smaller scale.

The Japanese monkey, Macaca Fuscata, had been observed in the wild for a period of over 30 years. In 1952, on the island of Koshima, scientists were providing monkeys with sweet potatoes dropped in the sand. The monkeys liked the taste of the raw sweet potatoes, but they found the sand unpleasant.

An 18-month-old female named Imo found she could solve the problem by washing the potatoes in a nearby stream. She taught this trick to her mother. Her playmates also learned this new way and they taught their mothers too.

This cultural innovation was gradually picked up by various monkeys before the eyes of the scientists. Between 1952 and 1958 all the young monkeys learned to wash the sandy sweet potatoes to make them more palatable.

Only the adults who imitated their children learned this social improvement. Other adults kept eating the dirty sweet potatoes.

Then something startling took place. In the autumn of 1958, a certain number of Koshima monkeys were washing sweet potatoes – the exact number isn't known.

Let's suppose that when the sun rose one morning there were 99 monkeys on the Island who had learned to wash their sweet potatoes. Let's further suppose that later that morning the hundredth monkey learned to wash potatoes.

By that evening almost everyone in the tribe was washing sweet potatoes before eating them. The added energy of this hundredth monkey somehow created an ideological breakthrough!

The most surprising thing observed by these scientists was that the habit of washing sweet potatoes then jumped over the sea to colonies of monkeys on other islands and the mainland troop of monkeys at Takasakiyama began washing their sweet potatoes.

It has been assumed that when a certain critical number has achieved an awareness, this new awareness may be communicated from mind to mind.

Now we humans in the room were of one mind and were sitting waiting expectantly, when the door opened and a rather distinguished looking elderly man entered the room. He stood by the hearth resting one foot on the grate and watched the flames while he lit his pipe.

"Hmm," He uttered. "So what have we here, a group of aspiring Adepts hey? Hmm" He quietly chuckled to himself. Francis and Raj entered the room and sat near the back.

The old man looked to Francis, "Come, come, you do the talking, I'm getting too old in the tooth for this." Then with a twinkle in his eye he sat in the large wingback chair.

"The bliss of striving, in essence, is illumination. The life of the Absolute is our life, there is only one life is there not? And this life is the life of all and it is no more in one than in another.

"The word Christ is a mysterious word to many and experienced by few, and this we must change, and so we strive to experience the Christ constantly and also permanently, and to be conscious at all times of the Christ working within us." Francis made His way to the fireplace.

"We look to this power within us for we individualise infinite power in proportion to our consciousness of truth. Gaining mere dollars is not spiritual supply. Greater savings do not constitute security; physical health is not necessarily a foundation for eternal life. These constitute merely an improved human belief.

"As one advances along the path all attempts to improve the human condition fall to one side in light of the true goal. I have little to say but these words, and I ask you to contemplate all or in part. You will have your own illuminations and this is theosophia, the truth." Our host then motioned behind me and an East Indian man spoke.

"Your thoughts are not my thoughts and my ways are not your ways. Here we are not attempting to gain more than one another, not to think better nor to think the same, but to expand and know the Divine thoughts and ways. At this level of thinking we realise it does not serve our cause to have concern for our own welfare but only for the concern of others in service to humankind, humanity." Then another person spoke.

"Daily we are provided opportunities to use what we are studying, mere words serve nothing. As we face each moment in the knowledge of the perfection of the law, we reveal more and more the light of truth and the Divine. The Master said, 'And ye shall know the truth and the truth shall set you free'."

This went on for some hours; we were presented with ideas and then given the time to sit in silence. In this silence we could just think about what was said, and the soul could then permeate an understanding. This was liberating wisdom instead of just data collection, and it came with ease instead of the constant struggle to follow a runaway train of facts fired up by an intellectual mind.

Words are symbols carrying great power, but these symbols have a limited spectrum and can create much confusion, and it is the soul when permitted that lifts the wisdom from the texts. From this place we could share with each other and this way of sharing insights meant we could make up our own mind literally.

It was getting late and hot chocolate was brought to us on a silver tray by the ghillie in the kilt who was outside when we arrived the previous day. As he was leaving he turned and spoke.

"We may live in the giving sense rather than the getting, the being sense rather than the attaining sense, and with this conceit and selfishness fade away. Have patience and forbearance with those still struggling, remember there are those who are ahead of the game with respect to yourselves and they too afford the same to you. Always be of service" He turned and walked out.

Now I'm ashamed to say my bottom jaw hung, for I didn't expect such from the chocolate carrying ghillie at all. Then our Host, a man of very few words, rose and departed. With Him went Francis and Raj, and like the others I departed to my bed. Strangely I dreamt of Africa.

# Chapter Twenty Four

*Reaching the end of my rope I tied a knot and hung on for dear life.*
Unknown

To the east the broad dome of the sky stirred. One could almost hear the whisper 'let there be light' and night, quivering a little, slowly obeyed. A ruby glow rose through ashen grey and leaked purple, scarlet, and gold, like a cracked egg across the sky. It was the birth of the day. A beautiful sunrise.

In the distance elephant's lolloped causing heat waves to dance in all directions, and through the haze I saw two figures slowly walking ahead like mirages in a desert. They stopped as I approached, and one of the figures turned and smiled. It was Beth, the mother of my best friend. She looked radiant but I wondered how I could be seeing her because she had passed away some years earlier.

"I'm walking the plains of Africa." Came the clear thought. The woman walking beside her then turned and I stood in shock. There was my own mother looking vibrant, though she too had passed over. A scene unfolded before me.

Four little girls, laughing and calling, ran towards the two women who reached out with open arms and then my familiar dark raven approached from nowhere. Expanding to an enormous size, and with satin wings, he enveloped the whole scene. The picture disappeared into a pitch cloak, and the moment was gone.

As I was about to leave, though I have no idea where to, for I was still sleeping, a rustling caused me to turn and my spectre was back.

Most people who come into contact with this awesome being surrender to him out of fear or pain, but I had no fear, only an overwhelming desire to show love though I'm not sure if it was because I had a concept of his loneliness. His spectral hand reached out to me and I took it.

All the stories and pictures that have been generated throughout the centuries describing his grotesque form and his dark mission does such a great disservice.

Visions flashed in front of me of those who had looked on him in horror pulling their hands away with terror, and I witnessed those who would rather perish alone than look upon him for any guidance. Such programming of the human has occurred over centuries.

He lived in the land of rejection, neither in light nor darkness, though he was brighter than any angel and so loved by those who truly knew him. His was a place where those who are lost linger. I knew his heart was bigger than all the sadness he had ever experienced and his heart was the heart of love.

How misguided I was, for there was no need to console him; *he* was the Master of solace and provided humanity with the greatest of services.

In this place where I stood his work was constant: always guiding those whose eyes were closed to the light 'til they could see. I was in his 'no-time' a moment only but I witnessed countless souls who struggled when first encountering him. Eventually they came to experience his enormous heart as they let go of the earthly life and became full of wonder at the beauty of the real life they were being guided into. This is what I had witnessed with these children on the plains of Africa when they died.

There are many like my mother and Beth whose short service it is to greet those just leaving this earth, how long they linger to do this work I have no idea for they too are in the process of 'the journey home'. They greet those transitioning with joy and peace and they are guided to their right place by the mind of him. The next thing I was aware of was daybreak in my room and I was pleased to be alive.

The days that followed were spent exploring and meeting other guests who were now becoming my dear friends, and in the evenings we would go to the library and attend little soirees.

Raj was still attending to work at the mine, and though I was aware he was an engineer I was also aware the mine was just a project. He had explained he was a student of the Ageless Wisdom, and as he put it so well, a student of life.

This evening after supper, like everyone else, I made my way to the library where Francis was already sitting in the high-backed chair. We all sat in silence.

A thought came to my mind, and though I say so myself it was quite a profound thought so I pondered it. I even came to a conclusion about it. Then another thought arrived at my station, eventually boarded the train and left, and this process continued. Suddenly I realised I was the stationmaster observing my thoughts as they came and departed. Who was the 'I' that was observing these thoughts? Then a woman sitting behind me started talking.

"Our souls are many but there is only one spirit. The same sun shines over everybody on this earth, and one and the same spirit shines over and illuminates every soul." Then the next person, a Hindu I believe, spoke.

"We are already master creators, however what we create is not always what we wish to experience. No one person is born with more power than another regardless of life circumstances. What one focuses on one generates. It always behoves a person to approach his moments with a positive attitude."

Francis turned from the fire and looked directly at me. I've always found it difficult to speak when eyes are upon me, but on this occasion, when Francis looked at me, I felt I would burst if I didn't open my mouth, so I did.

"Every moment we create by thinking, feeling, and doing."

He looked at a young man to my right and addressed him. "This topic is for you My Son."

"Yes," the young man answered.

I explained, "what I'm trying to get to is this. When interacting, with people or life, we engage our minds, our emotions, we act and react. When we watch a movie or television, we engage our minds, our emotions, we act and react.

"Is the law different for each?

"I've asked people why they watch movies of murder and brutality and the frequent response is, 'it's not real,' other responses are, 'it helps me unwind,' the big one for me is 'it's only entertainment after a hard day'.

"Is this entertainment? What does rape, violence and the suffering of others generate? Laughter, tears, indignation, anger, joy? Doesn't anyone think anymore?

"And I do become totally confused when the response is 'it doesn't affect me'. It *must* affect you, why would you watch it if you *didn't* get anything from it? As parents we don't let our children watch that kind of thing, and I ask why? I also give myself an answer, because it would be detrimental and disturb them. Aren't we all cosmic children? How does it not disturb us?"

I finished my rant. We sat silent awhile 'til Francis looked at me and laughed out loud.

"Well for one who has had little to nothing of a voice you fully engaged yourself there, and with passion." A wave of laughter moved through those assembled. The young man Francis had encouraged to respond shared.

"Karma is an exact science. It is entirely impersonal, and yet infinitely fair in its working. We live in three worlds—physical, emotional, and mental. We generate energies or forces as we act in each world. These energies bring about a corresponding result in their respective spheres. So you see, not only are there three worlds of action to consider but also there will be variations as to the degree of the energy engaged in the three worlds. Plus, one's motivation is always taken into account.

"Loosely speaking, physical acts create our physical environment; desires determine family and social links with other individuals; and thoughts result in mental abilities and tendencies.

"If our actions bring happiness to others, we will sooner or later, whether in this, or another embodiment, find ourselves in a fortunate environment, with an increased opportunity for spreading happiness and good will. If, on the other hand, we cause pain to others by our actions or our failure to act, we will find ourselves eventually in unhappy surroundings until we learn, by experience, a greater wisdom in living.

"The force generated on the emotional level is that of desire or feeling. To pursue desire aids in our development by binding us to the objects of desire. We may judge the wisdom of our desires by experiencing their results. Through the fruits of unwise desires, we learn to focus on higher ones and finally to be free from all desire. Through the happiness enjoyed from wise desires, we become illuminated and eventually learn to be happy in all circumstances. Desire also creates opportunities.

The mental force is that of thought. The force generated by thinking increases our ability to think clearly. Devoting some time every day to thinking deliberately and in a controlled way will increase the power of our mind as an instrument. Thoughts are things, quite literally. Our thoughts create and attract. Many thoughts are strongly associated with emotion and therefore bring the thinker into contact with other persons, in relationships, that are either pleasant or unpleasant. It is our choice at any given moment as to how we act and react. The only thing we have absolute control over is our attitude to these things.

Karma is a vast and exact science which cannot be addressed to the fullest in the time allotted, but keys have been shared here for you to study.

Sitting quietly for some time I just thought about all of this. I thought about my past actions, past relationships. Of course hindsight is 20/20, but I contemplated all I had created and stirred up in others and the ripple effect. Energy that *never* stops. *Never*.

It was now normal practice that after every interaction and expression of our thoughts we would have the time to sit quietly and contemplate all that was said. We didn't need answers, we were to connect to our higher selves for the illumination. A young woman, with a good London accent, broke our silence..

"Universal Brotherhood is not merely a noble and lofty ideal but an eternal fact in Nature. Personal desire, greed, ambition and lust are all forms of selfishness and selfishness is the great blight of humanity and a cause of human suffering.

"The path to the feet of a Master must be a path of service, with the chela ever seeking to serve humanity without over concern for himself or for seeking personal reward. This is the path every Master walks, and thank the Divine they are ever aware of the pitfalls and snares, always encouraging the sincere pupil away from these errors."

On the way to my room that night, Francis met me. "I am well pleased with all your efforts, and I tell you this to give you encouragement. Keep the goal ever in front of you and continue in all your efforts regardless of what life presents.

"The path may appear solitary, the path was never professed easy. It is fraught with snares, thorns, and pitfalls, and at times the heart will ache. But I promise you the goal of permanent bliss and love is attainable for all, and once earned will take that one to heights not yet dreamed of.

"The aspiring disciple must plough on in all weathers and conditions, in the winter of his discontent as well as in the seasons that feed him well. Remember trust." There was that word again. He departed.

I retired to my soft feather bed under the canopy, but it was a troubled night. I slept little, and what little I did manage was fractured with thoughts that disturbed me leaving me with a heavy and sullen feeling I couldn't shake off. It was still dark but I dressed and made my way outside and wandered down towards the loch.

Raj was due back and it excited me but even this was temporary and could not bring me out of the cloud I was under.

The castle loomed grey now and thinking it would cheer me I sat on the bench where I had sat with Raj. I watched the dull murky water lap monotonously onto the gravel shoreline, over and over and over. It sang a dark mantra.

In the distance the gong for breakfast sounded and I hadn't noticed that night had flown past. The gong for lunch came but I hadn't moved, and now I watched a storm brew overhead. This was a depression of my own making, but ignited by something I was yet unaware of. The funny thing was no one came to join me; I was alone in my moroseness. It was strange.

The day was gone and on the horizon the sun dropped into the lake taking with it the last remnants of any light. I heard a rustle and turned quickly expecting to see Raj but it wasn't, it was Francis.

"While there are some initiations set as solemn occasions, for which the candidate is prepared, it is our daily interactions with life that determine the true character of a person.

"These daily successes or failures show the real person, and how under extreme pressure he or she will deal with all aspects of life to come. If we fail these lesser daily opportunities we never get to the point where greater ones are offered.

"If we cannot bear momentary defeat, and this life is but a moment, then the defeat may be with us 'til the close of life. If a chance word finds us unprepared and we react with anger or retaliation, or if we give way to harsh judgments, or even if we remain ignorant of some of our most apparent faults, we do not build up that knowledge and strength demanded by natural law.

"Every moment we have a choice and moments are not set for any particular day or hour. We are the sum total of all our days and it may only be at the moment of death that the soul knows where he is and who he is.

"A Master does not set strange tests for you on a daily basis but watches to see how you conduct your daily affairs, and the result of all your days determine your standing."

Francis, like a father, placed his hand on my shoulder and it was then I knew. Raj had left, he was gone. He had gone.

So many thoughts were squeezing tight into my head. He was gone, not visiting somewhere, not working, but gone. I didn't know what that meant but I knew what it felt like, it felt too permanent.

Dear reader, spiritual words should accompany this, but I was washed overboard floating in a soup so bitter I couldn't taste any sweetness. More to the point, I didn't wish to.

I sat with Francis for quite some time listening with a dead brain and numb emotions. His strength and love swathed me in a cocoon of tenderness and compassion, and for this time anyway, I felt enveloped in soft cotton wool.

Strangely, my brain functioned enough to have some questions. Was it possible for one to just accept, blasé fashion, such a loss and thus feel no pain? Was this peace I was sitting in just a bubble of numbness? I didn't know, but it was a good place to be for now.

I stayed on my bench til night gently placed her mourning blanket around me. The moon, being only a reflection of light, shared nothing, but the stars shone as Raj had shone for me.

Francis made it very clear there were always gifts to be found when such suffering knocks on a door, and I needed to open this door and face what was standing there in order to find those gifts. He left my side and returned to the entrance of the building and then my lament rose.

Rocking helped to distract me from the twisting knot in my gut but the choice to control it was quickly taken from me. Now I needed Raj to hear me and to feel me, and I knew he could and would no matter where he was.

Tears surfaced and I cursed them, they were my tears, all mine. No one else had the right to witness my tears for him, no one, so I fought them back.

My head pounded, and any suffering that had visited me before in life was insignificant compared to what was now invading me. I didn't want anyone talking to me about him and Francis knew this. I was determined to stay by the loch for as long as it took. I didn't want anyone using Raj's name on their lips nor to have any vision of him, for he was mine. I didn't want to share him, not at this time.

The knot in my stomach now rose to my chest pushing so violently against my heart that I thought, if I kept it held there, I might die. Death was a wish I was now welcoming. Yes, death. Bring me death.

I knew him like no other for I had breathed his breath deep into me and our hearts had one beat. Then I was done, I-was-so-done.

In the dark by the lake, a guttural sound exploded from me so violently ripples reverberated into the air. Resting birds and small animals fled. My banshee call ripped forth tearing away at anything it could find, anything in its wake, and it continued over and over as my death wail.

Falling to my knees, I sobbed, cursed and vomited. The pain in my body reflected the pain in my being. Eventually I lay exhausted. I needed him to hear me now.

Through my grief poetry was born, poetry composed and added to by many true lovers who had gone before me.

"They tore you from me and now my notes wail through the trees. My body bursts Raj, striving to let my spirit free, so I too can be in the home where you are now.

"Hear my screaming in the stars My Love, in concert with those that weep on desolate planets throughout the Universe. Those who interpret my cries, and there will be but few, will be in sympathy with me.

"Let all who have not felt this fire of loss, that scorches such as this, be accounted as dead, dead, dead. I know my day will go on, but hand in hand with pain now Raj, hand in hand with pain.

"Through grief my days will be just sadness. Only those who feel the violence of such loss will understand. Oh love, oh madness, oh Raj!

As I closed my eyes, not caring about any spiritual path, I saw Francis in my mind's eye. I left my body to soar into another realm where the pain lessened and I heard poetry from my soul. It was then I felt My Love's reply.

"It is Love who heals our weaknesses, who is the physician of our pride, self-conceit and selfishness. O lover understand, it was love that gave you to me and it is love that bears me away. Have faith.

"When in love, the body, mind, heart and soul, don't even exist. Do not confuse your pain with selfless love, though it is there. You have experienced selfless love and in this love you cannot be separated from anyone.

"I am the Universe; I am not outside of you, look for me within. I am closer to you than your breath yet I am beyond the stars. I bathe you in the purest essence of my love which comes from a place of unimaginable beauty. Sorrow will dissolve if you surrender, surrender your heart to the touch of the Divine, surrender.

"Become the Alchemist who will light the fire of love in the hearts, minds and souls of all who read your words, let them read.

"Take our love to all, and even though you believe you are so small My Love, don't forget, your eyes have seen immense things. Remember these wise words, once shared by a great poet.

"Understand the world and you may serve it, understand yourself and you will serve humanity through your words.'

"I have always been so don't grieve me, and know that what you are seeking, is, and has always been seeking you. Know that though you may hunt constantly for me I am by your side, always. I have always been there waiting for you to know me. I took on form for you to see me and then to come to know my love.

"I see you and kiss your lips with the sweetness of everlasting honey, the honey of love. I touch your hand with the gentle breeze of the Divine's breath. I lay with you in my arms and my arms are the arms of nature as she folds herself around you and all life.

"Keep your attention on the prize not on the little desires of the human. I soar now as a bird searching the sky in so many directions all at once, for I am everywhere. Understand we never met somewhere my love, for we have been in each other all along.

"Those who don't feel passion like this, they sleep. Those who stay with only their words, they sleep. Don't sleep my love, be naked before truth, close the window on words and open the door on love."

All I wanted now was to be naked before the Absolute: for this I needed to dive deeply into this grief, but I was scared. I felt like the most solitary creature in the Universe, so alone in this pain.

Of course he was right, it wasn't his form I was in love with, beautiful though it was, it was his soul and spirit. Of course he had guided me like a Master into the arms of love, and with gentleness he reached me with the Divine's personal touch. He was my Lover who was the manifestation of Love.

As I came back to earth I felt only half awake, my symphony was odd, notes in my head played off key and hurt, and the terrible emptiness in the pit of my stomach only exaggerated the madness I felt.

I had no familiar place now. I was stranded with the broken wreckage of all my dreams, dotted as flotsam and jetsam around me. Nothing mattered because I still wished to be dead on the shore where he was.

The taste in my mouth was of sandalwood tinted with decay. Strange visions danced into my head and out again, visions of love, bloody forget-me-nots and knives.

I felt I was dying and then I breathed again and died again, and this continued until Francis touched my forehead. I remembered nothing until I awoke in my bed and the birds were singing outside.

# Chapter Twenty Five

*The first question which the priest and the Levite asked was: 'If I stop to help this man, what will happen to me?' But...the good Samaritan reversed the question: 'If I do not stop to help this man, what will happen to him?'*
Martin Luther King, Jr..

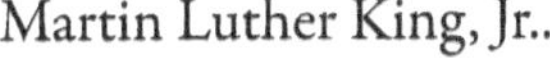

By the grace of Francis I was given a vision of the events that happened regarding Raj and his leaving. It was a drama that had been repeated again and again, over many lifetimes. and the players were the same but for one, Raj. He had volunteered. The whole scenario presented yet another opportunity for two particular souls to re-write their story,

I talk about this as if I was there: I was not, but I had been afforded a window into the happenings around Raj's leaving, for which I am ever grateful.

A storm raged in the sky that night, upstairs in the cabin, looking out onto the courtyard below, stood Raj.

The foreman, the brother of the lady who gave me the shawl, had received a call to go to the mine to check out something that was happening. Having completed his check and seeing nothing out of the ordinary he opened the gates to leave. Meanwhile behind a large tree lurked a dim shadow of a man that Raj could only see when lightning flashed.

As the foreman made his way back to the car, moving from behind the tree, but keeping well hidden, the man slowly made his way to the vehicle and his perfect opportunity. He raised his arm over his head, and when a streak of lightning lit up the area, Raj could see a large knife glistening.

Instantly - as Raj was able to do - he was in front of the foreman and, instead of the blade hitting its intended target, it coldly struck Raj in the chest and he fell to the ground. Terrified, the stranger ran.

The foreman, mortified and in shock, tried to help Raj back to the cabin but it was impossible. His last instructions were to do nothing but wait, no authorities were to be contacted. Then Raj slipped into a peaceful slumber.

Holding Raj close, the foreman waited as he had been asked to do, trying to contain his utter desolation.

A short while later, after the storm had rid its rage, the gate to the mine slowly opened, and there, drenched and sobbing, stood the assailant. Mortified with what he had done he knelt beside Raj's cold, wet body and begged forgiveness. Raj stirred and lovingly forgave them both.

Losing Raj was devastating, but I also felt saddened for the two men: one wreck of a man who shook with grief, and the other who shook with remorse. Raj had forgiven them both. The gift he gave that night would keep on giving, though I couldn't yet see to what extent. Francis switched my view as he always did.

"Success is not always seen by the physical eyes, though the physical eyes may behold the means. Love in action, Karma will present an opportunity in many ways to encourage one to make a better decision at a future time, one that serves the soul. Some of the best success stories have been the result of someone reaching a crossroad, usually the only place where one is coerced, to take a different road.

"The traveller may choose the path to his success or may choose to walk the path that leads to his demise. Either way, the path will reach another crossroad and again the choices will have to be made. It is never ending.

"Illumination is not always instant. It is by increments that we resolve and evolve and, in this particular instance, success has followed on the hem of a great sacrifice. The sincere remorse of those involved has given the gift of possibilities that are beyond your ken.

"The assailant notified the authorities himself, he volunteered the information regarding his deeds and his guilt in order to pay his debt, and this was something his heart was never open to before. It is a joyful outcome, though not one you may see today. Remember, change your thinking and you change your suffering."

A day later by the lake I listened further to Francis. I, too, had been given great gifts, many of which I had not yet unwrapped. Death is a big gift that opens onto a world of light, and hiding away was never going to illumine my heart, so I decided to unwrap the gift.

Earlier in my story when we were hiking, and a group were across the ravine where Francis had lit the fire, well one of them had been the author of the drama at the mine. I wanted to share this.

All of us write our own story, we make up scenarios in our head, then we engage our emotions, including me: rather like a TV show or movie. No one can ever avoid the roll of the cosmic camera. We will all star in our epic whether we like to or not, but wisdom would be to write our script consciously.

The days that followed were anything but calm. There were times I could be the observer of my life and this was due to my meditation practices, but then my monkey mind would remind me what Raj had done, my perceived loss, and then I would become absorbed in my own personal grief, my... my...my! But it was a process.

I felt I needed to feel my suffering. Why? Because then it would mean I was grieving enough, I loved him enough.

Then there was guilt, guilt around not giving enough and the letting go of pain. But guilt is an insidious rapist attacking the peace of truth, and like most people who have lost someone close, guilt creeps and seeps into the crannies opened by self-doubt. Did I give enough, did I show enough love? Was I unkind at any time? The list goes on.

There were times I wanted to go to a crypt and lie in a coffin in an attempt to be close to death's angel. God knows I had experienced this great being of late, more than once.

Then there was another side of me, a much bigger side that knew I wanted to honour him, to love him so much I could accept it all, to practise what he had taught me and let him go. I had to release him if I truly loved him. He once said to me, "only two things cause suffering My Dear, attachments and expectations." He was right.

When we lose a loved one we enter shock and grief but these two are part of the natural process. But there comes a time when we need to let that loved one go for it serves neither them nor us to hold on.

We grieve for our loss, our emptiness, and of course at times we grieve for the suffering our loved one may have endured before death. But they need to see we are getting on with living, and they need to go on living also.

Of course they are supported and greeted by many loved ones on the other side whom they feel totally at home with, and then there is a whole Brotherhood of Light, evolved beings waiting and willing to assist. Francis explained the law around the death process.

"First of all there is nothing to worry about. You will never die. The only part of you which will actually die when the transition commonly known as 'death' takes place is the physical body, and this is nothing more than your outer shell. Your overcoat.

"Your astral body will eventually disintegrate when the very last particle of the dead physical body disintegrates. Also the prana (vitality, life energy) which now animates your physical body and keeps you in physical incarnation will return after death to the universal prana. But still you – the soul – will never die.

"Raj and yourself have gone through many deaths so why would you feel a need to attach yourself so much to his physical form?"

Such a good question when seriously considered and it gave a different perspective to my aching. His form *had* changed in every lifetime.

"A few feet of flesh," he once said, "when there is so much flesh on the planet." It did seem a little ridiculous. No, the only way I was going to get out of this mindset was to function in my higher mind and connect with my soul.

So on a day by the lake, after Francis had discussed some personal things with me, He rose leaving me in peace, literally, and in that peace I closed my eyes. I thought I sensed Raj close and I whispered famous words said before by a great poet.

"One day my love, I shall be a lover like you." I rose with a smile that covered my face, filled my heart, and made my way to my room.

Selfless love is about the giving not the receiving and when we grieve we can lose sight of that. Gradually we let go but we never forget, and it is this letting go out of love that gently carries our loved ones back to us, and also carries us to them in another life. Love is the only permanently cohesive power in the Universe and we can never be alone in this love.

I decided to make my way to the library and there on the small table lay an open book, and on the open page on a golden piece of paper, in violet ink were these words.

'He who holds the keys to the secrets of Death is possessed of the keys of Life.' *Master K.H.*

'The end of birth is death; the end of death is birth.' *Krishna, The Bhagavad Gita.*

I then read the open page of the book and it said this.

The Master K.H. once wrote: "The man may often appear dead. Yet from the last pulsation, from and between the last throbbing of his heart and the moment when the last spark of animal heat leaves the body – the brain thinks, and the Ego lives over in those few brief seconds his whole life once again...

"At the solemn moment of death every man, even when death is sudden, sees the whole of his past life marshalled before him, in its minutest details. For one short instant the personal becomes one with the individual and all-knowing Ego.

"But this instant is enough to show to him the whole chain of causes, which have been at work during his life. He sees and now understands himself as he is, unadorned by flattery or self-deception. He reads his life, remaining as a spectator looking down into the arena he is quitting; he feels and knows the justice of all the suffering that has overtaken him. Does this happen to everyone? Without any exception."

That night I slept well, and in the morning true to form, we ate, drank lots of tea, and started on the journey south. Francis and a few others were to meet us at our destination.

# Chapter Twenty SIx

*Do not be afraid of your difficulties.*
*Do not wish you could be in other circumstances that you are. For*
*when you have made the best of an adversity, it becomes the*
*stepping-stone to a splendid opportunity.*
Unknown

Four of us had been assigned a driver for our car and it was quite the classic. Our journey took us down through southwest Scotland and into Wales where we stayed as guests in a country home, then past Glastonbury and into the Shires.

Southern England is beautiful and even more so in the area of our next stop. Our route was vague, as we seemed to go this way and that almost as if we were meant to be confused. It was as if we had all been given a blindfold and spun a couple of dozen times, then had the blindfold removed. None of us had any idea where we were and even the signs seemed to make no sense.

Upon arrival we slowly coursed down a long driveway lined with tall oaks standing like they were guarding a secret. Finally the car came to a halt at the door of a large Tudor house where under a weathered arch stood a butler.

Inside we were promptly served hot tea and the most delicious flat cookies that I later discovered were raw apricots, coconut and fresh juice. These were always on display somewhere for our convenience.

Once in my room I was content to sit on the oak window seat that followed the large bay. Deep red velvet with ochre brocade seemed to be the fashion of my room, and I have to say it all reflected a certain quality, a feeling I was extremely comfortable with. I looked out over a garden surrounding a small pond and the land seemed to go on forever.

There were nine of us at supper, and after eating and preliminary introductions we all settled in the large library. It seemed as if those who lived in these old houses always had large libraries and I felt quite comfortable now with this repeated format. I found a seat just as Francis entered.

"The library is at your disposal and I encourage you all to take advantage of the many rare books and documents waiting on the shelves. So now let us begin.

"There are three truths which are absolute, which cannot be lost, but yet may remain silent for lack of speech.

"The soul of man is immortal and its future is the future of a thing whose growth and splendour has no limit.

"The principle which gives life dwells in us and without us, is undying and eternally beneficent, is not heard or seen or smelled, but is perceived by the man who desires perception.

"Each man is his own absolute lawgiver, the dispenser of glory or gloom to himself, the decreer of his life, his reward, his punishment.

"These truths, which are as great as is life itself, are as simple as the simplest mind."

He looked over at a man who was sitting to my right and nodded to him and the man spoke next.

"Let me put it another way, this all means that God is good, that man is immortal, and that as we sow we must reap. There is a definite scheme of things and it is under intelligent direction and works under absolute immutable laws.

"Man has his place in this scheme and is living under these laws. If he understands them and cooperates with them, he will advance rapidly and will be happy; if he does not understand them, and if, wittingly or unwittingly he breaks them, he will delay his progress and be miserable.

"These are not theories but proven facts regarding the law of the Absolute, the Infinite, the Divine. We can at our present stage know nothing except that it is, and if we say anything, it is but a limitation and would therefore be inaccurate.

"All three of these Aspects are concerned in the evolution of man and also of the solar system, and this evolution is the Will of the Absolute, and the method of it is the plan of the Absolute also.

We sat for some time listening, but as the remaining talk dealt with more personal matters I am unable to expand any further. Needless to say I was comfortable in our new location.

# Chapter Twenty Seven

*We are such stuff as dreams are made on; and our little life is rounded with a sleep.* Shakespeare

Every morning as I awoke, I would give my gratitude for the opportunities afforded me. This was a new day and I was going to spend the open time I had wandering the grounds.

This place was filled with love and simple joy, but there was still a pain in my heart where Raj had been resting. Yes I knew he was still with me but I wanted his smile. I never professed I was walking on water and until I did, 'walk on water' that is, I felt sure I would still feel this emptiness at certain times.

But then something transpired which took my mind away from myself for a time, and it started with my cell phone buzzing. Sure enough there was a message from my friend Linda, and it read, 'coming to see you, can't wait, love sis'.

No one knew where I was, even I didn't know, so a lot of good that was. I messaged back to her that I was sorry but I didn't know where I was, and have a good time where you are.

Then the thought came that she might go to the place where my old friend had lived in Scotland and all for naught, so I looked around for someone to help me and bumped into the butler. He wasn't your normal big house butler, in fact he wasn't like a butler at all, more like a friend to everyone, but I asked for his help.

At first he looked at me rather strangely as if I had just spoken in some long lost African dialect and my marbles were running off somewhere new. Then he assured me.

"Anything regarding the Master of the house is always left to the Master of the house. No need to concern yourself."

He smiled and went off leaving me standing. Well funny enough it made me feel alright, and why not, anything that needed to be taken care of always was, and so I let it go.

That night we met again in the library, though I still had no idea who owned the estate. Francis was standing by the fireplace when we arrived, quietly talking with the butler who then departed. After a few minutes the door opened and there stood the butler again. Standing beside him was a new guest... Linda.

"Ah yes." Francis waved His hand, "true friendship is rooted in life's soil, watered by the nutrients of patience and selflessness, and accepts trust to rain down upon it." He smiled and continued. "We shall begin." Linda and I sat side by side.

"There is no such thing as death as it is ordinarily understood. There is only a succession of stages in a continuous life."

He stopped talking, rose, and suggested to us all that we continue our discussions amongst ourselves, which we did. A young man was the first to speak and we listened.

"When one passes over to the other side, one sees the absolute justice and fairness of everything that has happened in one's life. Everything proceeds exactly as it should, and always according to the unfailing law of cause and effect, action and reaction, commonly referred to as Karma.

"After reviewing one's life, the 'silver cord,' that which is connecting your physical body with its astral double, breaks, and with this process, physical death then occurs."

This was brilliant confirmation, for some of the books I had been reading in the library had referred to the law of correspondences.

They explained how the umbilical cord in the physical birthing process has a correspondence to the silver cord in the passing over process. A birthing into this world, as well as birthing into the next.

A young woman who had been sitting to the side of me spoke and I noticed a strong Irish accent.

"The Law of Correspondences is based on a holographic model of the Universe where the part reflects the whole. It suggests that the microcosm is the miniature copy of the macrocosm, and a general correspondence between 'above' and 'below' also."

Then another person added, and it seemed to me he was obviously very learned.

"Yes, to express the Great Hermetic Axiom. As is the Inner, so is the Outer; as is the Great, so is the Small; as it is above, so it is below: there is but one life and law.

"Nothing is Inner, nothing is Outer; nothing is Great, nothing is Small; nothing is High, nothing is Low in the Divine Economy."

We sat silently for about half an hour, and I needed that time I can tell you, just to assimilate that last sentence. But it is True. It was brilliant. Lastly, a quiet very feminine man spoke up.

"H. P. Blavatsky wrote how studying the law of correspondences will lead you to discover the greatest mysteries of life. One may study man the microcosm, by proceeding from particulars to universals. Or another way would be to start with one general view of all and descend from the universal to the individual."

This was a bit like the two books I had been given by the lady in the first library, The Secret Doctrine by H.P. Blavatsky. But by now my two brain cells were again trying to assimilate it all. Sitting by the large fire had made me feel sleepy and it seemed all the others felt the same, so our time was called to a close and we said our goodnights.

Sharing time with my friend, Linda, before retiring was important, so she came to my room and we sat on the bed and chatted. How she had found me was something I needed to hear, because I couldn't have found me if I had to.

"You see I bumped into an interesting man," she began. "He was walking along the beach in Cornwall where I was staying. As he approached I sensed something different about him and remembered what you said about meeting a Master and sometimes not being aware of it. Well as he came closer, I felt I had seen him before but couldn't quite think where. When he was right in front of me he said, 'Hello Linda'.

"Ellie, he acted like we were old friends, that was the confusion. Then he went on to say how it was good to see me again.

"Oh it got even better when he asked me what I was doing in town, and get this, would I like to share a pot of tea in the local tea room." She stopped and laughed.

"Anyways where was I, oh yes. Over tea he told me you had been in Scotland, but now had departed and was on your way to the Shires.

"Ellie, how did he know? Anyways it gets even better. It was him who invited me to join you."

She started to laugh again, and when I asked her why she was laughing she said that though this man had escorted her here, she had no idea where 'here' was. Even better, she still didn't know the man well, yet she trusted him.

We continued to chat and eventually both of us fell asleep on the bed.

The following night we were joined by our Host. Sir Geoffrey was a country gentleman and everywhere He went so did the big hound by His side. He wore a takiyah, which seemed a little bit unusual for a Brit, and perched on the end of His nose were a set of gold-rimmed glasses, though He never seemed to look through them only over the top.

He seemed a little aloof, but the moment He placed the gift of His glance on me, His compassion melted like warm butter into all the places within my soul and drizzled endlessly down into the crevices of my heart. This much I knew of Him, but nothing more.

He presented profound teachings, yet somehow I could grasp them. They say a pupil is only as good as his teacher.

On many evenings we were blessed with Sir Geoffrey, who would contemplate the fire for some time, light an old pipe, then talk as if He had been with us all the time. He would then conclude by saying, "Goodnight," rise, and leave with his hound by his side. He never minced or wasted words.

When Sir Geoffrey joined us, an East Indian man, beautifully dressed in plain white clothes and a turban who no one really saw arrive, or leave, would be present. Over the nights we met I went out of my way to try to see him arrive and leave, but something always, always, seemed to distract me just at that crucial time. I couldn't keep my eyes off this wonderful specimen, who I must say reminded me of Raj in many ways.

And so it was that on this particular evening, Linda and I gathered in the library along with eight other people waiting for Sir Geoffrey to arrive. At the back of the library stood the tall man with the turban again. This time it was he who initiated the discussion whilst making his way toward the fire, and it was just where Sir Geoffrey had left off the last time we met.

"So where did we finish, ah yes. You would do well to request of your surviving loved ones, not to try to contact you after the death of your physical body. This may tempt and drag you back to the physical considerations of earth life, keeping you bound to earth longer than necessary.

"Any type of lower spiritualism, lower mediumship and lower channelling is always detrimental, particularly to the people doing it.

"Many untrained psychics don't realise how it's only the astral shell they have any chance of reaching, for it will be impossible for the soul to be reached by those on earth.

"It is easy to mistake the soulless shell for the real you, because of its ability to automatically repeat certain facts, details, characteristics and information which you possessed during your lifetime.

"The life span of this shell will be prolonged as a result of such meddlesome interference, and undesirable situations and problems may potentially arise." With this the man in the turban walked to the back of the room and left. This time I saw him leave.

I wanted to know more about the place referred to as heaven in orthodox religions; I also wanted to know more about this enigmatic man in the turban. No sooner had I mentioned this to the person next to me, than Sir Geoffrey entered with His hound, and they both sat.

"Devachan or, as you like to refer to it, heaven, is not a location or a plane but a state, a state where consciousness returns. Though it has been referred to as a type of heaven, it is not the heaven state mentioned by your religionist, no.

"The heavenly state is a personal state to everyone, which they create for themselves. No one consciousness is the same, and no one heaven is the same. This would make no sense at all, no sense." He puffed on His pipe staring into the fire.

"Whatever you believed, hoped for, and even expected this heaven to be like while you were still alive, you will experience. It is of the utmost bliss, peace, and joy. There is not the faintest shadow, hint or even trace of sorrow, disappointment, suffering or pain. Everyone and everything you had hoped to be there will be there, because it is your own mental creation."

He rose, but then stopped and looked into the fire as if watching the flames rise to a waiting god. In my head, I heard him speak.

"He is indeed an Initiate and well-loved and you will encounter him again." He gave His goodnight and departed. On the way to the stairs I saw Francis.

"It is a blessing to be in His Presence, and what a blessing you have just been given." Of course, He was referring to our Host.

# Chapter Twenty Eight

*Let your life lightly dance on the edges of Time like dew on the tip of a leaf.*
Rabindranath Tagore

The following day we had a little free time so Linda and I got together. "Oh Ellie, it makes my brain hurt, all this thinking," Linda laughed. "But I get it, I really do, the teachings make so much sense."

"Lin, what we're studying answers nearly every question we've had about human evolution, the afterlife and the Universe, though I must admit, I felt the same ache in my head as I felt in my body when I first started to work out again at the gym." We sat together.

It was true. At times it felt like serious study especially when some of the science concepts were discussed. Eventually though it became so much easier and I feel sure, you, the reader, have had similar experiences yourself with studies.

"You know Lin, I won't lie, at first it was like sitting in a class for geniuses, but I swear all this listening and reading is releasing a sort of happy hormone, like when I eat chocolate, but without the calories and the fat.

"I don't mean to change the subject, but it's the staring into the fire that's fascinating me – they all do it. I've started doing it and it's almost meditative. I swear I heard some of the words He spoke last evening in my head. In fact, I know I did.

"There's something else, or should I say someone else who fascinates me, and that's the tall man in the turban. Who is he?"

"Ellie you're in my head." She smiled. Just then the door opened and he was there.

Motioning us to follow him, we did. We made our way out of the house and down through the forest. As we hurried along Linda looked at me and through her giggles whispered.

"This is fantastic. Bring it all on, hey?"

He came to a halt by a body of water, a small pond, the middle of which was a small island.

"Follow me," he said as he made his way onto what seemed like the water and toward the island.

Linda's face was a picture, for though she was up for most things his last two words brought out in her instant refusal, and with hard eyes she quickly turned to me.

"What's he saying, follow him, where, the water?"

He turned again to face us and repeated his request, and it was then Linda started to lose the plot.

"He's kidding right?" She glared and then she turned to him. "*Not happening,*" she shouted. "*Hello, can you hear me? Not happening*" I could see she meant it.

"It's OK, Lin, nothing's going to happen, you're safe." I proffered. But she looked at me as if she would rip the jugular out from my neck in one foul grab if I said another word. This Linda, I had never encountered before in all the years of knowing her.

"If you think I'm going to entertain that water, lake, that ocean, you can forget it!" She turned away as a deep voice carried across the water. "Come." I drew closer to her,

"Lin, I know it's water, but he would never bring you here if there were any danger. Trust, Lin, trust."

Thrusting her face so close that her breath steamed my glasses she locked her wide-eyed gaze onto mine. With her lips scant inches away she whispered through locked jaws, "****off. Don't you get it, this is not fear!" she seethed and continued her rant.

"It's terror Ellie, terror, and neither you nor some man who wears a turban because he's afraid to show his hair is gonna make me step out in that bloody water! Back off, right, *back off*. No one tells me what to do, *no one*!" she yelled.

But then she stopped in her tracks as if she had hit an imaginary wall and stood, not moving. Slowly she turned and looked directly at him, and he spoke again.

"There are two kinds of faith: blind faith and reasoned faith. Blind faith is based on ignorance and unquestioning subservience, whereas reasoned faith is based on solid spiritual knowledge." He held out his hands to her.

"Come. Behold, I stand at a door and knock. If you hear my voice and open the door I will come in to you."

As she walked towards him he spoke again.

"Though I stand at the door and knock it is you who must admit me into your consciousness. Come," he said again.

With that, a small boat moved its way toward us, though to be honest I have no idea to this day how it came there. Linda made her way to the water's edge and sat in the boat and I joined her. Sitting beside her I felt her fear but I also knew her faith. However that did not stop me hearing her constant swearing, despite the profound holy moment.

We continued across the water and stepped out of the boat and away from the lake. The pathway led us to a small house with a large veranda. The door opened and a beautiful man came out.

"You've admitted into your consciousness the power of resurrection child, even if only for a moment." He smiled. Linda smiled also.

"You have a question." He waited. Linda looked a little confused and answered.

"No."

We sat quietly for some time. It was a strange moment. It seemed our host was quite content to sit in peace and quiet until Linda piped up.

"Yes, I do, you're right." (Go figure) "I do and it's about my daughter and an experience, or was it a dream I had last night whilst asleep."

"What is real and what is a dream? Aye there's the rub." Waving His hand He motioned her to continue. She did.

"I don't wish to say I know something if it isn't absolute truth," she responded.

"Then you will be silent for many incarnations." He smiled. "Come come, let go of the fear for it will get you nowhere fast."

"Well," she began, "why am I telling you, I'm sure you know it all."

He said nothing but waited. And I sat there with my mouth open, shocked at her attitude.

"You know my daughter, of course you do, and obviously you're aware of the dark and troubled place she's inhabited for some time. Well no matter what I did I couldn't remedy the situation. I felt lost in a sea of constant failures with her.

"When we were together it felt as if I was constantly cutting down a vine that was sprouting from a deep root, and this vine was trying to strangle me. On my last visit to her I said the unthinkable, I told her I wanted her to die so that I could move on with my life."

Linda stopped her story and looked as if she were immersed in memories, and then she began sobbing. Gathering herself she continued.

"Of course we've all said words we wish we could take back but what had our relationship come to, more to the point what had I come to?

"I knew it went far deeper than either of us realised, but although rationalising it was easy, resolving it was not.

"Several weeks later she was admitted into an institution, and it was like she was dead to me, and I to her. I was fearful. I knew once she came out of this institution I would find it hard to control my urge to make things better. All I wanted was to take away her pain. And so I called a Master. Let me qualify that, I said a prayer of sorts.

"Whilst in my tormented place I also asked to be taken out of the equation. I wanted to die. I didn't wish to impact my life or her life any further. So not long after my call to this Master..."

She stopped her story, and realised, this may be the Master who had answered her call. He raised his hand for her to continue.

"After my call to this Master, I had a strange dream, or should I say, experience.

"It seems I'd been in service in a large house and had been raped, with the consequence being a pregnancy. Those were not the times for a girl in service to fall pregnant, even if it wasn't her fault.

"My parents couldn't cope with an extra mouth to feed, nor would they want the stigma, and I would've been discharged from my position had I gone full-term, so I murdered the child. The child, I believe, is now my daughter in this life.

"Back to the present. Once out of the institution her health began to deteriorate over the course of the year. Being her mother I began to interfere again. My confusion and hurt, mixed with her anger and hatred, created the stage for our past to become the present.

"We entered into a dance of going back and forth, me responding to her calls for help and her reaction being the rejection of me. Eventually it all culminated in her wanting to kill *me*.

"My love as a mother helped me to overcome such hate attacks, but I could see we had reversed our roles in this life, if my dream had been real. I believe I had murdered her in a past life and now she wished to kill me in this one.

"On one visit she finally demanded the end of our relationship, and vowed that even in the next life she wished zero association with me. In tears, I left.

"Strangely I had my first visit with her just prior to being invited on this journey and I'm absolutely sure it's no coincidence." She looked at the Master and fresh tears leaked from her eyes again. We sat silently for a few moments until the Teacher spoke.

"When Jesus spoke of the Christ within He was referring to the mystical voice, the personal divinity indwelling in man. Christ is not a person, but an embodied idea. This Christ is the power within to overcome all seeming adversity, and the power within to heal all wounds.

"How humanity struggles to achieve peace of mind, security and safety for themselves and their loved ones. Yet today we live in a world of less peace and security than has ever been experienced in history.

"Why is this, hmm? It is the Christ within who is the giver of lasting peace and sure security. All else is transient.

"One is resurrected by this impersonal principle we call Christ. It has been and always will be, the one constant. Naught can stay the same when it is pronounced, and this pronouncement is not with words, but with consciousness.

"It is this Christ principle that will wipe away all disease. If danger threatens it will be your everlasting protection.

"Do not pray with words or even thoughts, for this principle is not a word or a thought but the life that is you. Be still and hear my knock on the door of your heart, bid me enter to redeem and restore.

"Know you are the temple of the Divine, and that the name of the Divine is 'I Am'. When you have admitted the Christ Spirit into your consciousness and held it there secretly and sacredly, then at any moment you can close your eyes and just remember 'I Am' as your permanent meditation.

"Take all to the Highest within, the source of all life, and it will raise you up and perform mighty works."

He rose and we rose with Him. He then placed his hand on Linda's head, smiled and spoke quietly.

"And now it would seem you have earned your water-wings my child." He turned back into the house. The man in the turban motioned us to follow and as we did he spoke.

"This opening of consciousness to the Christ is contemplative, words are superficial. When you hold the truth of these two seemingly benign words 'I Am' as your first and only thought, you are contemplating truth, and you are one with the presence of the Christ for those moments, whether you realise this or not.

"The power of the Great Spirit is standing at the door knocking, waiting for your invitation to enter."

Neither Linda nor I spoke until the next day. We didn't wish to.

# Chapter Twenty Nine

*I am a little quill in the hand of the writing Ultimate who is sending a love letter to the world.*
Unknown

After breakfast, Linda and I went for a walk through the woods and found a spot to sit, hoping we would see something of the little island. I wanted to share and so did she.

"Lin last night whilst asleep, I'm pretty sure I travelled to meet the Master on the island again. He spoke about past lives.

"He said the obsession some have with knowing their past lives serves nothing and that the adoption of delusional attitudes, by those who are believers in reincarnation, have added ammunition to the disbelief of the unbelievers. He also said that the current obsession with past lives, by some believers, is self-centred."

We sat silent for a while, looking out over the lake, both of us were hoping to get a glimpse of something but there was nothing.

"Ellie, I do remember something from my sleep. Someone spoke of how those on a true path need to learn to control the fantasies in their lives."

This made me think of some leaders of the New Spiritual movements. There seemed to be an obsession with their own numerous past lives and that of the Masters they claim to know.

Now this may sound very harsh to those who don't take the time to think for themselves, but the question I ask is this - what use is it for us to know anyone's past life? It's the teaching that is important to our evolution, not the past lives of anyone. It's what we do, not the names we discover that matter. Is this ego?

Is all this focus a subconscious desire to be more important than the next person, or even a conscious desire?

In my research I noticed the Mahatmas of the Himalayan Brotherhood don't seem to harbour this egocentric behaviour. No, it would seem to be a human condition. H.P. Blavatsky who was in contact with these Master's, never made a thing of past lives nor of their importance, neither did, nor do, these Elder Brothers.

That evening after supper we all met in the library with the usual people who gathered, and Francis joined us to conduct the session.

"So who is going to start our discussion this evening?" He looked around.

"There is one here who has been relentlessly knocking at my door with constant questions, questions, and questions. Why, she has been taunting my peace for a time now" We chuckled.

"Me," said Linda. "I've a question that's been going over and over in my head and I think I need some help."

"Wise child." He said. We laughed even more.

"What is the difference between the soul and spirit?" she asked, "I get so confused" He sat quietly for a moment and responded.

"Spirit is your essential nature, pure eternal spirit. Spirit is your real self and the pinnacle of your being. This spirit which you are is not an individual thing but is formless and totally impersonal.

"There is only one Spirit. It is the Sun that shines over everything, over all, and from this Sun sparks are sent forth to manifest everywhere in this Universe and eventually return to the one. The spirit in you is the spirit in me, one spirit. This spirit knows no separateness, it is the supreme Atman." Francis stopped and motioned to me to respond and I did.

"The soul is a self-conscious individual. Before this human kingdom, there was no individuality, but now it has the 'I'. It's a permanent entity, but nevertheless an entity.

"It unfolded out of spirit, and not forgetting it will return to Spirit. The one. It incarnates again and again.

"Spirit has no direct contact with the physical form nor does it reside in the form, but above. It's subjective and has no relation to objective matter. It doesn't separate but is one, always."

Here Francis asked if anyone else would like to contribute and an Indian man spoke up. He had spoken before.

"In my country we talk about Yoga. Yoga is the union of soul and spirit, to practise yoga is to work towards this achievement. The soul's journey is to unite with spirit, to become at one permanently. It is a marriage, and this union is sometimes confused with today's modern understanding of tantra."

The door opened and hot chocolate was served. Before leaving, Francis suggested some topics we might discuss before we retired, and to do so among ourselves. He left us with these thoughts.

"It is naive to claim you know a specific past life. Do you know the location of that life, your identity, and your very nature in that life, ah, yes, your very nature? And can you prove what you know?

"Ask yourself a simple question, what would be your motive for telling others who you were, or should I say, who you think you were?

"Would it be an attempt to seem special in the eyes of others?

"What motivates one to desire to feel more important?

"Past life regression stirs subconscious fantasies, opening avenues into the collective consciousness, and how could you prove that a life you were 'tapping into' and claimed as known, was not the life of another in this collective?

"Have you ever asked yourself why so many are discovering they were Joan of Arc, Napoleon, Cleopatra, Queen Elizabeth I, and even King Arthur of Camelot?

"Ask yourself also, would you really wish to know who you were in a past life? Is it essential for you to know? What of those things that prove disturbingly violent and even traumatic, would you wish to know the details? And to what avail?

"Your overriding interests give you a good pointer as to relevant details of a past life, your psychological traits and characteristics and those things you become attracted to throughout this present incarnation. These are good pointers to your past. These are the things you may wish to look at in *this* life, and the most important in the estimation of your soul."

"Regarding Atlantis and Lemuria and other old root races, it is ridiculous and a romantic notion to claim knowledge of lives lived at that time. One is usually having immense difficulty knowing who they are in this life. Do you believe it is easier with a past life? Do you believe knowing your past life is more important than this one?

"Can you remember clearly what you did on this date last year or even the 11th of last month? I leave these questions with you." He concluded with this.

"There are times when a spontaneous recollection occurs, but this may stem from the soul for a very specific reason."

When He left the room. We continued discussing all He had asked of us, and it was in the early hours of the morning when we retired to our beds.

The following night we met again but only for a brief time, and we were left to talk amongst ourselves. It was as if we were to become proficient in functioning without the assistance of an Elder Brother, and then a rather tall woman started speaking to us all.

"A concept that may be a challenge for some, is the truth that when you pass over even your loved ones, whom you left behind on earth, will be there in your state of Heaven or Bliss as you refer to it.

"They will not really be there but they will seem to be there, and so vivid and realistic that you will never be inclined to question the matter or to doubt the reality of your experience for even one moment.

"Some of them will be having their own heaven experience at the same time as you are having yours, but the law of perfect justice and bliss requires that we each have our own personal blissful state, entirely of our own making.

"So there is no actual interaction or communication between departed souls, but you will be represented there, as real as life, in your loved one's Bliss/Heaven state just as they will be in yours." With this she stopped and pondered the fire and so did we.

Where Francis had come from I had no idea, but he was just in the corner by the far side of the hearth, and He walked over to speak.

"Think about this carefully, for the Great Spirit, besides being wise and loving is also the fount of logic, something your Mr. Spock would appreciate." We all laughed. Then He truly bid us goodnight and departed.

Later that week three more strangers, including the distinguished man in the turban, joined us and stayed at the back as usual. We never did see our Host again, but some nights Francis sat with us considering the fire.

I would like to say here that our days were like being in a school for Ancient Wisdom. It was very unlike my journey through the Rockies spoken of at the beginning of my adventure. But this is as it should be. One cannot always expect to be taken on so-called miraculous trips. Raj had pointed this out to me when I met him by the lake at Jane's home. No, this time afforded was for serious study.

One of these nights when Francis was sitting quietly watching the flames dance, He spoke again on devachan.

"When in this heavenly state, there is no awareness of having died or even a concept of death," He proffered.

"However, this being a temporary and self- created experience, it is nothing other than a type of dream, but it is a dream as vivid and as tangible as the life experienced whilst on earth.

"The duration of your stay in this Bliss will be in exact accordance with the amount and force of positive Karma that you accrued during the previous lifetime. This will naturally vary greatly from person to person."

At this point He stopped and viewed everyone in the room again then continued.

"Your blissful state will at some point draw to a close, and this will correspond with the process of reincarnation for your soul.

"With conception, your life will begin again, you will go through a pregnancy, which will finally culminate in the severance of the umbilical cord and rebirth on the physical plane will be complete.

"And the journey of inner evolution and spiritual unfoldment continues and it never stops. As Krishna says in the Bhagavad Gita, 'The end of birth is death; the end of death is birth'. Death is not the end and birth is not the beginning."

He stopped here and asked if there were any questions, but I feel sure he already knew the questions in the minds of those present.

A young woman who arrived with an older man, who I later discovered was her father, spoke up.

"Do any decide they don't wish to leave this bliss you speak of, this consciousness in the higher astral?

His eyes were forceful as He studied her deeply, then he spoke beautifully.

"Ah, I see you are interested in many things. Reincarnation cannot be refused or avoided by anyone, this is the Law of Karma and evolution. Even those who experience sudden death enter heavenly bliss, which eventually comes to an end and reincarnation is again experienced.

"It is a cycle, all life is a cycle. The only individuals who possess sufficient power and the ability to stay in the astral world for any extended length of time are Adepts, of either the 'good' or 'bad' variety, and examples of these are White Magicians and Black Magicians.

"An Adept in White Magic would only wish to stay out of physical incarnation if they knew for definite that by this action they would be able to serve and benefit humanity more effectively where they were in the astral."

At this point he stopped and turned to me with a look that touched me deeply. I felt I was to understand something, but I only heard in my head, "Patience Little One, you will understand." Then he resumed.

"But even they, because of Karmic Law, would eventually have to reincarnate and they would do so gladly. Such magicians live solely to benefit mankind and work only in the most suitable way with the Law of Evolution and Progress.

"An Adept in Black Magic however, would desire to put off for as long as possible the reaping on the Earth plane, the consequences of his past evil actions and abuse of the Laws of Nature." He stopped here and looked again piercingly at the woman.

"He would also have the desire to wreak as much havoc where he is and to cause as much harm as he can from the astral plane to the earth." His piercing look was still fixed on the woman.

"He may potentially be able to evade rein- carnation for many centuries but he can definitely not avoid it forever. Using his will to deliberately avoid reincarnation through such means and with such motives, he is creating even worse Karma for himself.

"Now an Adept when going through this whole process remains fully conscious, knowing and understanding exactly what's happening, This is not the case for the average person, and that is the only difference between the two."

With this, Francis bowed and then gave what I believe to be the head and heart salute of valour and self-sacrifice, and then departed out of the door.

# Chapter Thirty

*The Strongest principle of growth lies in human choice.*
George Eliot

I knew our time was coming to an end and I wanted to absorb as much as possible. Let's face it, the chance of having a third adventure was highly improbable. I had been gifted twice. How lucky can a girl get?

Linda and I spent time going over all the teachings and questions proposed to us. We laughed so hard at times as we recalled some of the ridiculous things that had happened.

She, like myself, felt elated, and how could one feel any different when in the Presence of such love and wisdom. Of course Raj was never far away from my thoughts and I still had much work to do around my perceived loss.

On this night, with us all around the fire, listening to Francis, it felt like we had become a family, truly a Brotherhood. He stared at the flames jumping high up the large chimney. What I hadn't realised, until the clock struck nine, was that I too had become engrossed in the same elemental dance. It had been two hours of silence and none of us had moved, well, not to my knowledge. What just happened?

"You have questions?" Francis asked. A voice to my right spoke up.

"You spoke at one time about psychics and the information they give as being inaccurate for the most part. Can you enlighten us more on this subject?"

Francis chuckled. "You have just spent considerable time contemplating. Hum? Let us see here."

Again He watched the flames and we automatically joined Him. It was then I heard Him, but not in the room. Surprisingly, I heard him in my head and later discovered we had all heard Him in our heads.

"Many psychics are unreliable but there are some who indeed have the capability to provide accurate information. This is attributed to the astral light, the psychic atmosphere that surrounds, and to some extent interpenetrates this physical plane. The astral light is like a Universal memory tablet, if you will, a giant android." He laughed then continued.

"It contains the records and images of everything from the past as well as the future. However, with regards to the future, the records and images are only for those things already sufficiently, and definitevely determined by one's own Karma. Accuracy on the part of a psychic means an ability to see to a certain extent in the astral light.

"However only an Initiate or Adept has the perfectly clear and reliable perception of everything *they* may need to see and know from all seven planes of the astral light.

"And, yes, to answer the question popping up in your minds at present, there are seven levels, planes, or degrees of the astral light.

"Why would you believe it necessary to try to find out from another what your future holds? It is so much worthier to attain that level of clarity yourself. Is that not the goal of all who embody? Is that not the goal of all here?

"Whatever the future may hold is of your own making, and thus has to be faced calmly and confidently, knowing that everything proceeds according to Law and that 'Law' is perfect justice." A man with a Russian accent spoke next.

"How does a soul know if he is still alive or whether he has passed on to devachan or heaven as some refer to it?"

Francis rose, went over to the hearth, rested his arm on the mantle and waited.

"Heaven, if that is what you wish to call it, is a state of such perfect and all-encompassing bliss that the soul cannot identify with anything less. Why, if it did, it would no longer be in bliss.

"The soul no longer has any awareness of death or suffering, it even forgets having passed through the process of death. This is what one experiences in this 'dream state' because it has created this for itself out of all the good. It's pure logic.

"The earth plane is so different from bliss, that just by looking at the world around you is sufficient evidence that at present you are certainly still alive on Earth."

"But what about the astral, which is passed through between physical death and entering the state of Bliss?" asked another, and Francis glanced at each person in the room individually.

"Come come, this has been explained to you. Simply by reason of your being here you have the means of contemplating these ideas for yourselves. We have no desire to mollycoddle you, or to indoctrinate you, but to present ideas for you to come to your own conclusions.

"The vast majority who have passed over only pass through the astral and in a predominantly unconscious state, and as such are not really aware of their astral surroundings. So this, too, should suggest to you that you are not in the astral currently."

Contemplation of the fire seemed to take us to an altered state, and this state seemed to make us more receptive. It became easier the more we engaged in the practice, a bit like meditation.

"Is it possible for a soul to be born and live in the astral plane?" Came the next question.

"The incarnations of a soul occur here on the physical plane and not on the astral or anywhere else," came His reply, "and the answer really depends on what you mean by born.

"Don't forget the astral is transitory – it is part of the cycle of birth, death and rebirth. So – no. And as far as an entire life, my first answer satisfies the second."

Where was Raj now, was he in the astral? Which I might add, I was now informed had seven levels, or was he in that blissful heaven place where it would seem he might be aware of me, but I would only be part of his dream of bliss?

"We are with those whom we have lost in the material form and far, far nearer to them now than when they were alive, and it is not only in the fancy of the person in Bliss/ Heaven, but in reality.

"For pure divine love is not merely the blossom of a human heart, but has its roots in eternity."

This statement brought some confusion for me, for I was not sure how in this blissful state referred to as heaven or devachan, one could be closer to loved ones than when we, or they, were on earth and still in physical bodies.

"When we take a wider sweep in our thought processes, we have a far more absorbing vista of eternal love, and a far more realistic viewpoint of the subsequent union between individual Egos as a result of that love. And here I am referring to Egos in the higher sense, not in a fashionable sense.

"Love 'has its roots in eternity', and those whom on earth we are strongly drawn to are the persons we have loved in past earth-lives, and also whom we have loved whilst in the blissful state of devachanic heaven.

"Coming back to earth, these enduring bonds of love draw us together yet again and add to the strength and beauty of the tie, and so it goes on.

"There is no separation between souls, though during earthly incarnation some may not always be fully aware of this or of the full law concerning this.

"The same people whom we come to love play so many parts in all the experiences of our lives and through many lifetimes, and each experience is recorded in the memory of the Soul.

"Esoteric philosophy teaches that death cannot touch the higher consciousness of man, and that it can only separate those who love each other so far as their lower vehicles are concerned.

"The man living on earth blinded by matter, feels separated from those who have passed onwards, but the one in Bliss, heaven, devachan, has a complete conviction that there is no such thing as death at all, having left behind all those vehicles/ bodies over which death has power.

"Therefore, to its less blinded eyes, its beloved are still with it. For it, the veil of matter that separated has been torn away." Francis rose and left.

Me 'ead 'urt, as my dad used to say, and it was time for bed, so like my companions I left the warmth of the library and tootled off to my four-poster.

Linda wanted to journal the following morning, so I checked if it was ok for me to take a wander around the grounds and whether anywhere was out of bounds.

A very jolly couple, who wove their conversations together rather like twins often do, informed me all areas outside were free to explore and offered to join me.

Down through a rose garden we entered a beautiful wooded area dotted with wild flowers seductively dancing with the whispers of the wind. A cappella of birds sang in rhythm with the stream which seemed to be chuckling along happily. I felt immersed in all this symphony, and all the while my two fellow strollers giggled like kids.

"I know," said one. "Everyone has the same response," finished the other. "We love it, guiding people here that is, and we never tire of seeing the joy nature gives to all who take the time to truly visit. We guess it's a little selfish really."

"But what is this place?" I gasped as we made our way to a bench and sat.

"Close your eyes and relax," whispered one of my companions, and no sooner had I done so than a choir of beautiful voices sounded all around. Arpeggios scaled to heaven as if with a single note.

"Now open your eyes," they whispered in unison. We were surrounded by crickets singing what I can only describe as a beautiful adagio.

"Nature is constantly praising, constantly balancing, constantly in service. By slowing your outer and raising your inner, you were able to perceive a little of the gift they are constantly giving."

Something had happened, this harmonic conversion reared in me the desire to sing, giggle and cry all at the same time. I wanted to go to the font and be baptised in this revival church of nature.

My new friends wished to show me more, so we departed until supper, ate, and then made our way for the evening's meeting.

As we sat in the library contemplating the flames again, Karma came to mind. It was a subject little understood by me really, and surely understanding it more would be of great value. You see, I was eager to become a serious contender for chelaship.

Let's face it, being a primary law that one cannot escape from, I needed to be well acquainted with it. Then a voice from the back of the room sounded forth and I turned to see our friend, the turbaned man.

"Karma is the first law. There is no Karma unless there is a being to make it or feel its effects.

"Karma is an undeviating and unerring tendency in the Universe to restore equilibrium, and it operates incessantly."

His voice was so clear at the front of the room, even though he was to the back, but he slowly made his way to the fireplace.

"Karma operates on all things and beings, even the minutest conceivable atom. Karmic causes already set in motion must be allowed to sweep on until exhausted." He stopped, turned and faced us.

"The effects may be counteracted or even mitigated by the thoughts and acts of oneself or of another. Every instrument used by any Ego in any life is appropriate to the Karma operating through it. Changes may occur in the instrument during one life so as to make it appropriate for a new class of Karma, and this may take place in two ways (a) through intensity of thought and the power of a vow." Here the turbaned man placed his forceful eyes upon both Linda and I, and we knew it was because of the letter we had written, and then he continued.

"And (b) through natural alterations due to complete exhaustion of old causes.

"Karma is both merciful and just. Mercy and Justice are only opposite poles of a single whole; and Mercy without Justice is not possible in the operations of Karma. That which man calls Mercy and Justice is defective, errant, and impure."

Upon finishing his last sentence he walked to the back of the room, stopped and turned to us all.

"May I add some final words from Neresheimer to this?" He smiled.

"Man is free to choose his actions in all circumstances. Whichever course he adopts from personal motive, whether good or bad, there will subsequently be corresponding reaction upon him, a reaction known as Karma, the law of cause and effect, action and reaction.

"Through want of compassion and lack of knowledge he often chooses wrongly, selfishly, inconsiderately; in consequence, the rebound which follows as effect, though the thought or deed has long been forgotten, is sometimes considered as being personal adversity and hardship.

"The law embodies the highest justice and intelligence, devoid of emotion and unerring in its compensation. Among the many pleasing incidents experienced in life, divers other things befall mankind such as sickness, poverty, as well as thwarted ambition, worry, discouragement, pain, misfortune, and various tribulations.

"All these are but states of mind, largely susceptible to improvement with a proper mental attitude. Adverse conditions may remain quite what they are, but one's mental relation to them can be altered in a moment or by degrees. If one succeeds in so doing, the aspect of an affliction will modify itself and often completely change. The Law is Compassion Absolute! Karma is its method. Reincarnation is its Instrument.

"The advancing cycle demands imperative change, the Teachers treading the Path of Compassion have been, and are, at hand for love of their fellow-men and sacrificing all else in leading the way. And your troubles? On another plane of consciousness, the plane of the soul, they are non-existent, except in the sense of a mere incident, just as one single letter might stand for an incident in a volume which contains many, many subjects.

"Hold to some lofty, impersonal subject which appeals to you. Brotherhood as a fact in nature, the unity of Cosmos and similar verities suggested in Ageless Wisdom teachings. Rise with them in the morning, letting them penetrate into you during the day, and retire with them, holding them as the last thing before sleep. Never fail in the performance of the least duty to the fullest extent of ability.

"Cease day-dreaming or letting the mind wander aimlessly into the past, or into anticipation of the future, instead, live consciously alert to the smallest thing connected with every thought and act, at the same time being discriminatingly positive as to what is proper and what is not.

"There is no universal prescription for meeting or brushing aside things that happen. Whatever occurs has to be met somehow, and therefore your mental relations to the circumstances determine the quality of the effect the happenings shall have upon you. If a broad enough view is taken, you may extract from adversities a valuable lesson.

"It is unwise to complain, or to mope or pray for better fortune instead of making an effort to fathom their meaning. Nothing ever occurs for which adequate causes are not in existence in man's atmosphere, whether generated in the remote past or in the present life. Calmly and courageously look on new conditions as opportunities for growth as this will promote individual self-reliance."

My two brain cells hurt terribly as they bumped from left to right trying to compute all He had said. Linda, as always, was more verbal than I, she had something to say.

"Are you serious? I thought when he walked to the back of the room he was going to leave us with his final words. He must be a comedian. I need sleep, I'm exhausted." We all laughed. The room cleared and I retired to my bed. to rest my head, with 'vinegar, and brown paper!'

Both Linda and I were due to leave the following morning, and on this, our last night at the stately home, I was asked to meet Francis at 7pm in the library. Thinking it was another of our group meetings, I rushed along eager to meet up with all those who had become part of my family.

There was only Sir Geoffrey and Francis in the room and I was asked to take a seat near the fire with the two of them.

There had been the journey into the Rockies and now this amazing journey, and yes, physical contact with a great soul is not what it is all about, but by golly it helps. Now, here in this old library with Francis and Sir Geoffrey, I felt at peace – utter peace. Sir Geoffrey looked over his glasses.

"We would encourage you to write further and also to use the Wisdom contained in older writing. We have been accused of plagiarism - tut-tut.. For in whose garden did those original lofty ideas germinate and whence did they arrive in full bloom? Plagiarism, tut-tut. Ridiculous!

"Be prepared, not all you have heard or encountered may be shared due to the personal nature and sensitivity of some of the subjects. As time progresses, the skills you are honing for the written word may be put to greater use. Kindergarten is necessary if you are to graduate." He seemed very 'to the point', and it was something I was comfortable with.

"We have spoken much on death this last while, something that's been on your mind for some time, yes? Many fear the word death. Won't entertain discussion! It is not dying that is painful, but living. However, it is in the living that one uncovers the illusions of death.

"And life, what of life? It doesn't become easier when you make the decision to write a letter, hum, oh no." He waved His hand through the air in dismissal.

"The climb is steep, the pitfalls many, and the trophy scars glorious. Is that not so?" He turned to Francis and smiled. Then He continued on.

"Faint heart, scattered mind and lack of faith are big boulders impeding that climb to the summit. When you see loss with the same eyes as gain, and service takes up permanent residence in your heart, you will suffer no more.

"Remember, attachments and expectations cause suffering, and these two need to be embraced to be Mastered.

"Have courage, dip yourself into daring, and at times be silent. Yes, learn to be silent. And though, at times, you may feel alone on that mountain, you have many who have gone before you to light the way."

This magnificent, benevolent man rose, smiled, and departed. Francis escorted me to the door and placed his hand upon my head like a loving father. I was so choked at having to say goodbye to Him I cried.

# Chapter Thirty One

*You can watch a clock tick.*
*You can witness a sunrise or a sunset, but that is not time. That is*
*simply movement.*
Zen Proverb

And so dear reader, you have an idea of the series of events that brought me to my 'Now'. Raj was now somewhere else, though I have no idea where, but at times his whole essence seemed to envelop me and that was a blessing.

When he had surrendered himself to this dharma drama, I didn't experience any funeral or celebration. I was only given the vision of the incident as the rest was irrelevant at the time.

Mourning over his shell was not in my consciousness now. It was the real Raj, if that is his name, that I loved and missed and wished to be with again.

Leaving England was not easy for myself nor Linda, but back home in my little flat I felt determined I was going to get my act together. So I embarked on a course of serious esoteric study. Days came and went, and yes, maybe at first I was expecting directions regarding my life path, but no one sent an email giving me details.

Linda had returned to her home, and we became constant telephone buddies chatting non-stop for hours at a time, getting further insights into all the wisdom shared.

But on this particular afternoon, whilst wandering, I passed some buildings just on the outskirts of my town, and slumped in a doorway was a man peddling for spare cash. I bent down to put some odd change in his tin and he pulled the mac from off his head and looked at me.

"How long have I got?" he pleaded. He must have thought I was someone else, but grabbing hold of me he pleaded again.

"How long?" I didn't know what he was referring to but he continued pulling on me.

"Stay with me, I'm scared." He cried.

These last words touched my heart and I crouched closer just as a familiar screech from a bird ripped the air. He shook. The sight of the bird told me what was about to happen.

"There's nothing to fear, a friend of mine is waiting to take you to where you can rest in peace." I said gently. "There will be old friends, and loved ones, and greater than that there'll be love you can't even begin to comprehend. I know, I've been there. And oh... ." his hold eased and he sobbed.

"But I'm guilty of so many things, I'm so sorry." I held him and whispered.

"There's no guilt where you're going, there's no punishment. You'll have every opportunity to sort the things you wish to sort, and you'll see clearly the reasons for everything in your life. You'll understand and you'll do so in peace." His face started to fade through my tears. "Embrace it all and trust that love will be there. Let go and trust."

He looked like a child, a little child fearful of an unknown stalker, but at that moment a surge of love powered through us and the familiar sound of raven's wings changed everything. With his struggling breath, he muttered.

"You know?"

"I've done this, trust." I whispered. "Death is my lover and I would willingly lay my body aside to be lifted to the place where you're now going."

He let go of his grip. In a whisper he departed and his lifeless body lay limp in my arms.

The ambulance arrived, and I sat and wept, not for his passing over, but for the fear he had experienced.

There was something I knew Raj wanted me to know about death. I just felt it. It became clear to me that whilst death remained such a big unknown, it gave the perfect opportunity for fear to effectively seep into all our lives.

We educate on the birthing process yet we avoid the dying process, and both are inevitable. We cannot run from death, so common sense alone would tell us education would bring great ease. We dread death like the devil, and children, by osmosis, assume it is the terror of all terrors and grow with the belief that this "devil" is always lurking in the background, waiting to pounce on his next victim.

This was one reason why death first presented itself to me in a bizarre form, so I could see what had been created by mass thought and then experience the unconditional love of its truth.

Now back to my story.

That night I retired to bed early and did something I had not done for a long time. I made a call to the Brotherhood of Light to take me in my finer body to be with my Teacher and also asked to meet Raj. The call compels the answer. Closing my eyes, I slipped into a twilight zone.

As I was about to doze off I felt my body quicken into the shadows. Voices muttered in the distance, then silence.

My whole body quivered like an arrow anticipating its target. I was being held back. Then like an arrow, I shot forward into the horizon. Quicker than sound to my ears came the rush of wings, the wings of a familiar companion. Huge but tender, he lifted me up and gently placed me on a shore of golden sands where a figure stood. It was Raj.

"Never send me back," I pleaded. "Hold me." He did, in his enveloping consciousness.

How can I describe this in words dear reader? It would be a bit like describing to someone who had been blind since birth, the colour red, or describing the taste of a peach to one who had never tasted fruit.

We spun as the sound of taffeta gently lifted away, then Raj lifted my head and smiled.

In the distance I heard voices and close by, I saw forms lurking in doorways and darkened silhouettes walking into buildings. This world was an alternate world, dim and heavy.

"What's happening, where is this place, who are these people?" I thought.

"Lower astral, addictions," Came his reply.

I looked over to a man sitting at a table continually pouring from a bottle and calling for more. Ahead of me was a bookstand which somehow didn't seem to fit into this place. I made my way over. A large book caught my eye.

"I can't read this, it's full of hieroglyphs. What does it say?" The figure turned.

"Take care," motioned Raj, "you are not encumbered by time and space here. Control your mind."

Gingerly, I looked at the words on the page, being mindful not to lend my emotions in any way, until one name caught my eye. A shard of light issued forth, which refracted into a magnificent array of colour, and instantly I was standing in a room of light beside my Scottish friend who had passed over.

"You must go, don't stay here," came my thought to her. She heard me instantly and replied.

"There are many who linger. Some due to their own earthly attachments and others because the earthly cling to them. It is always dangerous and detrimental to both parties concerned to try to make contact with the dead, and it carries great Karma." She smiled and was gone.

I wondered about all this, what was the book? Was it the book of life and death? Was there such a book? Obviously I was at the right place at the right time to complete something, and also to understand something. When I awoke that morning I knew I would get some understanding at some time, so I shelved it.

# Chapter Thirty Two

*First there is a mountain, Then there is no mountain, Then there is.*
Zen Proverb

It was Friday morning. The doorbell rang, the phone rang, and I didn't know what to do first.

"Hi Ellie, a question." It was Linda on the phone.

"Hang on Lin, the door bell's going nuts." was my response.

"Delivery for Mac." The man stood in the doorway.

"What, who?" was my confusion.

"Sign here. Have a nice day." The man departed.

"You there Ellie?" Linda was still waiting.

"Oh, Lin!"

The noises spilling out my mouth and down the phone, were of relief, sadness and joy, but also shock and stunned confusion.

A bunch of forget-me-nots had just been delivered with no note. Only Raj had ever given me these flowers, only Raj. Reclaiming my composure a little I became aware Linda was speaking.

"How about a visit to Calgary? Get on a plane and fly." Now reader, this was all too synchronistic and it involved Raj, so I literally caught the next flight to see her.

Calgary's frosty fingers grabbed me the minute I exited the airport. Linda arrived and we started on the road, not to her home it seemed, but to some outback she said I would remember well. And I did.

This was not something I was prepared to do, this revisiting. No. I was not going.

Needless to say Linda kept on driving and also driving me mad. We chatted our way to a little campsite where we were the only ones stupid enough to pitch a tent. Memories flooded back.

Nearby, a group of day hikers had lit a fire and welcomed us to sit and share the warmth of their friendship. They had hiked the area before, and shared their thoughts on a curious light they had seen coming from beyond the Foothills.

It was so interesting listening to them debate as to what it was, from the Northern Lights to aliens. Both Linda and I had our thoughts and decided to share some of them. They sat captivated.

Funny, years ago the thing was to sit around a campfire sharing ghost stories, but this night around a fire with strangers, Linda and I shared stories of strange Adepts, Masters, of encountering grizzly's that liked their tummies tickled, and it seemed to be captivating everyone.

Midnight blue is the 'tuck in blanket' of the Divine, a blessed wrap that spreads across our world covering everything in comfort. It keeps us cosy so our finer bodies may leave to wander into other worlds. So we said goodnight to our new friends and listened to the summons that the time to hunker down was upon us.

It was only on the walk to our tent that Linda decided to explain to me that we had no choice but to camp the night. We only had enough gas in the car to get us to the nearest gas station and it was closed 'til morning.

Once in my sleeping bag could I sleep? Absolutely frozen, not cold, but frozen, it seemed like I was on a rerun of an old movie: my movie. I couldn't warm up even with clothes over my PJs. I donned gloves and a bobble hat, and of course socks, however I couldn't stop shivering. Linda was shaking with the cold, and if I hadn't thought she was uncomfortable I would've pulverised her for this brain dead suggestion.

It was later into the night that I realised it was a seriously cold situation. There seemed no choice but to call to other realms for help, and by the time I got to the second line Linda had joined me. She started to cry and because of past memories I joined in, and hugged her, the sweet little girl, my friend. Through our snivelling we beseeched for help, and then got down into the bags as far down as we could go,

Some time later, I awoke from my unexpected sleep and felt wet trickling down my cleavage. I was so hot. My mind went into a mini panic, for the fire lit that night by our Calgary friends may have been left blazing and was out of control spreading to our location. But I noticed no light anywhere and soon realised it was I, burning up.

Linda was cuddled so close on my back, bless her, that her radiating heat was becoming unbearable, and to top it all she was snoring like an oversized, overactive adenoid.

The best thing for me to do was to get out of the sleeping bag and take off some of the gear. I tugged at the zip but it wouldn't budge. Being trussed up like a turkey in a roasting bag started my real panic. Breaking the zip proved impossible so I attempted to get one arm out, but I was truly jammed in.

In my manoeuvres I was able to pull off my gloves, rub off my socks and by bending my head down as far as I could I pulled off my hat with my confined fingers. It helped, but boy she was a heavy lump of burning coal. Then the snoring stopped. She slowly moved off my back, and though it was dark I knew she had gotten up.

"Ellie, are you awake now?"

"Well and truly cooked, but conscious." I replied.

"God you really snore, and boy you're hot!" she whispered.

Trying not to laugh at the compliment, I was still stuck in the bag, but I enlightened her.

"Lin, it wasn't me. I've been awake all this time trying to master the talents of Houdini. Look!" But of course it was dark.

At that moment we noticed the moon hitting the entrance to our tent. We watched a large wolf slowly exit.

On the journey home to Linda's we discussed the wolf and how it had saved our lives. We had also been perfectly safe which in of itself was quite the event and it was so gentle just lying there. Lets face it, what makes a wolf decide to enter a tent inhabited by two humans and lay between them?

I recalled meeting the bear, mentioned in the first part of this read, and the teaching Francis had given us, and we were both very grateful. We were also grateful that our calls had been answered.

Once back, Linda was faced with the news that her mother-in-law was extremely sick and her husband had to go to Ottawa for an extended visit. A thought came knocking on her door. She was always full of thoughts.

Life on this earth is but a fleeting moment and the bucket list long, so over a cuppa we made the decision we were off to India. We had the opportunity, the inclination, and all we needed to do was book the flight. After many pots of tea and phone calls, the booking was made. We departed two days later.

The drive from New Delhi to our first destination was through hell. It seemed the bus was going the scenic route, and two hours and one dead body later, I put a scarf around my eyes so I couldn't see the trucks approaching, trying to kill us.

I became complacent about the 500-foot drop beside the road, which the driver insisted on playing Russian roulette with. It all just added to the list of my possible death scenarios in this life.

Straddling my two feet on top of the seat in front of me, I lifted my body up and placed my hands under my coccyx to protect it from being smashed. All the while the vehicle bounced into potholes large enough to be used by spelunkers.

I sang as loud as possible, any song I could think of as well as songs that made no sense, in order to shut out the horns warning us of impending disaster. But arrive at our destination we did, a set of rooms close to the Red Fort.

On the banks of the Yamuna river sits a towering wonder of red stone, the Red Fort. Nothing can prepare one for the scale of this building, and to be honest, for me it outranks the Taj Mahal a thousand times.

While the walls, gates, and a few other structures in the fort were constructed of red sandstone, marble had been largely used in the palaces.

The 'Hall of Public Audience' was three aisles deep, and at the back of the hall was an alcove where the royal throne stood under a marble canopy.

Originally there were six marble palaces along the eastern waterfront, and behind, but separated by a court, was the Painted Palace. This painted Palace has a massive water-channel called the Stream of Paradise that runs down through it with a central marble basin fitted with an ivory fountain. It is said that one of the fountains in the easternmost apartment emitted rosewater. Yes, a rose water fountain.

Wandering around invited silent study and I was thankful Linda felt the same. It was easy to imagine rose water, warmed enough to create an aromatheric stream of infused love, cascading down the three-tiered pools from one level to the other.

In the distance a man dressed in white caught my eye. I was looking at the back of him but his movement and form I knew like my very breath. I had studied it over mountains, dales, valleys and hills. I knew that man and I loved him. My Michaelangelo's David, Raj.

Dusk threw shadows on the pathway as the distant figure moved further away. "No, no!" I shouted and kept shouting, but I was not fast enough to reach him. Then he was gone and I sat at the bottom terrace out of breath and despairing.

Linda, who had seen my frenetic behaviour followed me, and once she had reached me pleaded.

"What the heck are you all about?"

"It was him Lin, I saw him! I know him like my very hands. I couldn't possibly make a mistake?"

In a hidden place, a secret compartment locked away in my heart sat the last remnants of my grief, and this was the time and place my soul decided to let it out and let it go.

My standing and screaming for at least 15 minutes shook Linda, and around us people ran, some even screamed and ran. It wasn't long before officials arrived. In their awkward way, in a language we didn't understand, they wanted to know what was happening.

After much assurance to the officials, and then a lot of laughter from Linda, we were permitted to leave and went for curry in a hurry and bed with a head.

Sitting on our beds we chatted about our day and Linda pointed out that a little gratitude might be a good thing, and I was grateful. My grief had been bottled up so tight and the cork was released by seeing that stranger. Thank you stranger.

It was a balmy Indian night and in the early hours we heard singing outside the window. With both of us up, we went to the window to see where it was coming from. A man was sitting on a large rock chanting. This was India. Then through the trees Linda saw a figure.

"Look there's that man from Scotland," she mumbled, "you know that man, the one with the turban, the one who took us to the loch, you know." I didn't see him but she did, so we both dressed and went outside.

The warm air mixed a cocktail of exotic perfumes and those parts of nature that stay so hidden during the waking hours were out and living their best life. Then she saw him again and was off. Like a pet puppy I followed her lead.

Among the coconut trees stood a small stone statue of Buddha in a mudra, and a short distance away stood a man.

Some years ago a friend of mine visited the Far East, and on the last day went to a Buddhist temple. When she was about to leave, a monk approached and gave her a necklace, instructing her to give it to Ellie when she returned to Canada. It was a beaded necklace with a little Buddha in an enclosed surround. It was in the mudra I was now looking at.

The man moved towards us like a vision and said we were to go to Rishikesh. We didn't hesitate but returned to our lodgings immediately to pack, and left as quickly as possible.

# Chapter Thirty Three

*The obstacle is the path.*
Zen Proverb

"Rishikesh Ellie, where the hell's that? I think it's up somewhere to the left, but let's ask directions." We did ask and started on our way.

Geography was a subject that seemed useless back in my youth. Spain was a foreign land visited only two weeks a year, and we would pack pillows in the car if we were going to grandma's house which was two hours drive away. However, as I grew in years, I made the decision I would travel and have adventures, and as a result I was proud of my developed sense of direction. Ego? Yes. The reality check came quickly, Rishikesh?

Satnav proved the best and I soon became a master, not of wisdom, but of the cell. We reached a village about six hours from our destination and decided to stay the night, and after finding a room we ate, slept, and in the morning gathered everything together to continue on. Just as we finished our breakfast a knock came on our door.

A small man with thin-rimmed glasses smiled and indicated we were to follow him. Of course I had some apprehensions but I trusted. Fool!

About an hour in, we shared some of our concerns with our guide speaking with him like he was a deaf with only the ability to lip-read. Why do we do things like that, you know, assuming if someone doesn't speak our language we have to loudly act out every word with exaggerated hand and mouth movements?

In a most eloquent Oxford accent, he informed us we were off to the caves and not to be too concerned about the Divine's ability. He also said something very interesting.

"Be prepared for a clear out, it will be necessary."

Many times Linda and I have needed to change our views, clear out the old in order to let in the new, adapting to incredible changes. Just look at the journey we were on. We were prepared, or so we thought. We spent our day settling into our room and wandering.

The following day was a free day, so we decided to wander around this little village, hopefully meet some of the locals, find some of the temples, and make our way to an ashram that was recommended.

This place was in the past, incredibly beautiful and peaceful. Being strangers we stood out, but a kind family invited us to a gathering where we ate our fill and then made our way into the heart of the forest which they told us was special.

A mist of intoxication hung in the air due to the incense wafting up in praise to Shiva. We followed the deep guttural sound of chanting 'til we reached the heart of the sanga, and Linda sat.

Our guide had shared some information earlier that morning, which I needed to follow up on, so after a while I made my way back to find him.

During sleep that night I had woken up in a sweat, and when the morning came I asked our guide if there was anyone in the area who knew about herbs. He told me of an old woman who carried homoeopathic remedies, and being a homoeopath myself I knew that a little arsenic would do fine.

As the day progressed I realised my desperate need for her services, so I was pleased when I saw he was waiting outside.

Jumping onto his little cart I stressed my urgency, but by the time we came near her village I was already dripping with sweat again, and desperate for a loo. I stood on her porch in trouble. I was now a mess.

The door opened and a woman showed me to a small room, where behind some glass were an assortment of homoeopathic remedies. She handed me the remedy, I had a cold shower, and then she presented me with a sari as well as a plastic bag full of my smelly clothes. Grateful, I jumped onto the cart, and my guide drove me back to the ashram and Linda.

Through the forest I could hear Linda chanting but couldn't make out the words. I followed her chant and found her kneeling with a key in her hand seemingly trying to put a square peg in a round hole, the key was to the outhouse door. The intensity of her chanting increased, and the mantra was clear.

"Oh please no, oh please no, oh please no."

She had gone down with the sweats and diarrhoea also, but a dose of Arsenicum and a shower later, she too was feeling much better and we discussed the clearing out process and our blinkered understanding of what our guide had said.

Sleep that night was a blessing and a chance to heal our worn out bodies. When we awoke we hit the road not stopping until we reached Rishikesh.

# Chapter Thirty Four

*I searched for God and found only myself.*
*I searched for myself and found only God.*
Sufi

Rishikesh was an overnight sleep and then we were off to a place called Bareilly. India has a special sunrise you know, rare and earthy like the country itself. This Arian sun shouts "I'm here" and wraps its deep heat around a body quickly, and all this without a word.

In the heat we started on the long trek to the caves, our first stop Bareilly. It seemed like days we had been on the road, but our man informed us this leg of the trek was for a day only, and when we reached our destination we could rest.

Bareilly was a bustling commercial city, a city I had never heard of and, to tell you the truth, I wasn't that interested. I just wanted to get to the caves. Also my mind had been preoccupied with thoughts of my vision at the Red Fort.

Had it been Raj? No, he was no longer with us. However, I knew Raj and felt sure it was him. The mind can play such games and be so cruel at times. It can taunt a person taking over moments it doesn't have the right to take like a sneaky thief. Nevertheless, I couldn't stop thinking. The night was uneventful which was gratifying as both Linda and I were exhausted.

# TWO DINGBATS ON A SPIRITUAL QUEST

The next morning we were well fed, well tea'd, well rested, and raring to go. After a day's hike we arrived at a place called Rameswar, a holy place, where we stayed overnight. This was another blessing for little did we realise the journey forward from here was going to take every last bit of resolve, emotionally, mentally and physically.

Gangolighat Road, well what can I say? Mountainous hell, yes hell! I'm sure you'll understand my relationship with mountain passes by now. Not good. Narrow passes and high mountains cannot be something pleasurable in my book; actually they prove to me that there is a devil, for who would ever allow such an instigator of fear? God? Oh I know what you're thinking, God didn't create fear, but I'm using philosophical and poetic licence here to express my utter despair when I started to realise the *'Hell Road'*.

Stopping the whole cavalcade, I asked everyone if there was another route to our destination, it seemed not. I asked if anyone had sleeping pills and could they put me on a cart for the duration, and it seemed not. I wasn't joking. I made it quite clear, then and there, that I was not going any further. I sat on a large stone, arms and legs crossed, determined. Been there done that, not doing it again. Oh and tell me why I should. Um, hello don't bother, I don't need to know why.

Linda couldn't stop laughing at my attitude and the more she laughed the more I disliked her. She knew my terror and was therefore becoming a good candidate for carotid extraction.

"Ellie get up! Think of the things you've overcome in this life, think Ellie."

Yep, doing what she asked I did think...I shouted back to her four words, *"Watch My Mouth. No.."* She sat beside me and crossed her legs saying nothing. "I don't even have my love around to catch me if I fall." I was crying and she put her arms around me. A germ of courage rose and I responded to her plea.

"Come on, let's get there. Hey, I have you, my best friend, what else do I need?"

So we hit the path and stayed on it 'til we reached a place called Bhuvaneshwar where we rested for the night.

My night was full of visions, of dark steep places, high rambling paths crumbling too easily under my feet, and faces of monks and gurus. I was restless and decided to rise early and within about a minute Linda had joined me.

"I think this is going to be quite the happening Ellie and I'm nervous, in a good way, but will life ever be the same?"

I thought about it. Life was never the same after a journey like this. Life is never the same when you go to sleep and wake up the next morning.

Linda and I agreed that our journey since writing 'the letter' had taken us through what seemed like one incarnation after another in the course of a few years. We really were two dingbats on a spiritual quest.

If you could view *your* world in a 360 degrees circle, your partner, your family, your friends, employment, health, country, and your hemisphere, if you could view that world completely changed, all different, then you would get a small, very small understanding of how this little piece of paper has impacted our world mentally, emotionally, physically and spiritually. And I must say here that life has been an extremely crazy, happy, devastating movie worth discussing.

"Linda, we're not the same two women that started out and when we return home life won't be the same."

"We have little choice Ellie, standing still means reversing coz the whole shemozzle is rolling on."

The entrance to the caves rested at about 1200 metres up a rock face and the path to it was narrow and near impossible to see. Once in the caves we would have to descend into the bowels of the earth to reach the sacred chambers.

They say you can overcome your phobias, we won't discuss that. No matter how many heights I had traversed, it never became easier, the difference was that *I* had changed and was prepared to do it.

At the entrance our guide handed us over to another who also spoke fluent English. He explained the caves were extremely sacred but would soon be accessible to the public. We had seen no one on this last leg of our journey, other than those who were assisting us, and on this day no one was to be seen at the caves either.

He went in first and I followed with Linda at the rear. Inside, the stairway down was steep and slippery with a 30-metre drop to the side. There was little room to move and in this confined space both Linda and I became concerned. We sat down on our butts, lowering ourselves gradually, and the further down we went the tighter it all became. There was also a noticeable lack of good oxygen which made it very difficult to breathe, so we took it slowly.

This was definitely the day I was going to die, and this was going to be my place, I knew it. On my trip into the Rockies I was convinced it was going to be death by freezing or death by roasting, in fact, the list had grown substantially, and now I realised it was to be death by suffocation.

But it was Linda who froze. Her breathing was shallow, tight, and she shook her head – no more. She would not move up nor down.

When I tried to encourage her I received the glare I had received before when we were by the loch in Scotland, it was a look of, "say another word and I'll rip your gullet out, and while I'm doing that I'll dance the devil's polka." I just waited. Then I had to speak.

"Linda, you've overcome far more than I, and now it's my turn to say to you, think of what you've done in this life!" She was a courageous woman, she grabbed my arm and sideways we continued our descent.

When we reached the first chamber I had blood dripping from my wounds and Linda had blood under her fingernails.

This was the chamber of the large serpent, and it was no small creature I assure you. The floor resembled the spine of a large cobra with its ribs clearly defined on the hard but smooth surface. One could see the hood which was huge, and the large poisonous glands which were overpowering.

Our next chamber was the chamber of Ganesh, the remover of obstacles. One could see by his statue that his head had been cut off in the fight he had with Shiva. Above where his head should have been, was a lotus, and what is called 'life sustaining nectar' dripped onto his body. Beside Ganesh were two large lingams.

Our guide started to repeat a mantra and lit a little container of ghee. We joined in with him repeating every line he said. Peace oozed into the chamber like a snake, and it coiled its magic around us inducing a trance-like state. I was feeling a little heady.

Feeling a strong urge to leave this chamber, I quietly rose and, taking a lamp, made my own way to another. I stood alone in the quiet and closed my eyes.

Now I could feel him, now I could smell him, now the familiar essence of sandalwood wafted over me as a blanket of love. Warm, soft, gentle, his arms came around me from behind, and turning to face the beauty I knew, I met his dark eyes and I willingly sank into him.

My heart and mind became wrapped so privately in a cloth woven from love that I became convinced my alchemical abilities were manifesting my desire, Raj. Gently, my love took me by my hands into another chamber and proceeded to chant in deep Sanskrit tones.

What was real, what is real, was this an illusion conjured up by the hypnotic eyes of the cobra? I didn't care, for this moment was mine, and he was as real as Linda sitting in the other chamber. I looked at him and went weak, and yes, he caught me and held me tightly.

Time burnt the oil in the lamp, then he took me to yet another chamber, the chamber of the Divine Mother. Here there were more lingams, and in my head he explained how when the largest of these grows to touch the top of the cave it would be the end of the Kali Yuga.

Give up my eternity for him? Absolutely, but it could never happen and would never be asked. But I do surrender myself to him, and to the love that he is the embodiment of.

And this was his mission, to take me to the shore of pure love, encourage me to place the tip of my toes in the holy water, give me water-wings to help me float, then encourage me to swim deep without thought of myself. This is now a constant prayer in my heart and mind, though at times, I have to gasp for air. When I do, I swim to the surface and take another deep breath and dive again. He had achieved all he could with this small being; he had succeeded in all his earthly undertakings.

I had never seen his dead body, even though I had been given a vision of what happened that night at the mine, and no one had actually told me he was dead. He was gone and so I had only assumed.

One of the great pains I felt was not having the chance to tell him I loved him, though he knew, of course he knew. But now I had the chance to tell this phantom in my own, human fashion.

He smiled at me just at that moment, a truly benevolent smile, and drew me to him as he had done so many times in the past. This time it was in a gesture of fatherly love, and now I had touched all the aspects that were possible for me to touch of his Divine essence.

He held me for quite some time, and then slowly lifted my head to look deeply and seriously at me.

"My love, you know all there is to know about us, now take this opportunity to let go of your attachments. It seems somewhat violent, but you have been given more than most who travel the path of sorrow. Walk in faith and continued charity. You know the truth and now live that truth. Trust." Here was that word again.

"What you are generating is self-pity and it serves for naught. I have always been with you and will always be with you, I have said such and it is so."

He pulled me close again. I could hear his heartbeat and that startled me. I quickly lifted my head and stepped back.

"You're alive, Raj," but I don't understand, how can that be? You're my illusion."

He pulled himself to a majestic height and looked towards the sound of people approaching. This was the picture I hung in my heart that day, the one of this great soul. Then he looked at me, smiled and bowed. I turned to Linda as she entered the chamber.

As she approached she smiled at me and I was pleased, then our guide smiled at me, and I was pleased. I turned to share with them my love, and Raj was gone

# Part Three

# Chapter Thirty Five

*My soul is from elsewhere, I'm sure of that, and I intend to end up there.*
Ellie Mac

I stood and stared. Why had I done it? Why had I gone to so much trouble to return to the scene of our last parting? Of course I knew the answer was because of them, the Master and Raj. Even though I had gone to all this trouble, I still had no idea whether it was possible for me to enter their world again, but I had to try. Standing once again in the foothills of the Rocky Mountains I could sense myself on the threshold of something daunting, but what that something was, who knew.

I was Alice, just about to jump through the looking glass, and the world I was to enter, if the past was anything to go by, promised to inspect many aspects of myself and do so on many levels. For now, I had to face the reality as to whether I would be able to join them again.

The north wind whipped and I stomped forward in my combat boots. I was determined that nothing was going to block my route, not the elements, fear, not even death, whom I had danced with before on more than one occasion. Yes, I was ready and today I was going to wander here in my past record of events until I was permitted to go forward into my future.

Visions of the past entered my mind; scenes of campfires, hidden retreats and bears, there were always bears. The familiar smells of pine and fir mingled with earthy freshness tried to seduce me to stop, but I stomped on and smiled as the snow crunched, submissive, beneath my boots.

Fear did show up. What of those bears? What of death? What of? Fear loves to rear its tail in an attempt to whack the pilgrim off course, but fear was an unwelcome guest this day. I let it come and saw it go and closed the door as tight as I could behind it.

Francis asked me once to draw a line in the snow, which I did. He then asked that I place the word fear on one end and love the other, which again I did. He then asked me what was between them both and I answered the degrees of both. Then he asked me to mark a line where fear ended and love began, and I sat for hours with this.

My decision to go out this day had been initiated by love as well as two people, the old gypsy I had met in Victoria and the strange woman who had swept into my life with a bump.

"Take the cold road", the old gypsy had said, "Take the cold road," and Sam had also urged me to do the same. However let me go back to where this story began, just a short time earlier in Victoria, my hometown.

# Chapter Thirty Six

*If you understand, things are just as they are. If you do not understand, things are just as they are.*
Zen Proverb

It was that time of year when people who usually keep to themselves step outside and exchange common courtesies with strangers they rarely notice at other times of the year. It was just before Christmas.

The market buzzed with vendors touting and customers bartering, but then one voice seemed to carry over the airwaves leaving all the others behind.

"Want to buy a bunch of my lucky forget- me-nots lady?" the old woman looked directly at me.

What was that, forget-me-nots? No it's supposed to be heather, and I stopped. Across the road stood a wizened woman who glared at me, and I went over to her.

"What did you say, what did you call those flowers?" I asked.

"Want to buy a bunch of my lucky heather lady?" A scarf knotted under the old gypsy's face made her chin wobble as she spoke.

"You said forget-me-nots, I heard you." I insisted.

"No lady, your hearing's playing tricks. Wanna buy a bunch?" The old woman came closer and almost shoved the bunch up my nose. She grabbed my hand and turned it over glaring at the palm.

"Cross me hand with silver dearie and I'll tell you something."

Drawing my hand away, I rummaged through my purse looking for a coin and then she grabbed the ring on my finger that Raj had given me.

"That'll do lovey" she muttered, but I quickly retracted my hand and she laughed displaying the gold fillings that had taken up residence in her mouth. Grabbing my hand again she turned it so the palm was up and studied it carefully.

"Ah great journeys, great love, great loss. More journeys, more love, more..." she stopped as violently as she had started. Pushing my hand away she shoved her head close to my face and whispered, "you have to go back, go back."

Looking down at my hand I saw nothing but a map of lines going nowhere, five fingers, a palm and a wrist. I stood a while trying to see anything she could have seen, but there was nothing.

"Take the cold road, you know where it is Little One," came her loud voice in the distance. I turned to respond and bumped into a passer by.

"So sorry, I hope I didn't...?" came my totally disinterested mumble whilst picking up a large brown envelope I had knocked from a woman's hands.

"Not at all, just some tickets, no harm done," she smiled and walked on. By the time we had exchanged courtesies the gypsy was nowhere to be seen.

She had called me Little One and no one had ever called me that but Francis. Feeling a little discombobulated, I decided to do what is always best to do, have a cup of tea. I wandered over to the nearby tearoom and ordered a pot of good English Breakfast.

"So we meet again, may I?" I looked up to see the woman I had rudely bumped into and she sat down.

"Samantha, well Sam for short, do you live here?" She ordered a pot herself and placed the envelope I had wiped from her hands carefully on the far side.

"Yes I do now, originally from England, and it's Ellie." I always seem to put originally from England when asked, for more often than not the next question was usually, where are you from originally? Her tea arrived and she poured.

"I'm a tourist and wondered if you can recommend anything I may have missed?" her eyes went to the envelope.

"Well I'm sure you've done all the touristy things, what interests you?" then I found myself staring at the envelope also.

"Ah, now that's a good question" she whispered close to my face like we were best buddies from boarding school.

"I believe in synchronicity don't you?" She caught me off guard but she was growing on me.

"Yes I do and I suppose bumping, or should I say, me bumping into you, fits the bill."

"Talking about bills, let's get this one settled and walk" and we did. She put her arm in mine continuing with the old friend show and we ambled our way towards the ocean.

"OK Miss Ellie, where shall it be?"

We had a wonderful few hours, chatting, eating ice cream along the waterfront and it seemed we were pretty much into the same things. Our conversation went onto the metaphysical, and whilst we were seated on the prom, I happened to mention the Mahatmas, or Masters as we say in the West. She looked at me quite attentively.

"So where are these wonderful souls, these Elder Brothers Miss Ellie, where are they?"

I thought for a moment, after all she was a stranger and I had learned the hard way that it's not always wise to plough in mouth first. But she smiled and I blurted.

"Well I know for sure there are some in the Rocky Mountains and in the United Kingdom, and of course the Himalayas. Maybe I can tell you..." but she quickly rose.

"Oh my, time flies or stops, funny really when you think about it. I must away to the airport Little One." Little One?

Before I could say anything, she stepped out into the road just as a taxi approached. Without any delay she jumped in, closed the door and winding the window down, she motioned me to come closer.

"Goodbye my dear friend Miss Ellie, goodbye, and here…" she handed me the envelope, "this is for you, a gift." As the taxi pulled away she shouted. "Goodbye dear friend, and you must go back." Go back? I stood welded to the spot for quite some time.

Back in my little home I dissected all the parts of my day visiting them systematically in an attempt to discover what had happened. The last thing to look at was my envelope, the gift from Sam. Sitting at the table I stared from the pot to the cup, and back to the envelope.

It seemed as if the formula one racing car I had jumped into some time back in the first part of this book had gone into overdrive, and the track I had been driving on had just been extended. Don't get me wrong, I love the unexpected when it doesn't hurt me or anyone else, but life was changing again and at such speed that my other bodies seemed to be lagging behind.

Sipping the tea, I slowly opened the envelope. Pulling out the contents I viewed a ticket, a ticket to Edinburgh Scotland, the place of my saddest moment, the leaving of Raj.

# Chapter Thirty Seven

*When will you begin that long journey into yourself?*
Rumi

It was a week later when I left Victoria's warm weather to meet my first cold day in Scotland. The wind drove the rain as of a swarm of baby bees bent on stinging my face, and the damp sought refuge right through my clothes and into my bones. In contrast, the taxi was warm, the driver friendly and even the views through the driving rain were breathtaking.

The ruins of Rosslyn castle stood like a grand old lady guarded by her crumbling stone knights. They were frozen in time along with their countless stories and mysteries.

Close by were my modest lodgings where a jolly man greeted me at the door. Seeing how tired I was, he quickly ushered me to my room. Feeling delightfully weary I dropped my bags, flopped onto the four-poster and was lulled to sleep by the crackling fire in the hearth. Ah sleep; where the ingredients of my recent events and, unknown to me, my future events, slurped around like a hodgepodge soup, until a voice woke me.

"Come to me. Callanish." It was Raj and I sat up. All was silent. I felt sure it was him and waited for more words but nothing came. Eventually I drifted back to sleep. In that sleep a scene unfolded before me.

Twelve of us sat on the floor listening to a story being told by an old man looking like Methuselah. He was weaving a wonderful web with his words and we were all captivated.

"Each one of you will identify with a part of this story. It is an allegory. He walked slowly up and down as he spoke.

"The sky sifted snow like a master baker covering a cake in icing sugar, and the winds whirled white forms, which nestled on the earth like gossamer. It was a day for meditation.

"In a vast city, which the snow had claimed for its own, there was one who looked out through her window. Though she loved the storm, the thoughts of the poor, of little children with empty stomachs, crowded her brain and caused pain in her heart. She had a sense of helplessness towards such suffering she knew to be out there, dotted all over the planet. She knew there was a Divine Plan for all, but her thoughts would not stop whilst she was in the warmth and they were outside. She could not settle.

"By the warmth of the fire, her drooping eyelids hovered close together to doze, until a mysterious something roused her and she sat upright. There was another presence in the room, but whose? And how? The door had been closed all the while.

"Within the stillness, deep and almost mystic, she was greeted with a vision, and what a picture had presented itself! There standing, was the form of an eastern sage, graceful in bearing and earnest in his look. In one hand he carried a book-like parchment, and over his arm was thrown a robe that fell to the floor.

"Flowing dark hair mantled his shoulders and there was a delicious and pungent odour of sandalwood, which seemed to soothe her. His yellow Tibetan bodice glinting as he moved his position, and his voice, so soft and low, was heard for the first time as though spoken from afar and repeated through space. What is this strange phantom? was the thought this teacher saw photographed on the brain of the woman, and instantly he responded.

"There is no charity in the West for the unknown doctrines."

"What are the unknown doctrines?" Thought the woman. The stranger, smiling, answered.

"It is the essence of all doctrines, the inner truth of all religions, creedless, nameless, untaught by priests, because it is of the spirit and not to be found in church, temple or synagogue. It is the heart heard in the whirlwind and felt in the storm. You appealed to me with something stronger than yourself, with care and compassion for the helpless. Your heart breathed its prayer; your soul registered it in the atmosphere about you. Spirit was refreshed by so pure a light, which wafted from the lower kingdom to the higher, from the body to the soul, and thence to Shambhala."

And he continued with his words 'til very late, and he taught the mystery of man's being, his origin, his growth, and his destiny. This teacher visited often and instructed this willing pupil with the laws of life from the writings of the ancient volume he guarded so tenderly.

With gentle suasion he developed the intuition of the woman, but as time went on, routine matters began to absorb her days again. Weeks passed and the mysterious teacher returned only when opportunity offered, which was rare, and then one day the teacher came no more.

The illusions of the world took hold of her again, and the teacher then saw the futility of trying to train her in the Ancient Wisdom. However, he did not forsake his charge but sent a chela from his own hand who taught when times were possible. The chela answered many questions, which lifted her soul and planted aspiration and inspiration, and she developed a deep peace.

A day came just as the little forget-me-nots were showing their heads, when the chela's visits ceased also, and on that last day before leaving, he reassured her that in a distant foreign land, the Master awaited his pupil's coming.

But as every day life took up all her minutes, her teacher and his chela became a distant dream. Time passed, then one day, when in absolute despair, on the wall appeared a sentence as if by magic. "Tread the path and come."

In her heart she knew she was being called to higher things, but she also knew that to sever earthly ties and follow that calling was not to be taken lightly. Who would understand her if she were to follow? True, she felt this teacher of the East in the innermost fibres of her being. True, her love for the teacher was deep. Strange, that hesitation and fear and moral cowardice should now shadow her life. Strange, that so cruel a poison as doubt should rankle in the soul of the neophyte. What disappointment and despair doubt is able to produce!

Strangely, when her thoughts turned to those in need, doubt was hardly recognized. However, repeatedly it returned, until it came to be looked upon as an undesirable guest for her, and a sense of unworthiness crept in clouding her thoughts.

As years went by and the world lost much of its importance to her, her struggle and sense of loss intensified and her physical strength sank near to death. Why had the sage forgotten her? In this silence, deep inside her a still small voice whispered, "courage,"

Stirring her dying aspirations once again, lost and tired she spent her days and nights in internal battle, that, giving hospitality to doubt, was driven now to entertain despair. With two such houseguests how could peace or beauty be found? Deep inside her, the small voice still whispered, "courage."

She bowed her head over the writings she had preserved as sacred treasures, and her weary heart sobbed. All the while the listening spirit heard the heart, the mind, and the soul, and at last, as the breath in her body waned weak ready for death, it pushed forth. "Courage."

"With little strength left, she neared her last breath and gave a small cry and a murmuring sound like a tone from a bell rung on a high mountain. And on its tail came another note, clear and sweet, and wondrously like the teacher's voice, which had been silent for so long.

"Come." It called. "Come."

The call could not be misunderstood, and she lifted her head, lips alive with heat, eyes flaming with light. Gathering strength in every fibre of her quivering frame, she sent forth a shout, full of joy and expectation. "I come! Master I come!"

The story ended, I stirred from my strange sleep and looked around. I was still at the little cottage in Rosslyn.

It was requested of me to include that story in this book, as each reader will find his or her place in the allegory. I will leave it to you to make sense of it. But now on with my story.

# Chapter Thirty Eight

*As you start to walk on the way, the way appears.*
Rumi

The mystery around Raj's death had been a mystery to me. He had died in Scotland and seemingly resurrected in India, and now I was beginning to hear him, which made me either on the road to a loony bin or on the road to understanding the bloody workings of the universe. But all this was nothing, nothing, compared to what was to come.

Dressed, I went downstairs and made my way to the front door hell bent on my destination, this place called Callanish that I had heard someone call when in my room.

"You ok Dearie?" came a voice behind me. "I thought it best to leave you to sleep after such a long flight, my husband said you looked plum tuckered when you arrived. You go into the kitchen, I'll put the kettle on and rustle up a couple of coddled eggs." She was a warm sort and joined me by the open fire where she asked about Canada whilst I ate the welcome breakfast.

"Full of stories in these parts." She smiled. "Of course you will have heard about Rosslyn. Don't you go believing that everything's made up for the story books, there is much truth in myth." She poured more tea. "Why, when it comes to stories sometimes we can't tell what is real and what's a dream hey? She studied me, and I her. "So what are you up to today, lass?"

I asked about Callanish and if it was within walking distance. She looked at me as if she was about to burst something, and god knows I hadn't said anything that funny.

"You must be dreaming My Dear." She poured more tea, still laughing.

"Can I get there and back before supper?" I was serious and it was obvious she was not.

She leant forward and stared at me then spoke strangely, in a dialect that seemed a mixture of Scottish and Cornish with a bit of Somerset thrown in for good measure.

"Callanish the stone circle is far away in time and place, and the stones are our people mixed with quartz and hornblende crisscrossed with grain and crusted with lichens."

The more she talked the more she resembled the gypsy woman I had encountered back home. Then she leant back in her chair and spoke slowly as if she was recalling something special.

"At mid-summer dawn, before darkness lifts her skirt, folk go there to see the Shining One who walks the path," and she stopped, sat quietly and stared into the fire. Her staring into the fire reminded me of the last time I was in Scotland, then she continued talking.

"The avenue to the north was positioned 1,800 years before the Master came. Yes tis old, old."

I interrupted her. "Who is the Shining One?"

"Why the moon for some and for others it is the Master" she grinned and continued.

"The west row of stones show where the sun sets at the two equinoxes, and the line between the two stones outside the circle indicate the moon rising at its maximum, major standstill. This is an old lunar line and we celebrate Beltane and mid-summer there." And she stopped suddenly.

"Enough of my ramblings, you had enough to eat girl?" She started to clear things away.

I had but I had not heard enough about the Shining One. However her countenance now had a sign hanging over it "closed for lunch" so I rose and left.

Many things were going around in my head; the story told to me in my sleep, her reference more than once to my dreaming, and now thoughts of the Shining One. She never did tell me where Callanish was, but if I couldn't get to this place then maybe I could find an Internet café and research for myself. Famous last thoughts.

I discovered I had more chance of finding the queen of the fairies in this wonderful countryside than anything that resembled an Internet cafe. I gave up and spent my day, late though it was, wandering the countryside and viewing little old cottages, then returned home.

Tucked deep under the covers that night, I listened to the wind through my open window and stared at the shadows cast by the surrounding tors upon my walls. I was in love with Scotland, where the leaves, grass and trees create a whistling symphony that howls across the landscape and rocks one to sleep. The next thing I was aware of were tall stones standing in a circle, which made Stonehenge look like a model children would play with.

In the distance I heard a lament being played on a bagpipe as a tall figure stepped through the mists and slowly approached me. I held my breath when I recognized the ease and grace of the well-built form. It was Raj.

Like a being deprived of love for too long and with no inhibitions I rushed forward right into his opening arms. Lifting me as easily as a twig, he spun me around and echoed tones of love without so much as a word. On the periphery of my vision the stone circle spun and seemed to shatter into millions of pieces.

"Love is bright yet gentle on the eyes, don't you think?" He whispered. The whole moment was making me shake. "Until one becomes the sole, or soul, vessel of selfless love, Divinity will be an illusive courtesan permitting you only a sip of the nectar of life. Until then, one must sip when and where one can." Slowly I found my feet and still in his arms I felt his focused gaze upon me.

"My Dear, we are a means to a great end, whether in this or some distant future, and one day you will understand this. Take every opportunity to surrender everything of the personal to be of service to the many." And he was gone, poof, like the genie back into the lamp, gone. I woke up in my bed with someone banging on my door.

"Dearie, are you up dearie," came the voice on the other side.

"I am, hold on." When I opened the door there stood my landlady.

"There's a man here for you, he says he's ready and he'll wait in the garden."

What, could it be Raj? Was it true? I put myself together and nearly fell down the stairs and into the garden. I could see only the shadow of a man by the roses, and as I approached he turned bowing slightly. "I've arrived to escort you."

This commanding figure obviously had the wrong person for I had absolutely no idea who he was or what he was talking about.

"I think you're confusing me with someone else, but thank you I didn't book a tour and I don't have any idea what you're talking about. I'll get. ..."

"No need for that. Let me explain. I am to escort you to Callanish." He waited.

Of course, I'm not so crazy as to go off with any stranger who says he wants to take me for a ride, but he said Callanish, so I was more than ready. With goodbyes said to my old lady, I jumped into a waiting car with an unknown driver and was on my way to the big stones.

And what a suave gentleman he was, with obvious taste, for this was a vintage Morgan, yet carried that familiar smell of a new vehicle. Corners flew by as we sped on the open road, and boy could he drive. After catching my breath I asked him if they were sheep, bulls, telegraph poles, or just atomic blips we had passed.

He had a sense of humour too, for he laughed at my feeble attempt to be funny and assured me they were cottages and churches and not to worry so much.

Don't even ask me to explain how we covered such distance so quickly, other than breaking every speed limit on earth along with the sound barrier, but we finally reached the end of the road and only water lay ahead. This Morgan didn't float, so we, and the vehicle, boarded a boat. We were off to the Isle of Harris, destination Callanish.

# Chapter Thirty Nine

*You are not one, you are a thousand.*
*Just light your lantern.*
Rumi

They say these magical stones were at one time a council of pagan giants which now dominate the landscape as stone. As I viewed the whole area it was just as my vision whilst asleep. However, this was real and not some subconscious melodrama of a tired, wincing woman's heart.

The stones stood on a ridge above the waters of the Loch, shaped somewhat like a Celtic cross, with five rows of stones radiating from its central circle. It was massive. At the centre, a small circle of thirteen stones, a magical number, stood from eight to twelve feet high. Two rows of stones formed an avenue 273 feet long, and five stones ran south from the circle making a row 90 feet long. Ok reader, other than the fact I wish you to know how bloomin big this site was, I promise you that's the figures out of the way.

We were not the first to arrive, many had already gathered, and my guide, who obviously had done this before, whispered.

"It's a night of celebration in anticipation of the birth of new beginnings. Many have exalted Stonehenge as a ground of great ceremony, but in fact it is Callanish, the true northern light, which initiates the path not the Henge. Look around you." He pointed to the south.

"A low range of mountains sit to the south. See the shape of a woman lying on her back? Here you can see the uprising rock which provides the Woman of the Hills with the silhouetted visage of a pregnant belly." It was incredible, for she did appear pregnant.

"From where we're now standing, the Moon as it moves slowly on its journey in the sky will seem to roll along the body of the sleeping woman." He then ushered me away from the crowd to observe from another angle.

"Notice the rock formation here, how it becomes a pillow beneath her head, and the Moon will look to set just nicely into her crown. We will witness the various stations of the Moon's progression as it peers from behind the edges and tips of the different stones, and different stories will be told to different people in different places. This depicts the true path of the goddess, for she shares her wisdom child in different ways to different people."

This reminded me of something Francis once said, how at various moments in earth's history teachers have come to share with humanity the Ageless Wisdom, in many guises, for many cultures.

Meandering amongst the lively crowd I immersed myself in the celebrations now in full swing, and with utter abandon. Skirt swinging and boots stomping, I gave it my all as I twirled with strangers and shared my heart with Raj. Entranced by a spiral of movement, I entered the world of the dervishes and felt joy at being one with all present. People abandoned all restraints, until at last reaching a peak, they burst forth with ecstatic shouts of absolute delight.

Then silence reigned once more, for the outer festivities were now over and people departed as quickly as they had arrived. However my escort, now by my side, motioned me to enter the inner circle.

To the far side, a figure wove in and out of the shadowy stones reminding me of my dream, neither face nor form stayed long enough for me to see who it was. Silhouettes emerged through a thickened mist like ghosts from the past and gentle voices rhythmically chanted. As the moon hid behind a cloud the figure wove closer until I felt him by my side. I wished to turn, however something inside stopped me. I felt intoxicated by it all.

As the stars spun descending to the stones, the earth seemed to arch her back, heaving her belly to meet the heavens. The moon showed from behind the clouds and I remember nothing more. It was the smell of fresh baking that forced me to open my eyes.

Any bewilderment I had entertained before, when I thought I was lucid dreaming, bowed to the god of confusion that I was now facing as my mind tried to make sense of what had, and was, happening to me. I was freaking out, just a little.

Where were the stones of Callanish? What about the celebration? What about the stranger who had driven me there? More to the point, what about the old landlady who had knocked on the door to tell me the stranger was waiting for me downstairs?

The clothes I had taken off before retiring to bed hung across the back of the chair where I had left them, and this was my room in the guesthouse at Rosslyn. Had I dreamt it all? After dressing I made my way downstairs, but before I could say a word the old lady spoke.

"Oh dearie, you must've been more tired than you thought. That long journey from Canada really did a number on you." She placed tea on the table in front of me.

"I'm confused, how long have I slept? And not giving her a moment to reply I fired on. "Hang on a minute, you knocked on my door, you told me someone was waiting, I went off with him."

She shook her head, smiled, then poured more tea. Quietly I sat at the breakfast table. She must have been correct, it was due to the flight. The other alternative was I was losing my marbles and needed to visit the local asylum.

When she returned with more hot water for tea, I asked again about her knocking on my door and the man who was waiting for me in the garden to take me on a trip. She shook her head.

"Dearie, you slept for a long time. Why don't you just sit in the garden, put a blanket over yourself and I'll bring you more tea?"

I took her advice and for some time watched cute robins flit from branch to wall, and back again. It was chilly, but I needed a distraction. It was too beautiful outside to just sit, so I put on my coat, deciding to brave the world with a good country stroll to Rosslyn Castle and settle in the gardens close by.

Pilgrims had paid homage here for over 400 years. History and nature had embalmed the area with records and memories little felt in the newish worlds of North America. These special places in the sacred isles guarded treasures not forged with gold or precious metals, they held something more priceless, stories and myths handed down from one generation to another, riches from mouth to mouth, accounts far more valuable to human kind. This area held stories for sure, and I was soon to find out I had entered into the beginnings of a mysterious one myself.

# Chapter Forty

*Seek the wisdom that will untie your knot. Seek the path that demands
your whole being.*
Rumi

After leaving the gardens I turned past a yellow cottage and carried on along the country lane until I came across an old churchyard.

How many stories lay buried deep within that soil, how many tears had been shed, and by the amount of fresh flowers on the graves, were still being shed. I have had my losses, but through experience I have come to understand that there is no death, only the shedding of the 'worn out clothing' that the soul has used for a certain amount of time whilst on Earth.

As I say to my grandchildren, the bodies we are wearing are the spacesuits we use in order to navigate this earth whilst here. We discuss death in my family, for we can pass on fear to our children without even knowing by shying away from any mention of the one episode in life we will all have to face.

Further along in my wandering, I came across the castle ruins, found a stone bench by an old archway and sat to meditate. This proved impossible, as my mind had so many questions encouraging too many answers. So I gave up and decided to make my way to the chapel.

# TWO DINGBATS ON A SPIRITUAL QUEST

*Chapel Closed Till Further Notice. Please Respect The Reverence Of This Area. Thank You– Proprietor*

With the chapel closed I decided to wander back to my lodgings thinking maybe my landlady was correct, maybe the flight had affected me more than I realised. Once I returned, I decided to just sit by the warm fire.

"You have an invite for an evening at the chapel." My landlady poured the milk into a cup.

Of course I mentioned the poster on the door, but she repeated emphatically.

"Again, you are invited to come along, twill be a very informative evening. By the main doors, 7pm sharp." There was no argument from me. She poured the tea.

Much as I was getting to like her it was obvious she was not the full shilling, so I decided not to rattle her cage and just do what she had suggested in the first place, sit outside, rest and read, until it was time to eat supper and leave for the chapel.

By the time I arrived at the doors people had already gathered, and a woman with a shawl over her head shuffled by, unlocked the doors, and we were ushered in.

Dan Brown had made this place famous in his book "DaVinci Code" yet it had a history that didn't need trumpeting, it had been pulling in the right people since the dawn of time and would continue to do so in spite of all the books written.

Mumbling "sit" to all, she hurried to the front, stopped and dropped her wrap, and to my surprise I saw it was my landlady. We took our seats as the door opened and a tall man walked to the front to the welcome of all present.

He was regal, yet he had that indescribable humility which surrounds a great soul. The absence of a personal ego has to be experienced rather than explained. I have sat here and tried for over an hour to describe it for this book. Silence was not empty as we sat there, but full of the most wonderful feelings, then he began.

"Welcome, and I see we have a newcomer." He gave a slight nod my way in courtesy and went straight into it.

"Last time we met, I asked you to consider morality. Some may say that in today's world morality seems to have departed on a fast ship to Mars. Should we wish it back or should we hope it continues into outer space?" He stopped and seemed to be smiling at some personal joke we weren't privy to, and continued.

"Morality is a social disease that has reached pandemic proportions in the churches, and established deep roots in areas of commerce, society and the family home.

"Then we have another social disease, that of conventionality, some may refer to it as crystallisation, however this is too small a word for what I wish to convey to you. These two are closely linked.

"If we look at the mental bodies of very conventional people, we find their outlines to be rigid and hard. Usually their physical bodies follow the same rigidity. This hard, crystalized shell makes it difficult for those further along the path of enlightenment to penetrate it, and therefore give any form of direct teaching. Even whilst the body rests in sleep, in most circumstances, one may only be able to bring back a mere fragment of the teaching given on other levels, much to the distress of the student.

"The challenge is that conventional types will stick to the morals set forth by those around them, by society, nations and of course groups they belong to, and these change like the wind from group to group and country to country. But I ask you, what kind of morality is it that changes to suit men's needs, hmm?

"Fear motivates, and of course fear is a selfish emotion for it has self-regard first and little selflessness, if any. This fear is usually of what others may think and can be based on vanity, or fear of being hurt.

"Conventionality is also driven by superstition and superstition can be very subtle. Those on the 7th ray of ceremonial magic may have some trouble in this area, as this is the ray involved with ritual, and so the repetitive nature may engender even more superstitions. Very hard." He walked to the side and continued.

"Conventionalists rarely go against what the majority may think right, for they will have to deal with the rebuffs, and at times may be unpopular by going against the so-called norm. This is ever prevalent in some of the organisations around the world, whether they be political, religious, medical, and also in the arts and science.

"Conventionalists rarely go against the morals set by others and those morals may not always be of a standard required for discipleship.

"A man may be morally pure because he may find morality purely convenient, and this my friends is a form of morality which usually gives him acceptability in some form or another. To fear being judged by your neighbour is valid, however, this is also vanity and cowardice.

"Is it not true that when a child goes against the codes of the family the child is referred to as the black sheep? How many here consider themselves to be the black sheep?" Many hands went up including mine, and he laughed. "So, so," He walked back to the middle.

"So you see the morality of the masses is based in selfishness, whereas super-morality, something we shall open up now, cannot be so, for it cares not for the favour of others, nor for any form of status in society. It also doesn't give a hoot about popularity polls prevalent on the planet." Everyone chuckled but he continued talking.

"So I ask, where does this conventionality stem from? Morality is a brain function, and super-morality comes from the heart. The former is dependent on rules and conventions, the latter entirely dependent on the circumstances.

"I wish to share with you parts of a letter written by a Brother of the Himalayan Order.

"You believe I have never deceived a chela, correct? Do you believe I have never deceived you? Why of course there are times, when for the sake of the pupil the Master will deceive, especially in the probationary stage. This may shock many of you, and I can see it has ruffed a few of your pristine feathers already. Dear, dear, how sensitive you all are." He smiled. I will continue.

"Let me paraphrase further words of this Brother of mine, words that have already been shared." He wandered up and down and then continued.

"A Master is a great actor who rarely shows his true form. Imagine if you will, an Adept behaving in a manner congruent to his achievements, and yet you know the Master to be truthful, yes?"

As I looked around I could see agreeing nods as well as open mouths, and though I just loved all of this, I was a little confused as to his full meaning of super-morality.

"Can you imagine a Master or Adept ever showing humanity in general the love they feel? Why, they would be locked up and the key thrown into the depths of the ocean. And then what, I might ask? They would have to use their time and powers to free themselves from their jailers and depart to some hidden ashram in the Himalayas so as not to be found again by your head hunters." We all laughed. "I will continue.

"There are thousands of highly moral people on this planet with virtues galore, and they take great pride in letting others know it, but let me give you an example of a super-moralist in action."

He stopped to digress a bit here, and I was shocked when he asked me if I understood such a thing as super-morality. Not wanting to say no to the Teacher, I said "yes."

"Dear, dear," He responded "just think about what just transpired between you and I," and I got it quickly and blushed. He smiled very lovingly and resumed.

"Again I will paraphrase a story that has been told before. A chela approached his Teacher for help regarding his friend who was going through a very bad time. In fact his world was crumbling down around him, or so he thought. Due to a karmic condition the Teacher could not interfere with the life of the one struggling, and informed his chela to do the best he could to assist.

"Being a chela for some time he set to the task, putting aside all thought of himself and, of course, jeopardising his chelaship.

"When the chela visited his friend the following night, together they embarked on a determined path of partying and self-indulgence. In fact over time they visited and drank half of the local distillery away." Everyone laughed again.

"After some months of this constant indulgence the evening came when the chela needed to take action. Just as he was about to leave for home, in a taxi I might add, he turned to his friend and said.

"Why am I doing this with you? I've had enough. This stuff is terrible, it truly makes me feel sick and gives me a constant cracking headache, and to top it all, this constant partying is making life worse rather than better. Life is definitely not enjoyable anymore and so I'm going to stop, and I'm asking you to join me, dear friend, as I will need your assistance.

"You see, a little problem had presented itself, for the chela could not give up the stuff due to his karmic predisposition for addiction. Programmed behaviour is easy to establish. Now a monster had brewed within him. Please excuse the pun." Teacher ignored our laughter and continued.

"This chela took a great risk. He was aware of his karmic predisposition, and a pledge given to his Teacher not to indulge in any alcohol or drugs. However, by seizing this opportunity for selfless service, the karmic condition of genetic susceptibility was dispelled like smoke in the wind and they both came through the ordeal, and I might add, both with feet firmly planted upon the path.

"This chela showed no morals whatsoever according to the outside world, and broke a few of the laws set by chelaship, yet he was of the greatest service to his friend. He demonstrated true brotherhood with no attachment as to whether it was ever realised by another, including his friend. This chela demonstrated not only super-morality, he also demonstrated selfless service."

"There may be times when one is judged, yet appearances may deceive. No one knows from one moment to the next the work of the Master nor the reason anyone may feel, or be asked, to complete a certain task. And this brings me to truth, and the giving of truth by a Master." Here his whole energy changed as if he was communicating with someone unseen, then he resumed in a very formal tone.

"I will paraphrase the words given by an Eastern Mahatma if I may, taken from one of the Mahatma letters.

"Our Eastern ideas regarding 'motives' and 'truthfulness' as well as 'honesty' differ considerably from your ideas in the West. We believe that it is moral to tell the truth and immoral to lie; but here every analogy stops and our notions diverge to a very remarkable degree.

"What would you think of one, whose affable politeness of manner and suavity of language would cover no falsehood; who, in meeting you would tell you plainly and abruptly what he thinks of you, or of anyone else? And where can you find that pearl of honesty. ... All is lie, all falsehood, around and in us,..." He stopped and viewed us all, then continued.

"That is why you seem so surprised, if not affected, whenever you find a person who will tell you bluntly truth to your face; and also why it seems impossible for you to realise that a man may have no ill feelings against you, may even like and respect you for some things, and yet tell you to your face what he honestly and sincerely thinks of you."

He made his way to the centre, and smiled so benevolently it oozed warmth throughout the whole place. Then He continued in the same vein, placing his gentle but firm gaze on us all. "I will resume.

"And what of anger, for we know at least one of your Christian examples, the Master Jesus, who lost his cool, as you would say, in the temple?" Again He ignored our chuckles.

"Would you think more of an Adept, were he to conceal his anger; to lie to himself and the outsiders, and so deceive them by crediting him with a virtue he didn't have?

"If it is a good act to destroy with the roots all feelings of anger, so as to never feel the slightest paroxysm of a passion we all consider sinful, it is a still greater sin with us, to pretend that it's destroyed."

He continued on this subject and opened up for me a totally different way of looking at things. I began to realise what we in the West call virtues, values, morals and truth, are convenient standards used to navigate the world in order to be accepted and popular. However, He also said this is not an open ticket to cruelty, but just honesty, pure and simple.

Our time came to an end and I walked back through the landscape to the place I was staying. I found the old lady ready with hot chocolate and a warm fire.

"You do this often right?" I asked. She smiled and nodded. We drank our chocolate in peace and quiet, she looking over towards me at intervals, and me, well I just watched the flames and pondered. With eyes drooping I said goodnight and retired to my bed.

# Chapter Forty One

*No legacy is so rich as honesty.*
Shakespeare

My bed was cosy and it didn't take me long to fall asleep but I was disturbed by a sound.

"Come to me," a voice echoed, and I sat up in the bed. Though dark, I could see well enough to know my room was empty. Then I heard it once more. "Come to me."

I had no fear, though I did have a question. Where was I to come to? I fell back to sleep 'til morning and after breakfast wandered to the old seat in the village by the castle ruins. I sat, closed my eyes and quietly settled to meditate.

"I saw you there last evening at the Abbey. It was our second time." I was startled, opened my eyes and looked up..

She was demure, graceful, and her partner seemed to have stepped off a Jane Austin set. In a tender manner he touched her hand and they joined me on the bench.

"Sorry I was miles away" I said smiling, "I didn't expect to see anyone. It was my first time. Who was the teacher, do you know?"

He touched her hand again. "We call Him MJ" he said.

"Do excuse us, my name is Ruth and this is Lam. We arrived from India a few days ago. We have a message for you." She opened her small purse and lifted out an envelope, handed it to me, and they rose. I put it to my face and inhaled deeply. It was infused with a familiar odour, intoxicating and warm, carrying memories. I didn't wish to open my eyes, talk or be disturbed and they respected this.

"I don't wish to appear discourteous," I said. I wanted to rush away at this point, "I have to leave and..." Ruth giggled and Lam stood and bowed his head as gentlemen did in olden days, and as I left he said, "7pm at the chapel."

I rushed back to the privacy of my bedroom. Ritualistically I opened the envelope by first breaking the seal, then I used the tips of my fingers to lift out the edge of the folded paper, very carefully. Such a small sheet of paper, and it held my heart. This sheet of paper carried my dreams; this sheet of paper... must be from him, who else would write to me from India? I panicked. What if it wasn't from him? Please God, was there a God? Oh! but please.

"This is an invitation for you to join us. A vehicle will arrive at your lodgings at 9am tomorrow morning. Francis"

Francis had been my father and teacher in every sense of the word, and any disappointment was extremely short lived. I was to be in the heart once more of the Master whom I had loved forever. I read the note again, it said "us", and placing it to my heart in gratitude I rushed downstairs, down the lane to the bench, hoping to thank my two new friends. They were gone.

7pm came quickly enough, and I took my seat in the chapel. MJ arrived and opened the talk.

"We repeat many truths, so it will be little wonder that some of you have already heard or even read our words. Again I paraphrase the truths encapsulated in the letters written by the Mahatmas of the Himlayas.

"When under probation, a pupil is allowed to think and do whatever he likes, but he is warned before-hand, that he will be tempted and also deceived by appearances. The student may suspect his Guru of being 'a fraud'. More than that, the more sincere his indignation, whether expressed or boiling inside him, the more fit he is to become an Adept.

"He is free also, and not held to account for using the most abusive expressions regarding his guru's actions, provided he becomes the victor in the end. However, he must resist all and every temptation; and show that not even the promise of that which he holds dear, his future adeptship, is able to make him deviate from the path of honesty.

"It is the pupil who has the love of humanity in his heart, who is capable of grasping thoroughly the idea of practical Brotherhood who is entitled to the possession of our secrets. Such a person will never misuse his powers."

MJ was to the point, no wishy-washy dilly- dallying about him. He called it as it was and it made perfect sense that the neophyte would need to raise his or her game to reach the Master and not the other way around. What, in truth, does one think would be the point if we all stayed as we are and the Masters had to come to our level? He was how I wanted to be, he was an inspiration and my aspiration. We departed for the night.

# Chapter Forty Two

*Set your life on fire. Seek those who fan your flames.*
Rumi

Promptly after breakfast a car arrived at my lodgings and I was most surprised to see two other people already in the vehicle, Ruth and Sam. We were now en-route to our next destination, and within hours we entered an impressive Scottish castle.

Two large tapestries donned the walls in the grand entrance, one read "Ye temple of Honour' and on the other "Ye temple of Truth'. My two friends and I were fascinated by the heraldry that hung around a fireplace, but within moments we were ushered to our respective rooms just across the hall from each other. We were told by the Ghillie that a light lunch would be available at 1pm in the garrison, so I flopped onto a carved bed covered with tartan and dozed off.

At lunch, a sumptuous array of fruits, nuts, and breads were spread across the table, and to my utter surprise, familiar faces from my last trip to Scotland greeted me, all eager to share. A gong was sounded to summon us to the adjoining room and there, resting his foot on one of the two enormous cast iron hounds, stood MJ.

"A plethora of information on the dying process and Karma has been shared already, but I ask you, how reliable is the informant?" Wow, that was an opening!

"We have wisdom passed down by those we consider advanced souls, adepts if you like, as well as the written words passed to us by those lofty souls who have incarnated at different times in world history, however we ask the same question, how reliable are the informants?

"We have Jesus, Mohamed, Zarathustra, we have Buddha, a few who have presented the same truths by different methods. We have great minds such as Aristotle, Plato and our great Pythagoras, and in most recent years, modern versions of the Ageless Wisdom presented by Blavatsky, Mavalanka, Judge and others, all bearing the burden of the cross whilst doing so.

"In all nature and life there is hierarchy, and it is the hierarchy of light who have guarded occult truths down through the ages to be given out to humanity when the time presents itself.

"These teachings have been proven by every Adept who has earned the right to be so, for it is only by proving and not by dogmatic acceptance that one becomes the holder of this truth. And so it is that individuals at a certain stage in their evolution on the path of truth, will be called upon to present in his and her unique fashion these same laws to a new world.

"You may find some of the ideas we place before you controversial, however, that is not our concern. We place before you truth and it is for you to discern with your own intuition and by application of the laws. Intuition is not the mind illumining, nor the brain, but the soul via the mind to the brain.

"So we have our first question. Yes, Russia." A woman with a strong accent sitting just behind me spoke.

"What is the place I have heard referred to as devachan, and who goes there?" He smiled and I was in love.

"Of course it is a state" came his reply. "One, so to say, of intense selfishness during which an Ego reaps the reward of his self-less-ness on earth. In this state he is completely engrossed in the bliss of all his personal earthly affections, preferences and thoughts, and gathers in the fruit of his meritorious actions. No pain, no grief nor even the shadow of a sorrow comes to darken the bright horizon of his unalloyed happiness: for, it is a state of perpetual "Maya." So much so, that the happy Ego is unable to see through the veil, the evils, sorrows and woes to which those it loved on earth may be subjected to."

He stopped a while and we sat, happy to go into our own worlds to ponder His words. We needed this time. The strange thing was, whilst in this state I felt answers coming to greet my questions. So then I had a question.

"Is devachan the same for everyone?" He studied me.

"Canada! Yes good question, however, think child. I will paraphrase for you a letter which was written by an Elder Brother.

"There are great varieties in the devachan states. As many varieties of bliss as on earth there are shades of perception. It is an ideal paradise, in each case of the Ego's own making, and by him filled with the scenery, crowded with the incidents, and thronged with the people he would expect to find in such a sphere of compensative bliss. It is that variety which guides the temporary personal Ego into the current which will lead him to be reborn in a lower or higher condition in the next world of causes.

"Everything is so harmoniously adjusted in nature, especially in the subjective world, that no mistake can ever be committed by the higher Dhyan Chohans who guide the impulses."

I had another question, though I didn't wish to hog the floor, he looked my way and smiled.

"Canada, speak your mind, you have no trouble usually, come." The place rippled with friendly laughter and I felt totally at home.

"Who are these Dhyan Chohans?" He looked to the class and asked, "someone?" Ruth spoke up.

"There are many Chohans of various degrees, all of whom form part of one hidden Esoteric Brotherhood on Earth. I would like to quote from a book I have here that I am just reading. It has the writings of Madame Blavatsky and the Mahatmas.

"The highest we know, the Dhyan Chohans, are of pure intelligence, whereas the Ma-Mo Chohans are of destructive intelligence. The latter are not devils but imperfect "Intelligences" who have never been born on this or any other earth or sphere no more than the Dhyan Chohans have. The former preside at every waking up of the Universe, which we call a maha-manvantara or big bang. The Dark Chohans preside at the going to sleep of the Universe. All in this Universe is contrast."

He smiled at her. "Well put. I will continue with teachings from the Brothers of the Himalayan Order

"You may not understand this at first, how- ever think well over it and you will.

"The Law of the Dark Chohans is darkness, ignorance, destruction etc., as that of the Dhyan Chohans is Light, knowledge and creation.

"The Dhyan Chohans answer to Divine Wisdom and Life in blissful knowledge, and the Ma-mos are the personification in nature of Shiva, Jehovah and other invented monsters with Ignorance at their tail."

Well that said it, for sure, and I feel certain some people will have something to say on that. This is the very thing I loved about my time with these amazing Teachers; they provoked thought, not followers.

Cocoa was served at this point and we all mingled chatting over what was said. Being still a little confused I went over to Ruth to ask further.

"Ruth, I was under the impression that a Chohan was rather like the teacher of a Master and can incarnate on this earth, so what did you mean?" She wrapped her arm in mine and escorted me to the corner sofa.

"We were referring to the highest Dhyan Chohans who are directors of pure intelligence at the beginnings of a Universe."

We sat and chatted for about an hour and I realised I knew so little, but decided this was going to change. I wanted to know more, as much as I could take in. So let me share what I discovered briefly in my own words.

There are definite laws and structures to the Universe and also regarding our own journey through time and space, and there are those who have gone before us who have struggled the same as us and understand our struggles. They are always ready to assist a soul along its path to truth because they have gone through the process of proving the wisdom they have found and know it to be true. These truths never change.

Every now and then a great soul incarnates and gives that truth in a different way, through a different culture, and it's the crazy humans, with our lower egos, who mess it up. There I said it.

We create a church, a following, a sect or new group. We place a person at the head and we hang on every word they say, call it what you wish we worship them. This happens also in the New-Age movement, let's not kid ourselves, and it's a big pit fall. New priest, new guru, it's all the same. Man know thyself, but you'll have to do the bloody work to get there, if you want to get there, that is.

So why trust what these Teachers, Masters of the Brotherhood of Light are sharing? Because they have proven the laws and the truths for themselves and share the same truths and laws given by all great teachers of light who initiated all the world religions in the first place. But, here's the difference, it's up to us to prove these laws for ourselves. The Brothers are not going to do it for us.

By now, our Teacher had already departed and the gillie entered announcing the following evening would be a ball and anything we needed could be supplied if requested.

# Chapter Forty Three

*Your task is not to seek for love, but merely to seek and find all the barriers within yourself that you have built against it.*
Rumi

I had my docs, a skirt and a blouse and my tartan shawl gifted when I was last in Scotland. Whilst the whole place was in preparation for a joyful evening I was struggling with a tsunami of memories which swept their way to my heart, and I was drowning.

There was the memory of my first waltz with Raj, his grip around my waist, the look, his kiss. Just then a knock came on the door. My heart seemed to stop, and in the gap between it stopping and starting again I re-lived moments like a movie on a deathbed. He had stood in the doorway and smiled, as his earthly goddess, me, stood before him in a fine gossamer gown with thick winter socks and heavy Doc boots. Yes, he seemed to love that quirk in my personality. He had taken me into his arms and then placed a ring on my finger to signify our bond, and this was for my sake, never for his. Yes, this knock gave me hope, then a second knock came and I rushed and turned the heavy iron handle.

"Are you ready, we're going down?" Ruth asked as she viewed me tenderly. She mentioned nothing of my red eyes and swollen snot girl face. No, she took my hand as a best friend would and together we went down the stairs to a vision of Vienna.

Couples whirled under chandeliers whose crystals droplets shot rainbows onto all the inviting surfaces. At one end, raised up behind a garden of flowers, a tuxedoed orchestra played polkas. At the other end large glass doors opened wide onto a veranda, and drew in fresh air from the hills of heather.

We were captured in a warp of splendour and my energy lifted. Music and colour gyrated together like the couples entangled on the floor and I found myself swaying in sync though I was only a bystander.

The music waned and finished, then, with one heaving swell, a waltz filled the room, to the delight of everyone. Instead of sadness I felt elated, grateful for opportunity, for love, for him and it rekindled the fire inside me.

Making my way to the big open doors, I found a secluded spot on the veranda overlooking the forest below. I welcomed the cool caressing air, and with my eyes closed I travelled back in my mind to the night of my first ball.

With no effort, I conjured him behind me and felt his arm slowly come around my waist. He tightened his confident grip. The odour of sandalwood enveloped me as if he were a returning genie and I the lamp. In my little world we were one. By inhaling deeply I attempted to satisfy my hunger for more, and the waltz played louder. I sank willingly into this wonderful ocean of madness and I gave in to every ounce of passion I could summon up. What did I care for onlookers?

His breath caressed the back of my neck, and I turned willingly, becoming part of all his movements. Then, like a feather caught on a breeze, he pulled me closer and we danced as we had before. Wrapped in a mosaic of movements I soared 'til love exhausted me, and oh! the exhaustion was complete and fulfilling.

He pulled me closer, his lips brushed my forehead, then over my cheeks. I couldn't breathe, my body dropped as a lead weight, and the music faded.

Later, I was informed I had passed out with the heat on the balcony. Someone had found me and taken me back to my bed leaving me to rest.

It was a lesson well learned regarding my little attempts at alchemy. I had used my mind, summoned my desire, and directed the will. Pity I didn't use a little more wisdom.

Looking out the window of my room, I saw for the first time an incredible array of little blue flowers pushing their way up through the soil. They were forget-me-nots. As I turned in order to commence my day I realised that in my clenched hand I had a handkerchief and embroidered on the edge was a name, Raj.

The next day was a free day and I wandered through the gardens and out into the wild countryside, grateful that nature never fails to share her peace with anyone. Whilst wandering a call came in on my cell, which I was certain I had left in my room.

"Hiya stranger, have you had any weird and wonderful things happen lately? It was Linda.

"Oh crikey Lin, I'm so happy to hear from you. So much has happened and I'm not sure if I'm all here, or even compos mentis. She laughed, but I was serious. She had questions.

"What's been going on? I've been trying to get hold of you for ages, but either no signal or no reply."

We chatted for quite some time and I told some of my story so far, but I was not aware of just how much I could divulge.

One of the things I have learned, since my travels began in The Rockies, is that a student is "To Do, To Dare, and to Be Silent." I was not sure if I was an accepted student, a bona fide chela, but I was going to keep my mouth shut. But Linda was Linda and she had things to share also.

"Well, I've gotta tell you girl, I had a dream last night, and in that dream you were saying to me, he's alive, I tell you, he's alive. I thought I was in some revival church of Billy Graham's and you had gone all religious on me, like, joined the great hallelujah chorus. Then you told me to call today at this exact time and I would get you, and look at what I did."

I knew nothing of what she was saying but she interrupted my thoughts with, "I'm on a flight today to Edinburgh, wanna pick me up?" Of course I did.

# Chapter Forty Four

*Run from what's comfortable. Forget safety.*
*Live where you fear to live. Destroy your reputation.*
*Be notorious. I have tried prudent planning long enough.*
*From now on I'll be mad.*

Rumi

Later in the afternoon, before going to the airport to pick up Linda, there was a soiree. We gathered as usual, and MJ entered, made his way to the big blazing fire, sat on a high backed chair and swung one leg over the arm.

"So let us talk on the subject of chelaship and the path." He lit a cigarette and puffed like a good-un.

"Why do 'would be students' with such intense personalities, force themselves within the enchanted circle of probation! Ah well, such as it is."

There was a feeling of discomfort in the room, for this was not the behaviour we were used to.

"So what is Theosophy, you may well ask. Well in the words of a great soul, it is that ocean of knowledge which spreads from shore to shore; unfathomable in its deepest parts, it gives the greatest minds their fullest scope, yet, shallow enough at its shores, it will not overwhelm the understanding of a child."

"It is truth, and is not something which has been invented by anybody at any time. These truths were originally prepared in systematic manner in past times by Great Seers. It has come down to our own times tested in every age by generations of Great Souls. This formulation today is what we refer to as Theosophy." He threw the cigarette he was smoking onto the fire.

"Many people borrow truths." He started to laugh at this point and lit another cigarette.

To be truthful I was concerned about the smoke and thought of opening a window, though it was not my place to do so. Then he threw the cigarette on the fire. I was now feeling so uncomfortable I was shuffling in my chair. Other people were looking around, yet none of us said a word.

"Back to what I was saying, or rather, what this Great Soul was saying in the past.

"Some have their truths on loan, they pay their deposit and hire it for a time. So it often happens that an individual who has a truth on loan discovers it doesn't always satisfy him. Usually when he is put to some great test or when he happens to be in a crisis, his hired truth doesn't serve him. You see, he doesn't own his truth.

"Each individual must find his own truth, go his own way, a way he must learn to tread without antagonism, condemnation, and denunciation of other people, full of respect as to the ways of others.

"Yet people need to come together in the mutual desire for Brotherhood, for this must start if this planet is to evolve through her initiations smoothly."

He stopped talking and took the time to look at each one of us before he resumed. I was becoming concerned, though like the others, I still kept quiet.

"Each one ought to take advantage of all the truth that surrounds him from all avenues, and all should take advantage of each other's truths. Not in order to copy, but in order to study the causes and the effects of the truth as lived. Think carefully about this last sentence, for there is great truth to be revealed to the one who takes the time to own it.

"I will now share more of the insights given by the Brothers of Light.

"Over the years there have been leaders who have held their truths almost like bludgeons, and they are the borrowers, gathering information which can never establish itself as part of them.

"We have today people who insist that their particular interpretation of truths or their particular theosophies, philosophies, religious, and scientific beliefs are the only truths, and they dogmatically teach it as the only truth from their positions of authority, negating other avenues. That is not only dangerous, but it is almost untruthful.

"It means that the individual who insists upon his own particular way, indoctrinating his own beliefs and interpretations upon another, does not possess his true path but is possessed by it, is obsessed by it, is enslaved by it.

"It is perfectly clear to me at all events, that we have to understand and appreciate, to encourage the truths of others, to shine upon our way, in order to illuminate our own path more clearly.

"For whoever you are, there is always change, and truth which is less is constantly giving way to truth which is more. Until, that is, we come to understand the Truth of the Ancient Wisdom.

"Your most cherished opinions which you hold most dear, which give you the courage and the hope of peace, all of them, are far less than that into which you are destined to grow. There is Absolute Truth but we only see in part.

"Thus is it that one should hold one's truths lightly, and use them while they are usable, and then allow them to go below the threshold of the ordinary consciousness into the storehouse of experience. The time will come when you shall turn from that facet of truth you understand at present to another facet. What then, who holds the key to the door then?" He stopped and lit his third cigarette.

"Now my friends, this may have been the longest ramble of words I have ever given."

We all laughed, and with that He asked that we share any questions we had. I had one, but, watching MJ puffing away on yet another cigarette, I stayed shut up. Then a man sitting on one of the sofas spoke up in a good Scottish tone.

"So tell me if I hear you correctly, Theosophy is a way of life? I was to understand it was a society one joined, and followed, like joining a church."

MJ was obviously enjoying another cigarette, though God knows what He did with the last one. He nodded His head, rose from his chair, walked up and down, well sort of swaggered really, returned to His seat, and plonked His leg over the arm again.

"This is a misnomer if I am permitted to say so. It was the desire of two Mahatmas that people come together with a common goal of Brotherhood, and so a society was formed to encourage Unity and to enable a base for sharing, and this society still continues to grow. But a society does not make Theosophy, Theosophy is a way of life. I cannot stress this enough."

"The motto of this society worldwide is this. 'There is no religion higher than truth.' That speaks for itself. There need be no more said on that subject and I suggest you go away and consider the deep meaning of that simple motto."

He threw the remains of his cigarette on the fire and bid goodnight, whilst the rest of us stayed behind and discussed the weird events around the talk. Later that evening, I picked Linda up at the airport, and being tired and jet lagged she went straight to her room and I retired to mine.

Sitting on my window seat my thoughts went over our most recent soiree, and although I had been given insights I just couldn't get my head around it. The teaching was magnificent, as always, but MJ was not the image I was used to.

Then a knock came on my door. I turned the heavy handle and opened it to Linda. She couldn't sleep. Sitting on the window seat, I shared with her most of the events I had experienced so far, and I also shared the strange events of the soiree.

"Lin, He was smoking cigarettes, and not just one, but a whole bloody packet. Chain smoker I tell you, truly one after another, and He inhaled!" She laughed.

"He even swung his leg over the arm of the chair, laughed like a docker, and was, I don't know how else to put it, like, crass. How can that be?"

We eventually exhausted ourselves and fell asleep together on my big high bed.

# Chapter Forty Five

*In each moment the fire rages, it will burn away a hundred veils.*
*And carry you a thousand steps toward your goal.*
Rumi

The morning was quite uneventful compared to my journey so far, and the soiree that afternoon took on a more personal nature. We were all aware that our time together was coming to a close and we would soon be returning to our respective homes.

I had made the decision that upon returning to Canada, I would head to the Rockies and attempt to find someone linked with the Brotherhood who may help me resolve my questions around the loss of Raj.

The teaching earlier in the evening was given by Francis and other than some aspects appertaining to humanity as a whole, which I may be able to share at a later date, the remainder was of a personal nature and not to be shared in a book.

Late evening we came together as a cosy group with few in attendance, and it was MJ who greeted us. Linda and I sat to the side and before we could even settle into the chair she elbowed me in the ribs and gave out a shriek.

"Crikey Ellie, I don't believe it. Look at that, you were right." MJ had lit a cigarette. He didn't react to her outburst but carried on with the talk.

"One body," He puffed away, "and yet man sets against man, which is ridiculous, and it's childish.

"When you injure your foot, without even thinking, you quickly extend your hand to comfort and assist it. It's automatic. You use one part of the body to comfort and assist another part of the body when it's suffering.

"Yet, when many see their brothers and sisters suffering, instead of automatically extending the hand in brotherly assistance, many detach themselves leaving that part of themselves to struggle alone.

"This action has its ramifications. This is a big error. It is not logical and, if nothing else, our teachings are logical and have some modicum of common sense. We all wish to feel happiness, so does it not seem plain common sense that one would extend oneself to assist another? We are one body, I repeat this, we are one body."

At this Linda piped up. "Jeez Ellie, if we are one body, then he is smoking for all of us and doing a darn good job of giving us all some terminal illness." I cut her a look and we sat quietly. He continued.

A very delicate young man put his hand up and asked if he could say something. I noticed him join us a few nights earlier but he kept to himself and seemed rather timid.

MJ changed. His manner became brusque; He took on an air of coarseness, something quite contrary to what I had experienced, even considering the former night. He walked over to the chair where the young man sat, deposited himself on the arm, and slapped his back like an old chum.

"Come on old chap, speak up, I cannot hear you well." But the young man just sat mumbling to himself. Taking a packet of cigarettes out of his pocket, MJ offered him one.

"Here, have a cigarette?" He said. as He puffed His way into a fire hazard.

Linda became verbal, thinking only I could hear her and blurted out.

"What's all that about hey?"

MJ glanced her way with a slight smile just as the boy attempted to speak up.

"Well, um" he started.

Lighting the cigarette, MJ handed it over and slapped him on the back once more.

"Spit it out, you don't need to apologise for living. Look here, you are one of us, or, should I correct myself, we are one." And He burst out laughing. MJ stayed on the arm of the chair puffing. The room was now becoming decidedly thick and I didn't wish to be the first one to draw attention to the fact that we could all soon die by asphyxiation or instant cancer. Then MJ spoke again.

"Come on my man, spit it out for goodness sake. Take a deep breath, expand that chest, and just give it."

With that, the quiet, delicate, apologetic boy stood, and with some indignation and a lot of determination in both his demeanour and voice, directed his attitude towards MJ.

"I've been cornered, I can tell you, and on those occasions I always put my head down and found my own avenue of escape. However, note I say escape." Here he became louder, he was getting quite worked up.

"Though I may have avoided some physical pain, I have not avoided inner suffering, and yes, I have had inner suffering. So now I have a question for this illustrious teacher here." He pointed to MJ and moved closer to his target.

"With your obvious decorum and manners, you tell me how I can be in this happiness you love to speak of, hey, hey? You tell me Oh Great One." With this the teacher stood and gently placed his hand on his arm and then his head.

"You have taken on a personality in this life my son, which has given you the maximum opportunity to find that happiness. Those who squeeze you in this life are your greatest teachers, thank them.

Karma is a loving teacher. Thank Karma and them. Find gratitude and happiness will ooze from every cell within you. And look, you have just found your voice for the first time in this life and it is a good one at that, and from now on you will exercise it more, yes?

"Things always change when you decide they will and I believe you've reached that time my son.

"Now let me share a story." And with this MJ threw not only His cigarette, but the packet into the fire and requested the windows be opened.

"There was a great boxer, Mohamed Ali, who had a goal and he trained constantly, torturing his body. His body pain didn't matter to him, his goal was the only vision in his mind through all his training. Well, he reached his goal.

"Later on in his life his body, as well as his mind, broke down as a result of all the gruelling punishment it had undergone." He placed his hand on the young man's arm again. "But he succeeded. He succeeded with no thought of what may happen to his body. And so it should be. Forget your physical comforts and strive for the goal. What better goal than to have the vision of enlightenment and leave all the trimmings in order to reach that goal?

"I also add, enlightenment is unattainable without Brotherhood, I request you think on this one aspect seriously, for without Brotherhood you cannot advance further along the path." He rose and the young man sat down with a look of calm resolution.

As folk were leaving, the young man went over to MJ and placed his arm on his and thanked Him. As he turned to leave, he returned the pat of friendship on Teacher's back. Teacher smiled and nodded.

"Whoa, did you see that? That was bold of him" Linda whispered.

"We have ways to encourage, and our ways are not always your ways, or should I say, conventional." Linda listened as it was to her He was speaking.

"We assist those who are persecuted, those who persecute, those who sit in judgement and also conventionalists who need to be shattered out of their old thought patterns." That was us.

He laughed, and I must say to be in the presence of a great soul laughing is like being lifted into a place of utter joy. It tingles throughout the body, the sound giggles through the mind and links with the soul where all joy resides. From the soul it reverberates down to the open heart and rushes through the veins like a youthful elixir of everlasting life.

Am I being too gushy here dear reader? Yes maybe, but I do wish to share the feeling, which is very real.

As He turned to leave He stopped, looked directly at Linda and studied her with a smile on his face. I was expecting some great words of wisdom, but he made what I thought was a very comical comment.

"Smoking is very bad for your health, remember that." He left us. Back in my room, both of us sat on the bed, chatted and laughed.

# Chapter Forty Six

*There is a life-force within your soul, seek that life.*
*There is a gem in the mountain of your body, seek that mine.*
*O traveller, if you are in search of that, don't look outside, look inside*
*yourself and seek that.* Rumi

Today we were departing. By the main entrance stood the ghillie, the wise man we judged at first to be a servant, and he had already said farewell to those whose transport had arrived. Then there were four, Ruth, Lam, Linda and I, and we stood silent whilst the gillie just looked at us. Then with a strong Scottish accent he whispered.

"So what's all this gloom and doom emanating from your faces, have you not learned anything since you've been with us?" He eyed us individually and no one spoke, 'til Linda put her tuppence worth in.

"Seems a bit weird to me gillie, for no sooner do I arrive to join the party than I'm shuffled off to the airport to do the transatlantic again. What's that all about?"

Our vehicle arrived, the bags were put in the boot, and we said our last farewells through a window as we pulled away.

Teacher had spoken the evening before about looking at someone, or something, we perceived as an irritant as our greatest teacher. He mentioned how we would fare far better if our irritability could move towards an attitude of gratitude. With a turn of the dial labelled "perspective" we could, if we chose, switch so called negatives into opportunities and also create the habit of doing so.

Someone said to me recently that the teachings were all so mental, that there was so much to contemplate. This may appear to be so but that person missed the point.

The teachings are the seeds that get us to think and it is thinking that opens the connection to our higher self. It is the connection to our own fount of wisdom that truly cements us in our own truth. MJ spoke of borrowed truths, well this teaching may assist the guru junky.

When we understand the laws that govern this world and our universe, the causes and the effects, it is power. It defuses ignorance and smashes down the walls that keep humanity from peace and happiness. Ignorance is *not* bliss; it is a curse, a blight that keeps us bound.

When we understand the laws that govern any plane/or level, we can become master of that plane and this law applies to all the planes of existence.

I am laughing here talking about planes. By understanding the laws of gravity, mechanics and dynamics, by studying and applying what we now refer to as aerodynamics, hundreds are now able to fly in a long metal tube with little wings across the sky, from one destination to another.

Look at the possibilities, look at what can and will be achieved if, and when, we understand the laws governing different planes, and I don't mean the flying ones now.

This is something a Master has achieved; on the physical, mental and emotional planes or levels, and this is the difference between us and the Adept. If we know how the law works, then we have more control over ourselves and our environment, and we can pass that along to others as an Adept does to humanity.

Another thing I had learned was to test the teacher and the teachings honestly and with love, a bit like being a spiritual scientist. It is intelligent if nothing else, that if the result of our decisions and actions are peace and joy, then we may be assured it was truth, and law, that we were following. If we find that it is not so, that the results are contrary, then we have a choice.

Our own testing is no different than that carried out in a laboratory, we become the scientist of our own lives and conscious creators in our own world.

# Chapter Forty Seven

*Start a huge, foolish project, like Noah... it makes absolutely no difference what people think of you.*
·Rumi

We were so wrong about our destination. How can one assume so much and get it so wrong? We were not en route to the airport, and our miserable anticipation, whilst waiting with the ghillie, had served nothing other than to lower our energy and also our light. Considering the talks of late our attitude seemed pathetic.

We travelled several hours and this gave us the opportunity to view so much more of the more of the more built up areas. However both Linda and I were happy to once again look at Scotland's stunning glens and heather as we entered into a more rugged area of Scotland.

We wound down more of a path than a road until we passed through large iron gates, down a long winding driveway, and arrived at the front door of a magnificent Gothic style home.

Inside, the entrance hall was adorned with family portraits and memorabilia, as well as a blazing fire half the size of the wall.

I was appreciating of late, that anyone could be a Master, even a gillie, so I wasn't going to assume the butler was a butler, if you see what I mean. The man showed us to our room.

There was a certain feeling of familiarity about the place, and a fragrance that was almost intoxicating at times. A thought came to my mind of how fragrance has vibration, and if it had vibration it must have colour and sound. A strange thought, I admit.

My room was just as one would expect in a stately home, though it wasn't gratuitous or overstated. As the view was so beautiful I thought I would pass some time before supper in the garden just outside my window.

That evening after supper, Linda, Lam, Ruth and I met up and wandered the halls and the grounds together, mindful of the west wing which we were informed was out of bounds. Then we retired to our beds for the night.

Down at our first breakfast, Linda and I made plans for the day, which we had free, however things changed when the man who had greeted us when we arrived came over and handed me a note.

*Burgundy room 10am. – make no plans – soiree at 8pm.*

"What's up sis?" Linda saw the note.

"I have to go, though when I'm done I'll come and find you."

Along the oak panelled corridor hung the framed faces of history. Who they were, I had no idea. I wondered if they had studied the occult, whether this country home had an occult lineage, or whether they were just lords and ladies of the past.

"Come in" a strong voice echoed and I opened the door. This was the familiar energy I had experienced upon our arrival; it was Sir Geoffrey's aura, his Presence. He was standing with his back to me looking out of a large bay window. Just as before, his pillbox hat was on his head, his companion, the large hound, was by his side relishing the attention his master was bestowing upon him, and then I saw Francis, my own teacher smiling by the desk. Sir Geoffrey turned peering over His gold-rimmed glasses.

"Sit, sit." I sat and our host turned again to look out of the window. I had the impression he was a great thinker rather than one who used too many words. He turned and spoke directly to me.

"Our Brother here tells me you've been writing. Yes, the seeds of writing are sown, and they promise some fruit. It matters not how many read the words, but who. We ask you to keep writing, for how else can one hone skills needed for a distant future? There are many great books in these libraries and we suggest you take advantage. Use the wisdom given and weave it into the fables you so love to share." I interrupted.

"But, I don't have the ability to do that, I have..." Here Francis raised his hand, requesting I listen.

"Already, you have shared some of your experiences and travels, and we trust that, in your own unique way, you will share more. What better way to share these truths you have been given than with the telling of a story? All life is a story, all life. So play." Sir Geoffrey turned and viewed me over his spectacles and continued.

"'Til one has left maya behind and discarded all the stories, 'till then, let us tell a good one, and one that may inspire. Hmmm."

How could I possibly do justice? What about the ethical use of another's words or teachings? I voiced these concerns and Sir Geoffrey offered his response.

"Nothing is new, truth has been shared in many different ways, and this will continue. Do you think for one moment anyone writing anything worth reading is writing anything new?

Now you have the opportunity to reach those who are not yet established firmly upon the path yet thirst like yourself." He was right and I had a good idea.

"Well here's my thought. What if we. ..." Francis threw his head back and laughed so hard and Sir Geoffrey smiled over his rims.

I stopped, and thought quickly about my attempt at bartering with these two Great Souls and felt a little embarrassed, and started to laugh also. Francis was still chuckling as He ushered me to respond.

"Well yes, people will always read. I think I get it. Like, why not share some of the truths I've gathered, limited as they may be at present. I like it."

Francis laughed again and our Host looked over his glasses at me as if astonished, but of course I knew he couldn't be.

"Hmm, many words. A writer you think Brother? He smiled at Francis. This will do." He didn't say another word.

Now my dilemma was to do or not to do. That was the question, but of course it would be to do. What is story telling if not a challenge to incorporate one's own experiences with those of true wisdom? Weaving my own experiences with the words of others would be a unique way. I could only *Try*.

# Chapter Forty Eight

*I have neither a soul nor a body, for I come from the very Soul of all souls.*
Rumi

No formal gatherings were to be held for four days, so Linda and I decided to go camping. Whilst I had been engaged in the meeting with Sir Geoffrey and Francis, Linda had been wandering and rummaging. In an outbuilding she had discovered all the gear needed for a small adventure. After speaking to the cook, who put together some food, we packed warm clothing and set out.

We weren't concerned about our safety because we were confident we had two big things in our favour. Firstly, Scotland wasn't as big or as wild as the North American Rockies, and we had survived that, and secondly, we were under the protection of highly evolved souls who would never permit anything untoward to happen to us. How inflated can little egos become and how wrong can two people be.

We ambled up hills and down glens like two explorers discovering for the first time the wilds of Africa. Linda shared her "look at that bird," as a crow flew by, and I shared my "look at this flower." We were in our element creating a world we both loved to inhabit.

With our first night drawing in, we erected our two-man pup tent, which wasn't difficult, and hunkered down 'til morning. We rose with the sun and started our day.

A few hours later we realised that the altitude we were climbing took us into weather we were ill equipped for, and terrain we were not expecting. The executive decision was made to plod on until we reached a crag we could see in the distance that overlooked a small lake. There we would hunker down for the night. Once we arrived I sat on my back pack shivering.

"We should light a fire, Lin, It's cold" She was shivering also.

We gathered twigs from the few trees in the area and attempted to lay that darn fire, over and over. All of the matches, and most of the dry wood later, we huddled together and didn't speak for quite a while. Neither of us had much to say. Nobody knew where we were. We had no matches, no wood, low food, and I felt totally disheartened.

"I can't do this again Lin, I can't. This is no more than a rerun of the Rockies. Who does this over and over again?" She hugged me for a long while, that precious girl, my best friend, and said all would be well, though I knew by her face she didn't believe it any more than I did.

Slowly drawing backwards through a dark tunnel, Linda became a small figure in the distance. Her mouth was moving, and she looked distressed as she clung to a limp body slumped by a dead fire. It was me.

The dream I was all of a sudden falling into felt freeing, but seconds later, I was drawn back through this tunnel to my friend, at least I thought she was my friend, who was in my face shouting, whacking me violently.

"Get off." I screamed, pushing her. "Leave me alone, stop." but she didn't. Again the tunnel drew me in, and she was a distant memory.

Blackened wings expanded to create magnificent darkness, the coldness in my body melted into radiant warmth, and memories rushed through my mind. I was only slightly conscious of life and not yet sure of death, but I was cosseted in love. It was my Dark Angel.

He could send a shudder through anyone who didn't know or understand him, and now his long bony fingers reached down, as oh so gently he lifted me out of my dense clothing, and effortlessly we soared towards another shore, a shore with some light.

There were seven, though I could not make out who they were, but there were seven lights, and I felt keenly that I was the topic of discussion.

Raj was standing before them, and try as I might to get to him, I was locked in the arms of my Angel of Death. To my amazement Linda was standing near Raj. What was she doing here?

"Ah, I know it now, I see it all now" she exclaimed. "It was her *spirit* that escaped my hands, and as I stand here I see what awful learning lies hid' in the ignorance of the heart! What *realm* have I entered that shows such as this? Oh, what secrets you divulge when you decide to show your hidden worlds."

I had never heard her speak in such a manner, in fact, though I was confused by the whole scenario, Linda speaking like a female version of Will Shakespeare on crack, was doing my head in.

"The heart," responded the light standing in front of her, "for all time has held the mysteries of creation and the heart. This is why time and space have been afforded the soul."

Raj responded to this. "Yet our solemn rites don't deceive me, for the shadows, dark, still predict that even in this place and before death's dark angel, I, I have the power to save her." And the being flashed light like a laser, then spoke to him sternly.

"But at some unimagined and most fatal sacrifice to yourself." Nobody moved. Raj waited and spoke again.

"To myself, yes! But there is no self in love and I will go through this alone. I want no other guide, only the instincts of compassion and pure love to guide me. No dark cave, no solitude to conceal her and those like her who cry out for compassion to show its loving heart."

At this point I felt the seriousness of the situation, I felt something was hanging on a thread so delicate it could break, and my love would break with it. All this was not about me at all, it was about him, Raj. I had become a witness only. Raj continued.

"Though my attained path fails me, though the stars regard me as nothing now, and space, with its shining masses, will again be to me but the sapphire abyss, I return to love, and hope, and to try. I return to the mortal world. When have love and hope ever failed to triumph and to save?" Then Linda spoke again.

"Let me forgo *my* attainment, small though it may be, for a path where I can serve what I feel is true and right. Take me and let my sister live. Take thou me." Linda's Old English was now freaking me out. The whole situation was freaking me.

"Alas brother," a light came towards Raj, ignoring Linda.

"My brother, did you think that the bond between the survivor of ages and the daughter of a day could endure? Are you now seeking, among thy solemn secrets, safeguards for her? The phantom that served you has power over the lives it taught you to rescue. You know this dark bright one?" I saw Raj step back and felt a strange sensation.

Linda turned to Raj. "I feel it is the shadow of the dweller that stands before you, not light. Do you see, do you see?" she shouted. Then Linda addressed the seven again.

"Oh beings of seeming light, cast thine eyes of compassion onto one who has given his heart in service. Have mercy."

Now this attempt to meld the characters of Portia, Romeo and Shylock, seemed rather dramatic from where I was being held, and I started to laugh, though no noise came from me. Even Marlow and the Bard of Stratford could not have done a better job at creating such a 'tragedy of errors'. Raj seemed to be surrounded by a shadow now and spoke quietly.

"Humanity, with all its sorrows and its joys, is mine once more. Day by day now, I will be forging my own ties again and they will take me by the bands of my love to earth. Exiled from the bliss visible to the most abstract senses, the grim dweller that guards my threshold has entangled me in its web. Yes he says I have failed, but so I must for love. And—" He stopped and turned to the Dark Angel holding me in his arms. "In *this* hope, I triumph; for I have the supreme power of love for this dear life. Insensibly my soul speaks. You know because of the pure spirit of her, this ordeal has no terror for me. Shall I regret the finer kingdom that vanishes moment to moment from my grasp? No, I regret nothing for the Master of Love." Raj raised his head to the light above him and away from the seven.

"My Highest Self, whose vision is still clear and in peace, look deeply into those realms shut from my eyes and counsel me, please counsel me. I trust that enough power remains to me to overcome my dweller. Oh Brothers of Light, counsel me." The whole scene darkened and I felt I was losing myself into another tunnel, but then Raj spoke again.

"Answer me, for in the darkness that now veils me, I see only the pure eyes of my love. I hear only the low beating of my heart in the world again. Answer me, you whom I know to be pure love itself"

I managed a sound. "No." Raj looked directly into my eyes and spoke

"Her soul has not yet formed enough to travel this world, for while she fears, she cannot soar. See how she fears." The being now in front of him seemed to show less light, and it spoke.

"You, who have relinquished this bliss, I offer you the heavenly stars for more earthly days. Do you not see that to love is to fear? Do you now see that the power of which you boast over this one is already gone? It awes, it masters you, it will mock you and will betray you. Lose not a moment to come to me. If there can yet be sufficient sympathy between us, through my eyes you shall see, and perhaps guard against the perils that loom through the shadow. Come from all the ties of humanity, they will only obscure your vision." Raj stood tall.

"Oh tempter, for that is who you are, you show now your darkness, you speak of all that I cannot follow, for love is my heart, my being, and it is to love I surrender in all its forms. Let it be that I fall, let it be that I fail, I must surrender to all love in whatever form it may take." Raj fell to his knees and I struggled. Linda stood upright.

Pain seared my heart. This pain I would endure forever though, if it were to take even an ounce of suffering away from the world Raj was in.

The last remnants of light departed and in its place stood a hideous monster. Many faces, each becoming more grotesque than the first, arms flaying black tar, sounds spewing forth as the cries of thousands of life forms, who had succumbed to its manipulative illusion, tried in desperation to escape. Raj now stood as the brightest light, so bright I could not see him clearly, then he was gone.

Thump. Again I was back at our camp looking at Linda, an angry pretender shouting undecipherable words. Things became worse when she started to take off her clothes and then take off mine, and I started to fight back. Crazy woman got crazier and I became weaker, but then she huddled up close and wrapped me with her warmer body.

"Oh please Ellie stay with me." As I drifted, she shouted trying to keep me awake, and this continued for I don't know how long.

# Chapter Forty Nine

*Friend, our closeness is this: anywhere you put your foot, feel me in the firmness under you.* Rumi

Being released from hospital with me was a list. Don't do and do, keep this and that, take this and that. I had been there a few times before, and now I just needed to get back to my centre and away from all the sterilised routines of a hospital bed.

Linda and I had a few quiet days in our Scottish retreat, and I waited before saying anything about what happened. You see, when out there, I had a dream. It was of Raj and Linda and of seven lights, and sitting one afternoon on the window seat with Linda, I broached the subject.

"When that happened out there in the Highlands, what was it like for you?"

Linda continued to look out at the garden. As she turned to face me, she had tears.

"There were seven lights, Ellie, I counted them." She had given me what I wanted and I knew then that my dream was real.

"Oh Lin, what happened?"

"Well most of it, you know. You had a heart incident again, and this time I too was compromised due to the cold. It seemed I lost consciousness. We both stayed silent for a while.

"I thought you were my friend" I said humorously, "you were like a friggin Rambo woman thumping me. I still have the bruises."

She placed her arm around me. "Sorry for that." She paused.

"He is a great light Ellie and, dreadful as it all was, I do believe I witnessed something very good. From what I could make out he was definitely facing his demons, his dark night of the soul, who knows. The lights were trying to fool him, to coerce him to their way of thinking, but he didn't waver, he saw them as they truly were.

"Ellie, I do believe he surrendered his bliss to come back and serve humanity. He made a choice." She sat quietly thinking and continued.

"The last thing I remember was that I came back to my body, we were rescued, and the rest you know."

I started to laugh. "I have to ask you Linda, what was it with all the Shakespeare dialogue? I had no idea you spoke Old English."

"It came so naturally at the time, but blooming heck Ellie, when I relive it all and listen to myself, well..."

We sat and talked and laughed, and then we went down for supper and our first soiree in the library for four days.

# Chapter Fifty

*If you could get rid of yourself just once, the secret of secrets would open to you.*
*The face of the unknown, hidden beyond the universe, would appear on the mirror of your perception.*
Rumi

It was so good to be alive and now both Linda and I were ready to re-focus on serious study again in the library. We gathered as usual and chatted amongst ourselves then Russia spoke up.

"There have been many questions about the validity of Shambhala and I would like to share some things, if I may?" She continued, "It is the secret home of the great Brotherhood of Masters, and from this centre, at certain times in the history of this humanity, decrees for spiritual and intellectual work come forth to be shared."

Linda had a question. "Is it an actual district, like a place?"

"Oh yes," Russia responded, "surrounded by a range of the Himalayan Mountains, which no force can penetrate, for akashic barriers protect it. It's been held inviolate against aggression of any kind. There, surrounded by the greatest and most evolved human beings, the Silent Watcher of the earth has His invisible abode."

"Who is this Silent Watcher Russia?" came a woman from Lebanon, and Russia answered.

"He is the 'Initiator' called the 'Great Sacrifice'. Just then the door opened and the ghillie entered.

"Teacher will be delayed and so we will continue without him, and if permitted, I will share a great truth." With this the ghillie walked to the front.

"The Silent Watcher sits at the summit of the Spiritual Hierarchy and is one who, through evolution, having practically gained perfect knowledge of all that he can learn, remains on the periphery of this world in order to help the multitudes of less progressed entities coming up behind him. There he remains at his self-imposed task, waiting and watching and inspiring. Hence the term Silent Watcher. He has renounced all individual evolution for himself out of pure compassion for those still evolving.

"It is under the direct, silent guidance of this great Guru that all the other teachers and instructors of mankind have come. These include Buddha, Jesus, Krishna and other teachers we refer to as the Hierarchy of Compassion. It is through these Great Teachers that infant humanity received its first notions of the arts, sciences, as well as spiritual knowledge; and it is they who have laid the foundation-stone of those ancient civilizations that puzzle our modern generation of students and scholars."

I sat and could do nothing but wonder. Then I turned to Linda, she was in tears. We were all silent. The gillie walked across the front of the large fireplace.

"The Hierarchy of Compassion serve as channels for the spiritual energies coming to every planet, and shed light and peace upon the pathway of all humanity from the compassionate depths of their own being.

"They have made the great sacrifice, giving up all hope of their personal progress, in order to remain at their appointed tasks in service of the world. They work steadily on, watching others go past them as a river of lives sweeping along in unending flow."

I was now a snot girl, and the ghillie stepped forward and handed me a large handkerchief.

"Consider the achievement as well as the wonderful work of those who have preceded us. They are revealers in the sense of unveilers, for they are the initiators, who pass on light from age to age." I passed the cleaner part of the handkerchief to Linda. Just then, the door opened and MJ entered.

"Ah, I see you have carried on without me. That is as it should be, for who knows about time, hey? So where were we, ah yes." The gillie left the room and MJ continued.

"From this Wondrous Being originally comes our noblest impulses through our own higher selves: the aspiration we feel stirring in our minds and hearts, the urge to betterment, the sense of loyalty, all the things which make life bright and beautiful and well worth living." He stopped for a moment and we all sat for a while, then he gave us his final words.

"I address all here. Your calls were registered in Shambhala. They were not made with idle words nor with the desire towards psychic phenomena. It was noticed how each one present made these calls, consciously or not, with one thought, to serve. It is humanity that must be in your hearts and not the self if you are to progress along this path and become one with those whose whole being is service.

"This is our last evening and I bless you with love. May courage and fortitude show on your banners and may the motto on your breast be "To Do, To Dare and to be Silent." He departed.

Needless to say, it was also our time to depart. We were sad to leave but also joyous, as we were far more anchored in the truths we had been given and also buzzing with the experiences we had shared.

Linda and I were flying back home, but we knew we would still be in close contact and would, with passion, continue on our spiritual quest. This was our very nature.

# Chapter Fifty One

*Karma is the man that is.*
*Broadly speaking, he may be said to be the continuance of the nature of*
*the act and each act contains within itself the past and future.*
Unknown

Our plane touched down in Calgary giving me the perfect opportunity to have a visit with Linda and then proceed to Lake Louise alone. After a few days of tea, constant chin wagging and no sleep, I departed, my destination was the mountains.

Lake Louise looked the same, however I had been transformed since being found in the Rockies near to death. My quest now was to find Raj, or at least some definitive answers. I was Lady Galahad with my sword raised.

Up the side of the lake ran the path which I had taken to return home after being with these Adepts for many months, and now I was walking it again in the hopes of finding them. Halfway up, I took a breather and studied it, the path that is. It had a sad feature, it had brought me home and away from Raj. But, I had also witnessed Francis, my teacher, inviting others to join him. All on this very path.

Find this old path, if you will, or another, and sit quietly with it. We can learn much from a path, rather like Siddhartha did from the river he sat by. Today, my journey along this old friend felt different. I was holding onto the three words I had heard three times in my recent travels in Scotland. "Come to me." So, leaving the last of the tourists behind, I started my slow ascent.

The far side of the lake showed nature's genius with symmetry and order as well as beauty, as she merged mountains and the waters edge in a sacred geometry of colour and shape. She furnished proof that everything, though it may present at times otherwise, was in perfect order. Around two hours into my stroll, I planted myself on a log and took stock. It all seems a little silly now, my stomping like a spoiled brat demanding answers. And I had.

Why had I done it? Why had I gone to so much trouble to return to the scene of such parting sadness?

Of course I knew the answer, it was because of them, the Master and the Lover. Even though I had gone to all this trouble, I had no idea whether it was possible for me to enter their world again but I had to try.

I felt like Alice, about to jump into the looking glass, and the world I was about to enter was going to reflect, inspect, and perfect many aspects of me on many levels. Maybe I wasn't going to be able to join them again, but, being a determined old broad, I had to try.

Walking through the wooded area I began to appreciate the silence as it gave me the chance to reflect. I've had such joy throughout my life, but I've also experienced extreme pain, physically, mentally and emotionally. When I replicated the old letter I had found, little did I understand the ramifications. If one requests, in such a way, to be given all the Karma one can be given, then do trust that what you ask for will be given. The good, the bad, and the ugly.

So I had already pled my case to the Universe, and today I was going to continue here, in my past record of events, until I was permitted to go forward into my future. Visions, like scenes from old movies, played in my mind; scenes of campfires, hidden retreats and bears, always bears. Familiar smells mingled among the pine and fir, creating an intoxicating perfume, but still I stomped on into the snow smiling to myself as it crunched beneath my boots.

Of course I felt some fear, but in quests like these fear loves to rear its tail in an attempt to whack the pilgrim off course. Fear was an unwelcome guest this day, and I let it come and saw it go, and closed the door tight behind it.

Francis asked me once to draw a line in the snow, which I did. He then asked that I place the word fear on one end and love the other, which again I did. He then asked me what was between them both, and I answered, degrees of both. Then he asked that I place a line in the snow where fear ended and love began, and I sat for hours with this puzzle.

My decision to go out this day was partly the result of two people, the old gypsy I had met in Victoria and the strange woman who swept into my life with a bump then left me just as suddenly.

"Take the cold road" she had said, "take the cold road." Nothing now was going to make me turn back. Yes, this was going to be the day.

"Hello friend." A tall man walked towards me.

"Bloody hell you startled me, I didn't see you coming." He sat beside me on a log.

"There are many things we don't see coming." I shot him a look and he just smiled. Then trying to be a little gentler, I responded.

"Funny, I have just spent the last few hours thinking of how none of us truly view things the same way, and we can never truly predict what will happen next."

He looked straight ahead, and we sat a while in silence. Was this someone I was supposed to meet? I felt unusually comfortable considering the circumstances. Then he turned and spoke again.

"What a blessing we don't have a view of the future. Both the past and the future distract from the present and the present is the only gift that can be unwrapped and appreciated." He kept looking at me whilst taking off his jacket.

OK, maybe this wasn't an emissary of light, maybe he was a nutcase and his stripping heralded a threat.

"Who are you?" and I was just about to follow this question with another, when he responded.

"A fellow traveller along the path. Would you care to join me?" Of course I said yes. Then I noticed his dog collar.

Though I was not one to follow a religion (excuse the pun) there was something OK around the man, so I continued. We chatted about life in general, then a few hundred yards into our walk he started to veer off the path, and I stopped.

"Well, time for me to go now, enjoy the rest of your hike" I smiled and turned to go back.

"That's the problem, you are always going back and I am here to take you forward." He continued walking and I ran after him.

# Chapter Fifty Two

*Karma is the force that will make men pursue the ethics they have in theory.*
Unknown

The next hour flew by, and we chatted about science and philosophy, two subjects I relish. Ahead we came upon two large trees of incredible beauty, standing like a gateway, and we passed between them. There stood a cabin.

In the first part of this book, I had been taken to a cabin just like this, and now the memories were flooding back. My new friend picked up my thoughts, and lifted them with precision out of my head. Before I could open my mouth he shared.

"You are revisiting many old thoughts and missing the present being handed to you. What a waste of time, space and energy. While contemplation is commendable, going over ad-infinitum dead ideas is childish and there comes a time to let go of the old play things and visit the new."

He was doing my head in, and my face showed it. Who was this person? I knew enough from the past to realise he may have something to do with Francis, but there was still a 'but'.

"When you engage the mental or the emotional body there is always a result, and that result is what you refer to as a good or bad effect. Whatever one thinks, feels and performs, whether good or bad, must necessarily be enjoyed or suffered. Karma is the man that is. Think, Karma is the man that is.

We entered the cabin and he went over to a table where sat a pot and three cups. He poured tea and it was piping hot.

"Every effect which can be realised from an act must be hidden in the act itself or it could never come into existence." He smiled at me and I really wanted to understand.

"Stop, I need to get all this, it's too much, too quick. It's deep, and I love it. More please, and not just tea." I drank and he poured another cup.

"It must be evident that not only is there a relation between the cause and the effect but there must also be a relation between the cause and the individual who experiences the effect. If it were otherwise, any man would reap the effect of the actions of any other man."

He looked over to the door, yet went over to a window near the back of the room. Seconds later I heard footsteps and anticipation caught my breath. Could it be Francis? There was a third cup on the table. I went over to the door and opened it.

"Oh dear, excuse me," she said, "but I wonder if you could help? I need to find my way back to the path. I seem to have found myself lost."

Our host had his back to us and did not turn but responded. "Can you explain please, how you can be found and lost at the same time?" We both just stared at him.

He laughed, then asked her to enter and sit for tea first. She seemed a little unsure at first, but as I had some questions, I just carried on where I had left off before the knock.

"Sorry, but I need to go back to what you were saying. Can you just finish explaining about Karma?" But she rudely interrupted whilst he poured her tea.

"Oh I'm not sure about all that Karma stuff. It's promoted by a lot of self-styled gurus, fooling people who have lost their way."

"You mean a bit like yourself? I smiled. She didn't seem to get it, but continued her ramble.

"I was raised Roman Catholic, though in my adult years I was never a churchgoer. The priests were always telling us what we should think and what we should do. Believing anything someone tells you seems a little ridiculous to me, and this new age notion of Karma and reincarnation, well, that's really out there. Belief in such things is a farcical game the mind plays as it stretches to see something that isn't there. I want evidence, good scientific proof before I believe any of that twaddle."

Our host joined us, and she nearly choked when she saw his religious dog collar. He smiled.

"What is proof? Don't you see that the only way to get proof of a thing is by thinking it through to the end? And while you may be wrong, it is still the only way for thinking human beings to get to that proof. Don't mistake evidence for proof.

"If I have a receipt which shows that a thousand dollars has been paid, does that prove the money has been paid? Any lawyer will tell you it's not proof. It's only evidence substantiating a possible fact that a thousand dollars has been paid by so and so to so and so; but it may be a forgery.

"But if an individual hearing detailed circumstances about a thing, sifting the evidence laid before his thinking mind, is convinced that X has paid Z a thousand dollars, then that evidence substantiates it making the conviction more strong." This guy was mental.

"Even the world of science substantiates the law of Karma, referring to it as 'cause and effect', 'action and reaction'. You've heard of Newton?" He smiled kindly at her.

"And reincarnation is accepted by more human minds than the number of those who don't hold with it. Even those who profess to be atheists may be heard to say, in my next life I will... This may be said in humour, but it is something that is becoming mainstream, along with other terms associated with the Ancient Wisdom. In the early Christian church reincarnation was known and taught. Christians should remember that Jesus was a Jew who thought his mission was to Jews. He must have known the doctrines held by them, and they believed in reincarnation.

"For them Moses, Adam, Noah, Seth had returned to earth, and at the time of Jesus it was currently believed that the old prophet Elias was yet to return. Jesus never denied the doctrine and on various occasions assented to it, as when he said that John the Baptist was actually the Elias of old whom the people were expecting."

I held my cup up for another tea, there was still more in the pot and he still had more to say.

"It is very clear that Jesus approved the doctrine of reincarnation, and following Jesus we find such great Christian fathers as Origen and Synesius.

"We have Solomon saying that when the earth was made he was present, and that, long before he could have been born as Solomon, his delights were in the habitable parts of the earth with the sons of men.

"The church now says in effect, that Jesus did not know enough of a doctrine taught in his day, which was brought to his notice and approved by him.

"Christianity is a Jewish religion and this doctrine of reincarnation belongs to it historically by succession from the Jews, and also by reason of its having been taught by Jesus and the early fathers of the church.

"If there be any truthful or logical way for the Christian church to get out of this position, excluding, of course, dogmas of the church, I would like to be shown it. Indeed, I hold that whenever a professed Christian denies the theory, he thereby sets up his judgement against that of his/her Master, Jesus, who must have known more about the matter than those who follow him."

I clapped bravo, for he had presented something I was always tongue tied over, but he didn't know when to stop.

"Alone in reincarnation is the answer to all the problems of life. I ask you, what loving parent would impose hardship to a portion of his children and look on as they floundered. How much would the epitome of love abhor such favouring?

"I tell you these things to assist in breaking down the foundations that you have, which you may use to construct your future beliefs."

He had spoken sense and it had stirred questions, but she wasn't the only one with questions and I voiced one of mine.

"Who the hell are you, because you're not the ordinary run of the mill minister or priest?"

He laughed so loud. "I'm not a minister or a priest." Then he took off his heavy sweater realising we had misread his clothes, and showed us that the top of his polar neck sweater wasn't a priest's collar.

"Make yourselves at home," he chuckled, and left us both to get acquainted.

She sat quiet, then, as I was about to say something she chirped up again. They had a lot in common, my two new friends, they both loved to talk.

"Who the frig are you people?"

Pouring tea, I briefly shared how I met this man, as well as some of my experiences in the past whilst hiking these parts.

As best I could, I shared my hope that an incredible door may have been opened to her, and myself, and though I kept it to myself, there was a maybe, just maybe, our host was a nutcase. They say con-men are very clever at their game. When he returned she was raring to go.

# Chapter Fifty Three

*Karma the child, is the father of the man.*
A Great Soul

She never stopped talking, and when she wasn't talking she was humming. She was a non-stop tape of noise, and nature seemed to run away from her, as *I* wished I could. I was blocking sounds as best I could. Vision seemed the only sense worth having, but even that she invaded.

"Oh god look at that, isn't it fabulous." Followed by, "wow, did you hear that echo? Go on, try it yourself, it's just like you're in the Swiss Alps." Then she would start yodelling and practising her audition for "The Sound of Music".

My peaceful countenance took flight on the wings of the last bald eagle trying to escape the border of Canada, and all I wanted to do was throttle her. I couldn't seem to distract myself either; for the more I tried to push her over a cliff out of my world, the more she invaded my space. Then something happened.

We were walking in a wooded area, and she stopped quite suddenly, a contrast to the 'Sally invasion' I had experienced 'til this moment. Her head darted one way, then another, like she was listening, then she rushed to the base of a tree some 40ft away. Crouching down, she lifted the top half of a deer onto her lap and held it close.

As I went forward toward her, our guide motioned me to stay. It was eerie, one of those moments when nature seemed to be holding her breath. Nothing moved. Then life stirred, and a breeze started whipping up mini tornadoes causing leaves and fine dust to disturb and rise. As suddenly as it all started, it all ended.

Sally seemed at home with nature as she laid the deer's head back on the bracken. Then she rose and stood silently looking ahead. I could see she had been affected and I moved forward and put my arms around her. I liked this woman, and it took this incident for me to see it. The deer slowly rose and left.

Paul shared that Sally was a healer very close to the Devic kingdom though she was unaware what that meant. I was so blessed to have witnessed this amazing healing.

"I haven't even asked you your name yet!" she said, looking past me towards our host.

He responded "how about Paul? He was a holy man, a minister to the public."

"You say how about Paul, have you forgotten who you are? And I'm Sally by the way" she interrupted, before he had the chance to get another word in. He smiled and she happily skipped off.

Her enthusiasm for everything was contagious, and I soon found myself signed up as her newest cast member as we rambled together singing "the hills are alive with the sound of music." Our host kept his distance until we stopped to rest.

"Why do we reincarnate then?" she queried. He looked over to me as if I knew the answer. I felt I did have some idea so I responded regardless of whether I knew or not.

"Reincarnation gives us a further opportunity to get our act together, and Karma gives us the basis for growth within that opportunity.

"The first result of karmic action is a desire for birth in this physical body. The birth seeking entity, consisting of desires and tendencies, presses forward towards incarnation into the surroundings most in harmony with its karmic tendencies and the effect of actions contained in that Karma.

"All life is the reaction to an action, and this continues until the soul, the re-embodying part of the individual, has reached that stage where it steps off the wheel of birth and rebirth." Paul continued, "Karma the child is the father of the man. The 'old being' is the sole parent, the father and mother at once, of the 'new being.' It is the former who is the creator, and far more so than any father in flesh. Each man's life is the outcome of his former living." She was quiet a while, then responded.

"Is Karma just another name for fate then. Is there no possibility of escape? It makes me feel a little trapped and powerless." I too had a question.

"To what degree can one affect his own Karma and in what manner?" He didn't reply immediately, but looked around.

"Although at first it may appear that nothing can be more fatalistic than this doctrine, a little consideration will show that in reality this is not the case.

"Karma, broadly speaking, may be said to be the continuance of the nature of an act and each act contains within itself the past and future.

"Fate has nothing to do with it, for you create your futures with your thoughts, words and deeds. Being conscious of this and acting accordingly is where your freedom lies

"You may both wish to accompany me. I'm off to a meeting, where the answers you're looking for will be presented to you. There seems no need to concern yourself any further regarding your safety, nor your conversion" he was attempting to be funny here. Of course by now we both wished to continue onward with him, and to learn more. We travelled further into the mountains for some while in relative silence. Oh what peace! Then Paul stopped.

"When a heart is lifted it sees the world through different eyes." Turning to Sally he said. "Look to the first ridge in the distance, what do you see, Sally child?".

She looked and shrugged. "Mountains, beautiful mountains."

"Look beyond. He motioned her to look again. She pushed her head forward and squinted her eyes.

."Even when we think we see, the eyes can still present illusions," he said. Look again my dear."

"Oh there you go," she shouted in triumph, "over there, it's a building." And she was right. Around an hour later we approached the ridge where we could clearly make out an entrance carved out of the rock.

"Wow, who the heck lives here?" Sally whispered as we approached the entrance.

"Francis," said a woman as she approached us.

"Excuse me, did you say Francis?" I was shocked. Had I succeeded in finding my teacher once more? Had my persistence payed off? I was excited.

She smiled and escorted us inside to a larger area where a few people had gathered. It was then I felt a poke, quite violently in my lower back, and turning, I came face to face with Linda.

"Well we're back and it's been quite the journey so far sis, hey? We started out as two dingbats on a spiritual quest and we're still two dingbats." I felt emotional.

We were all guided through a doorway to a study, and finding our seats we settled down. By the door on the far side, in the shadows, was a tall man speaking with Paul. He was of similar build and countenance...but no, I had done this before at the Red Fort and I was not going to go down that road again.

I feel we've all had those times, when we think we see someone but it's just a memory playing with the mind which fires up the emotion of the heart. This was a perfect example for me to really implement what I had been studying. Take control of the monkey mind Ellie, take charge of your emotions Ellie. Become the conscious creator of your world Ellie.

Linda and I looked at each other and shared some thoughts, and she pressed my hand in companionship, that dear little friend of mine who had been with me through the highs and lows. We knew our journey was coming to an end and we wondered what our lives would be like once we returned to the 'real world'. Then the presentation began.

# Chapter Fifty Four

*Love came and became like blood in my body.*
*It rushed through my veins and encircled my heart.*
Rumi

"Karma and re-embodiment are the means by which all humanity will develop love." Paul continued.

"As a mother, even at the risk of her own life, protects her son, her only son, so let the disciple cultivate love without measure towards all beings. Let him cultivate towards the whole world, above, below, around, a heart of love unstinted, unmixed with differing or opposing interests. And let a man maintain this mindful love whether he stands, walks, sits or lies. For in all the world this state of heart is best. These teachings were given by the Buddha.

"The law of love will work, just as the law of gravitation will work whether we accept it or no. And just as a scientist will work wonders out of various applications of the laws of nature, even so a man who applies the law of love with scientific precision can work greater wonders. For the force of non-violence is infinitely more wonderful and subtle than the forces of nature, like for instance electricity. The man who discovered for us the law of love was a far greater scientist than any of our modern scientists. Only our explorations have not gone far enough and so it is not possible for everyone to see all its workings.... The more one works at this law the more one will feel the delight in life, the delight in the scheme of this universe.

The talk ended and we all departed to our rooms to prepare for an informal meal together.

"You up?" came Sally's voice at the door. Here we go, Sally's enthusiasm was at a high. She entered and flopped onto my bed.

"Oh what an amazing talk." she sighed. "and I met a fascinating man as we departed, he was so regal."

"Ah yes Sally, that would be Francis, he is my teacher. She looked at me questioningly.

"No, I'm talking about Raj." Before she could get another word out of her mouth a bell rang announcing ten minutes before food was served and she departed as quickly as she came.

Gathering my thoughts that were now scrambling wildly throughout the room and bouncing off walls, I made my way to the door just as a knock came. Grabbing my cardigan I opened the door, stumbled, and Raj caught me, as he always had.

His hand stroked the back of my head as he pulled me close to his heart. I sobbed. This time he was for real. In the flesh. My Raj. His eyes searched deep inside me, then he smiled. Closing the door gently behind him, he kissed my forehead and brushed my lips, he held my gaze with his dark eyes and sandalwood curled around me. There was a regal feeling about him, an energy that I had encountered with the Great Souls I had been privilege to meet, and I recognised it. It was an initiation he had been through and He too had become a Master of the Brotherhood of Compassion.

He once said to me, love is the only cohesive energy in the Universe, and time is an illusion of the mind. Oh my love, Raj, had truly taken my hand and literally guided me along the road called love. He had dipped me into a small particle in the cosmos of reality.

Once my feet were firmly in the world again, Raj took my hand and without words we made our way to the library. He escorted me to my seat and departed.

Francis and the Egyptian Master entered the room, accompanied by Raj. We all fell completely silent.

"The study we are about to embark on tonight is part of the Ancient Wisdom of Egypt. The source. The fount. Those with ears to hear will hear, all others, another time will arrive."

# Chapter Fifty Five

*These are the golden stairs, up the steps of which the learner may climb to The Temple of Divine Wisdom.*
H.P. Blavatsky

The evening was in preparation for the serious studies on the Occult Wisdom we were to be presented with the following day, and although we were not told directly, there was a buzz going around that the Egyptian would be the one teaching it all.

These teachings, which I have started in this book, have been told before in different ways. But it was made clear to me, when I had the interview with Sir Thomas and Francis on my recent journey to the UK, that I was to weave them into my story. I have attempted to do this.

In the room were approximately 30 people from a variety of backgrounds and among them there were a couple of familiar faces.

My role on this journey was to be the scribe, to gather as much of the teachings as possible so as to share with those ready to read. I knew that at the same time I was being given the opportunity to grow myself and to do so with my greatest Teachers, The Brotherhood of Light.

Raj was part of this Brotherhood, the Brotherhood of Compassion, but I had no illusions about being the only one in his heart, so was humanity, indeed all of nature. It was Raj who stepped forward and spoke.

"The talk today will be multi-layered and steeped in symbolism. This is the nature of all occult work and as such, I will lay the foundation upon which the walls of the pyramid will be constructed.

"Our purpose is not the enunciation of any special philosophy or doctrine but rather to present to you statements of the Truth that will serve to reconcile the many bits of occult knowledge that you may have acquired, which are apparently opposed to each other and which often serve to discourage the beginner in the study."

"Our intent is not to erect a new Temple of Knowledge, but rather to place in the hands of the student that with which he may open the many inner doors in the Temple of Mystery through the main portals he has already entered.

"Contemplation on these teachings will stimulate a part of your mind that will take you beyond the abstract nature of that given and divulge a much deeper meaning only attained by the serious student.

"The fundamental and basic teachings embedded in all esoteric philosophy of every race, can be found encapsulated within these teachings shared with you.

"Even the most ancient teachings of India have their roots in the original Occult Teachings and from the land of the Ganges many advanced occultists wandered to the land of Egypt and sat at the feet of the Great Master.

"From him they obtained a Master Key which explained and reconciled their divergent views and thus the Secret Doctrine was firmly established.

"Nevertheless, the original truths taught by him have been kept intact in their original purity by a few men in each age. From lip to ear the truth has been handed down among the few.

"All in attendance, as well as those who read these words," he looked over toward me and I understood, "have earned the right, by serious study and selfless heart, to be given this opportunity and then make a choice. One cannot serve two Masters.

"There have always been a few Initiates in each generation, in the various lands of the earth, who kept alive the Sacred Flame of the Sacred Teachings and such have always been willing to use their lamps to re-light the lesser lamps of the outside world.

"There were always a few to tend faithfully the altar of Truth, upon which was kept alight the Perpetual Lamp of Wisdom.

"These men have never sought popular approval, nor followers of great number. They are indifferent to these things. They reserve their pearls of wisdom for the few who recognize their value.

"When the ears of the student are ready to hear, then come the lips to fill them with wisdom.

"The lips of Wisdom are closed, except to the ears of Understanding. Think upon all these statements.

"Each layer is revealed according to the student and the time. Revisiting these truths given, contemplating the words, will eventually reveal all these layers.

"There are those who have criticised this attitude and who have claimed that the proper spirit was not manifest in their policy of seclusion and reticence.

"But a moment's glance back over the pages of history will show the wisdom of the Masters, who knew the folly of attempting to teach to the world that which it was neither ready nor willing to receive.

"There are certain Sacred Teachings which, if publicly promulgated, would bring down upon the teachers a great cry of scorn and revilement from the multitude, who would again raise the cry of "Crucify! Crucify.

"In the time we have had together, and will have together, we have endeavoured and continue to give you an idea of the fundamental teachings, striving to give you the working Principles, leaving you to apply them yourselves.

"If you are a true student, you will be able to work out and apply these Principles. If not, then you must develop yourself into one, otherwise the Teachings will be as "words, words, words" to you. And so enough. We will convene after lunch." He departed with no more words.

Linda and I took the time over lunch to ask each other our questions and share our answers, and then it was back to the hall for the commencement of serious study.

We sat together and chatted until the gong sounded, then Raj and Francis entered. Without any introduction or pause Francis addressed us. What was shared with us came from the original teachings taught to the initiates in the temples of Egypt. I hope at some time in the future, I will be able to bring this wisdom forward to you, but until then, I encourage all who have read this journey so far to call to the Master that resides within you, connect to your Solar Angel, and prove all teaching for yourself.

# Chapter Fifty Six

*The minute I heard my first love story,*
*I started looking for you, not knowing*
*how blind that was.*
*Lovers don't finally meet somewhere.*
*They're in each other all along.*
Unknown

Bringing this book to a close is heavy, for I am trusting I have shared enough of my many experiences to have done justice to the journey. I trust you, who have read these words, will be adventurous and embrace your journeys with great passion and reap to the fullest what all true Adepts have placed before humanity and are still placing. This will take determination, for all that has been shared by these Elder Brothers of ours, has layers. As you study the words, these layers will dissolve into enlightenment.

Linda and I spent the following day quietly sharing our thoughts and visions. Mid morning on the last day, Linda prepared to leave, not by choice but by time and circumstance.

This brought my own return closer. Looming in my mind was the question of Raj and I, but by now I was coming to realise that all would be as it should be until it changed.

The last party left the entrance taking the narrow path down to the place where Sally and I had looked up and spied the retreat for the first time. I watched as the group disappeared into a line of trees around the mountain's edge, and my last vision was of Linda turning back and blowing a kiss to her best friend, me.

As I turned, before me stood a tall vision of strength and purpose. Raj. His head tilted slightly to one side causing his dark hair to flow a little and his piercing eyes were focused upon me. He beckoned me into his open arms and I entered the armour of his peace. His energy caused me to quiver and I let it run up and down my spine gently. He held me for some time. A voice rang like a faint echo hitting one canyon and then another.

"The journey has just begun, just begun." It was Francis.

I sobbed from my soul yet had to smile and look up to Raj. He too was smiling. He took my hand and escorted me back through the doors I had entered when first arriving, and they shut behind me for the first time.

www.ingramcontent.com/pod-product-compliance
Lightning Source LLC
Chambersburg PA
CBHW031440160726
47994CB00005B/1807